WILLIAM GOLDING

a critical study

Also by Ian Gregor

THE MORAL AND THE STORY
(with Brian Nicholas)

THE GREAT WEB:
THE FORM OF HARDY'S MAJOR FICTION

WILLIAM GOLDING

a critical study

MARK KINKEAD-WEEKES
and
IAN GREGOR

faber and faber
LONDON · BOSTON

First published in 1967
by Faber and Faber Limited
3 Queen Square London WC1
Reprinted in 1968
First published in this edition 1970
Reprinted in 1975
Revised in 1984
Printed in Great Britain by
Redwood Burn Limited
Trowbridge, Wiltshire

© 1967, 1984 by Mark Kinkead-Weekes
and Ian Gregor

British Library Cataloguing in Publication Data

Kinkead-Weekes, Mark
William Golding—Rev. ed.
1. Golding, William—Criticism and interpretation
I. Title   II. Gregor, Ian
823'.914   PR6013.035
ISBN 0-571-13259-6

Library of Congress Data has been applied for.

Contents

Preface

In 1967, when the first edition of this book was published, we thought of it as having a double purpose. It provided a series of detailed readings of the five novels which Golding had then published, and it sought to describe the evolving nature of Golding's imagination as it had revealed itself step by step in the process of their composition. The manner of our book was more exploratory than judicial, more concerned to describe the changing nature of the fiction than to attempt any overall judgement of strengths and weaknesses (though we had something to say about these in particular cases), or to 'place' the work in a wider context of contemporary literature.

As a view of an imagination in process, taken from a point immediately after *The Spire*, the enterprise seems to us to have its own argument and consistency, of which both its date and its limitations are part. We have therefore allowed it to stand, unaltered, in this new edition.

Since then, however, Golding has published three more novels, *The Pyramid* (1967), *Darkness Visible* (1979), *Rites of Passage* (1980); and taken together, these would seem to provide sufficient occasion for looking at his career as it has developed after *The Spire*. In adding a new chapter, we have adopted the same kind of approach as before, concentrating on the evolving nature of the imagination, and hence on the interrelationship between one novel and another. Again we offer readings of the individual works, but this time we felt (particularly with *The Pyramid* and *Rites of Passage*) that such readings could perhaps be more selective than we had allowed ourselves to be in discussing Golding's earlier work. If we are adding to the original book, it is not in the spirit of annexing more rooms to an existing structure. Indeed, the later novels are seen as rather different architecture, whose juxtaposition with the previous building produces new sightlines.

The critical reading of a contemporary is not merely a matter of sensing the evolution in the work, but of becoming aware of the evolution in our own responsiveness as readers. If a contemporary writer has sustained our interest for nearly thirty years, this becomes a substantial part of a reading lifetime, in a way that is different from our response to writers who belong to history. We change towards

Preface

them too, but are less aware of *them* moving, than ourselves. But the career of our contemporaries obviously moves faster than we can follow: we see their work as not only incomplete, but as not (yet) offering the full curve from which the point of view for a complete conspectus could be chosen. It seems then that we are bound to talk in terms of process, evolution, exploration; and, though we must constantly be seeking the outline of a pattern, it will be in a way which contrives to suggest fluidity, temporality, as well as order. To write about our contemporaries is to make the date of our writing (in 1967, in 1983) an inseparable element in what we have to say, and the way we attempt to say it.

M.K.W.
I.G.
Canterbury, 1983

I

LORD OF THE FLIES

(1954)

I

Lord of the Flies has become a compulsory stop on the route of any surveyor of the English novel since the war, an addition to the canon of writings prescribed by school examination boards, the occasion of a volume of critical essays published in the U.S.A., and an award-winning film. Such popular success has eluded the four novels which followed. They have received wide and sometimes generous notice, but it is the earlier work that has guaranteed them their respect. They have achieved virtue by association. Yet Golding's novels are unmistakably all of a piece. Among themselves they reveal a family resemblance, a unity even, that gives the phrase 'a Golding novel' a readily understood meaning. Why does the first occupy so unique a position?

What distinguishes *Lord of the Flies* is its powerful and exciting qualities as narrative, and its appearance of extreme clarity of meaning; the later works are more difficult both to read and to understand. *Lord of the Flies* fulfils most effectively the novelist's basic task of telling a good story. It also meets Conrad's prescription: 'by the power of the written word to make you hear, to make you feel . . . before all, to make you *see*'. It was not surprising that it should have attracted the attention of the film director, providing him with an unwavering narrative drive, and also with an unbroken series of intensely visualized scenes. On the other hand, at every point and with a kind of inevitability that is as impressive as the story itself, we are made aware that much more than this story is being told; indeed a clearly focused and coherent body of meaning appears to be crystallizing out of every episode. A reader can feel that he possesses this novel in an unusually comprehensive way, and that he could give a lucid, even conceptual account of it. The book has high polish, and seems to present itself for our contemplation as a remarkably complete and solid structure. This of course may not always be regarded as a strength. Many readers may feel the book to be too crystalline, too insistent, too manipulated to be acceptable, but it seems likely that it is this combination of narrative momentum and thematic clarity that explains the popular success, which greater Golding novels have failed to achieve. Whether the art *is* so clear and crystalline, however, is perhaps open to question.

Let us consider the finding of the shell, which provides the title for the opening chapter. We watch the conch, we might say, liberated from ordinariness, grasped, filled with meaning:

' "What's that?"

'Ralph had stopped smiling and was pointing into the lagoon. Something creamy lay among the ferny weeds.

' "A stone."

' "No. A shell."

'Suddenly Piggy was a-bubble with decorous excitement.

' "S'right. It's a shell! I seen one like that before. On someone's back wall. A conch he called it. He used to blow it and then his mum would come. It's ever so valuable—"

'Near to Ralph's elbow, a palm sapling leaned out over the lagoon. Indeed, the weight was already pulling a lump from the poor soil and soon it would fall. He tore out the stem and began to poke about in the water, while the brilliant fish flicked away on this side and that. Piggy leaned dangerously.

' "Careful! You'll break it—"

' "Shut up."

'Ralph spoke absently. The shell was interesting and pretty and a worthy plaything: but the vivid phantoms of his day-dream still interposed between him and Piggy, who in this context was an irrelevance. The palm sapling, bending, pushed the shell across the weeds. Ralph used one hand as a fulcrum and pressed down with the other till the shell rose, dripping, and Piggy could make a grab.

'Now the shell was no longer a thing seen but not to be touched, Ralph too became excited. Piggy babbled:

' "—a conch; ever so expensive. I bet if you wanted to buy one, you'd have to pay pounds and pounds and pounds—he had it on his garden wall and my auntie—"

'Ralph took the shell from Piggy and a little water ran down his arm. In colour the shell was deep cream, touched here and there with fading pink. Between the point, worn away into a little hole, and the pink lips of the mouth, lay eighteen inches of shell with a slight spiral twist and covered with a delicate, embossed pattern. Ralph shook sand out of the deep tube.

' "—moo-ed like a cow," he said. "He had some white stones

too, an' a bird cage with a green parrot. He didn't blow the white stones of course, an' he said—"

'Piggy paused for breath and stroked the glistening thing that lay in Ralph's hands.

' "Ralph!"

'Ralph looked up.

' "We can use this to call the others. Have a meeting. They'll come when they hear us—"

'He beamed at Ralph.

' "That was what you meant, didn't you? That's why you got the conch out of the water?"

'Ralph pushed back his fair hair.

' "How did your friend blow the conch?"

' "He kind of spat," said Piggy. "My auntie wouldn't let me blow on account of my asthma. He said you blew from down here." Piggy laid a hand on his jutting abdomen. "You try, Ralph. You'll call the others."

'Doubtfully, Ralph laid the small end of the shell against his mouth and blew. There came a rushing sound from its mouth but nothing more. Ralph wiped the salt water off his lips and tried again, but the shell remained silent.

' "He kind of spat."

'Ralph pursed his lips and squirted air into the shell, which emitted a low, farting noise. This amused both boys so much that Ralph went on squirting for some minutes, between bouts of laughter.

' "He blew from down here."

'Ralph grasped the idea and hit the shell with air from his diaphragm. Immediately the thing sounded. A deep, harsh note boomed under the palms, spread through the intricacies of the forest and echoed back from the pink granite of the mountain. Clouds of birds rose from the treetops, and something squealed and ran in the undergrowth.

'Ralph took the shell away from his lips.

' "Gosh!" '

The whole rhythm of this seems one of transformation—the unliving thing is disentangled and given a new social purpose. It announces man and summons men together, this 'Sound of the

17

Shell'. As the novel proceeds this meaning becomes more and more sharply defined. 'We can use this to call the others. Have a meeting . . .' It is his association with the shell rather than his size or attractiveness that makes the children choose Ralph as their leader; and having been established as the symbol of assembly, the conch becomes identified with its procedure, with democracy and the right to free speech. It becomes a symbol of immense suggestiveness. Every time a boy cries 'I've got the conch', he is drawing on the funds of order and democratic security. We take the point when Jack blows it 'inexpertly', and when he lays it at his feet in rejection. The conch helps both to trace the trajectory of plot, and to establish character. Nowhere does Piggy's role seem more economically and poignantly expressed than when he prepares to confront the Tribe and its Chief with 'the one thing he hasn't got'. Then the conch in Piggy's hands becomes no less than the basic challenge to the Tribe to choose between democracy and anarchy, civilization and savagery. The answer comes in unequivocal terms: 'The rock struck Piggy a glancing blow from chin to knee; the conch exploded into a thousand white fragments and ceased to exist.' The shell, whose sound began as a summons to society, ends as a murderous explosion on the rocks. It traces out for us the swift tragic progress of the tale, and condenses its meaning—or so it seems.

But will this kind of reading satisfy, when we stop talking about the book from a distance and really look at the texture of the writing and the kind of experience it proffers? What will strike us most immediately is surely that the episode is far too long and circumstantial for any purely symbolic purpose. When we investigate the nature of that circumstantiality, what it reveals is Golding's concern to hold back rather than encourage the conceptualizing or interpretative intelligence. The counterpointing of the two boys shows this very clearly.

It is Piggy who is first excited by the shell, but only as a curio. It is Ralph's consciousness we live in, and he hardly listens to Piggy. Not one of the fat boy's sentences is heard to a conclusion. What is important about Ralph's 'day-dream', moreover, is that intelligence and social memory are laid asleep, while the physical senses, alone, remain sharply aware. Hence the description of fulcrum and lever, weight and resistance; the interest in how the shell is physically disentangled from the weeds. In fact the 'civilizing' intelligence is kept at bay while the actual conch in its strangeness and beauty is made real to the senses. Suddenly Piggy's babble stops, while he too strokes 'the glistening thing that lay in Ralph's hands', wet, reflecting light, strangely beautiful.

The second half of the scene elaborates the contrast. Now Piggy invents the idea of the meeting, giving the shell a social purpose; but again the life of the passage comes from Ralph, and he is only interested, as any schoolboy would be, in finding out how to blow it. Again Piggy moves into unison, the shell is primarily an object of play for both of them, and the simple vulgarity of the farting noises fills them with equal delight. The imagination at work is profoundly physical, and what it seizes is, precisely, the *sound* of the shell. It is made real to us in its context of salt water, brilliant fish, green weed; then in its own strange cream and rose spiral, embossed by an art other than the human; finally in the harsh otherness of the noise which shatters the peace of the island and terrifies bird and beast.

Physical realities come first for Golding and should stay first for his readers. Other meanings are found in and through them, as the man-breath passes through the shell's spiral to emerge as signal. But we must not translate the shell into the signal. What comes out is far from simple; and the human beings will be as taken aback as the animals and for the same reason. If we really look and listen, what we shall see and hear will be the harshness of human self-assertion as well as the signal of human sociability; will be the sound of irresponsibility and childishness as well as of forethought and intelligence; will be the fragility of order as well as the impulse towards it. As the sound penetrates the densest thickets, while clouds of birds fly and 'something squealed and ran in the undergrowth', man-sound prefigures stuck pig and stuck Ralph squealing and running for their life, as well as the assembly and the rules. Golding's symbols are not in fact clear, or wholly articulate, they are always an incarnation of more than can be extracted or translated from them. Even at this early stage, when the fiction seems to offer itself so alluringly for conceptual analysis, it is always richer and more profound than the thesis we may be tempted to substitute for the experience.

It is not a question of rejecting such meanings, so much as developing a delicacy and tact in handling them; a sense of how limited they are in themselves and how far they fall short of accounting for the density of the fiction. We need similar tact with the characters. Even from the finding of the shell, for example, it is easy to see how one could extend Piggy's point of view until he came to stand for something like 'rational humanism'; and many of his physical deficiencies might seem to express Golding 's critique of the humanist. We certainly cannot see him as simply a fat boy. Yet he is much more complex than such a formulation could account for, and often inconsistent with it; we would have to mutilate Golding's boy to fit him to so Procrustean a bed. If we respond to what is on the page we shall find in the novel less the pummelling of humanism than the growth in stature, in credibly boyish terms, of the 'true wise friend' who on the last page is almost the tragic hero. Like the other characters Piggy does embody meaning of various kinds, so that we become aware through our imaginative response to the boy of wider horizons and deeper problems beyond him. On the other hand, he is too diminutive to support an acceptable representative significance, just as Jack cannot be Satan or the Power Urge, though he may reveal truths about both to us, and Simon is both less and more than the Saint. Indeed, if we became less eager to confine Golding's creations to a crystalline structure of meaning, we might be rather less worried about the ability of the island and the boys to sustain the weight of a full statement about 'the human condition'. We ought to admit more readily the limitations of the insights Golding can legitimately embody in so select a situation, while at the same time pointing to the fact that his fiction is far richer and more ambiguous, even in *Lord of the Flies*, than it looks. Both too much and too little has been claimed for Golding's first novel. That is why it is often so difficult to be fair to it.

Finally, and on the deepest level, it is now possible to see that there is a sharp irony in the temptation to translate the fiction into an unambiguous emblem: this does worse than simplify, it subverts. It is exactly the tendency to convert and reduce complexity into simplicity which Golding sees as the root of evil. This was not perhaps easy to see when the novel appeared, though it was always there, and there is no missing it now. For in novel after novel Golding has attacked on the same front: the way that 'homo sapiens' makes Neanderthal man the image of his own evil; the way that Christopher Martin and Sammy Mountjoy recreate real people into the shapes of their own need and lust; the set of emblems that must be cleared from Jocelin's mind at the moment of death and replaced by the vivid and complex physical truth of the Spire itself. For Golding, the Evil Tree grows in the human brain, in human consciousness, and emblematic and conceptual reduction are dangerous manifestations of the Fall. So, in *Lord of the Flies*, it is the way in which the children look for an external manifestation of what is really in themselves that releases the sin of Cain. Evil exists, but not as a Beast. There is an analogous truth about the conch. What the Sound of the Shell really is . . . is a sound. Like the whole island, the shell is a unique, physical existence whose being is its meaning. Yet it can reveal man, as the shell shows forth all the implications for good or evil of the human breath that resounds through it. Only it is fatal to forget, as the children and many readers do, that the meaning is in the boys, not the shell. The conch's symbolic meaning depends on the state of the children's minds. Once power becomes more real to Jack than the rules, the conch is meaningless; but when he raids the camp for fire, Piggy thinks he has come for the shell. Though Piggy reaches his greatest stature at the moment of his death, it is also the moment of his greatest blindness, rendered for us at a level far deeper than his lost spectacles. For he holds out as a magic talisman what is, literally, an empty shell. It had a more inclusive sound, and if the boys had been able to understand that sound fully instead of reducing its complexities there would have been no tragedy.

II

The island gives the children freedom to reveal themselves. We listen with increasing attention to what it is that the Sound of the Shell announces about these human beings. Golding re-occupies R. M. Ballantyne's *Coral Island* and declares its portrayal of those idealized British boys, Jack, Ralph and Peterkin in their tropical paradise, to be a fake, since boys are human beings, and human beings are not like that. Or, rather, he does not 'declare', he shows the falsehood by producing an island and boys that are more convincing than Ballantyne's, and then gradually revealing what the difference implies. The structure and technique of *Lord of the Flies* is one of revelation.

At the beginning the most obvious element of the Shell, its strangeness, its glamour, its beauty, parallels the first response to the island itself. Disaster has brought the children there: an atomic explosion, an evacuation by air via Gibraltar and Addis Ababa. Their aircraft has been attacked, probably over the Sunda Sea, and has released its detachable passenger tube to crash-land in the jungle of a convenient island while the plane itself flies off in flames. There is a great storm, the jungle is loud with crashing trees, and the tube, with some children still in it, is dragged out to sea by wind and wave, while the rest scatter into the thickets. It is a terrible experience; but it is not one we share. Indeed, that story has to be pieced together from scattered hints in the boys' conversation. For, once they have slept an exhausted sleep well into the day, the experience has left virtually no scars on their consciousness, though they may have nightmares later. What Ralph is conscious of, and what occupies our delighted attention too, is the *Coral Island* glamour, the unspoilt beauty and excitement of trees, rock and beach. The fact that there are no grown-ups is primarily 'the delight of a realized ambition'. And as Ralph takes in the marvels of the island: the strange green shadows crawling over his body under the coconut palms, the surf breaking on the coral reef across the peacock-blue lagoon, the incredible beach-pool with its ready-made diving ledge, 'here at last was the imagined but never fully realized place leaping into real life'; the perennial boys' dream of which the worlds of *Coral Island* and *Treasure Island*, and the lake islands of *Swallows and Amazons*, are only shadows.

The first chapter resounds with 'the deep bass strings of delight'. The children gather to the casual summons of the Conch, they elect their leader, draw up laws, divide out function and prerogative; but we ought to be sharply aware of the inappropriateness of this kind of terminology. It is a wonderful game played under perfect conditions in perfect surroundings; and though it acts out memories of grown-up order, it can go on all day with no interference from grown-ups. There are the tensions that there are bound to be in any game, between Ralph and Jack and Piggy, but they are containable because the game is large and splendid enough to have acceptable parts for everyone.

There is not only 'government' but 'exploration'. A specific reminiscence of *Coral Island* occurs as Ralph and Jack, talking over the top of Simon's head, set off to explore their domain, and the aura of glamour is strong.

'They turned to each other, laughing excitedly, talking, not listening. The air was bright. Ralph, faced by the task of translating all this into an explanation, stood on his head and fell over.'

There is also something of the fairy-tale: 'The coral was scribbled in the sea as though a giant had bent down to reproduce the shape of the island in a flowing chalk line . . .', but, best of all, there is no giant, no ogre, it all belongs to them.

The 'glamour' is set, however, as it was not in *Coral Island*, against a real jungle, dense, damply hot, scratching. This is not a stroll through a nineteenth-century English wood with different trees. Demonstrably, discomfort and joy authenticate each other:

'Here, the roots and stems of creepers were in such tangles that the boys had to thread through them like pliant needles. Their only guide, apart from the brown ground and occasional flashes of light through the foliage, was the tendency of slope: whether this hole, laced as it was with cables of creeper, stood higher than that.

'Somehow, they moved up.

'Immured in these tangles, at perhaps their most difficult moment, Ralph turned with shining eyes to the others.

' "Wacco."

' "Wizard."

' "Smashing."

'The cause of their pleasure was not obvious. All three were hot, dirty and exhausted. Ralph was badly scratched. The creepers were as thick as their thighs and left little but tunnels for further penetration. Ralph shouted experimentally and they listened to the muted echoes.

' "This is real exploring," said Jack. "I bet nobody's been here before." '

It is the same with the rock-rolling, which is a specific comment on the scene in *Coral Island* where the boys are taken aback as a huge rock thunders down the mountain side. We are convinced that boys, faced by poised rocks like this, would behave as Golding's do, and there is a realistic sense of mass and force. The boyish argot and happy wrestling, the sweat and dirt and scratches, the shining eyes, all act with one another to make a world that is both solid and boyishly glamorous.

On the other hand, the darker elements we heard in the Sound of the Shell are not forgotten, though they are for the moment submerged. When we look more closely, we can see that the glamour is shot through with more sinister suggestions. Mirages are created for us as one of the physical realities of the South Seas; but we can never be unaware of the deceptiveness of appearances afterwards. The marching choir, and the way Jack treats it, recalls an army world of authority, arrogance and callousness, rather than the holy singing their uniform suggests. Jack's angry blue eyes and his habit of driving his sheath-knife into a tree-trunk hint at a capacity for dangerous violence. Hidden in the games there might also be an irresponsibility which has wider reverberations. When Ralph 'machine-guns' Piggy, or the 'enraged monster' of a rock crashes down 'like a bomb', we are perhaps primarily aware of a kind of 'innocence'. This is obvious in the episode of the piglet, where even Jack cannot kill 'because of the enormity of the knife descending and cutting into living flesh; because of the unbearable blood'. Gun and bomb are only a game, or a schoolboy phrase. But as soon as we replace game and cliché within the context of the situation that brought the children to the island, we may feel less assured; there is certainly blindness, perhaps something worse. The glamour of the 'natural' is also ambiguous. On the one hand there is pleasure in ripping off the clothes that speak of discipline and regimentation at school, the pleasure of nakedness in sun and water. On the other, it needs only a little of Piggy's 'ill-omened talk' about the realities of the situation to make a school shirt 'strangely pleasing' to put on again.

It is however worth pointing out that Golding in his opening chapter is seeking to re-imagine the Coral Island more truly. To imagine fully is, for him, to reveal indications like this existing naturally within the glamour; they are not simply put in like sign-posts pointing out a fore-ordained road. In retrospect, Ralph's standing on his head can be seen as a warning signal, but it is doubtful if any reader has ever taken it as other than a lifelike movement of joy at the time. It is perfectly ambiguous; that is its success. The diarrhoea might seem to invite allegorical translation —the body of man is no longer fit for Eden—but it is, no less, a realistic comment on the effects of eating nothing but fruit. The snake-clasp speaks of Eden too, but, more than any other detail, it is also eloquent of British schoolboy uniform.

In the first chapter, then, the coral island glamour is the dominant note in the Sound of the Shell, but there are one or two more sinister undertones if we really listen. The second chapter reverses the over- and undertones of the same concert. Glamour and game are still strongly present in the second Assembly, as rules are made up and Ralph's simple confidence in rescue out-weighs Piggy's fear.

' "This is our island. It's a good island. Until the grown-ups come to fetch us we'll have fun."
' Jack held out his hand for the conch.
' "There's pigs," he said. "There's food; and bathing water in that little stream along there—and everything." '

But 'everything' means more than glamour. When the idea of making a fire as a rescue signal takes hold, the coral island element of fun and adventure is still high, and one notices particularly what a sense of community it gives the boys. In this there is irony for the future.

'Ralph found himself alone on a limb with Jack and they grinned at each other, sharing this burden. Once more, amid the breeze, the shouting, the slanting sunlight on the high mountain, was shed that glamour, that strange invisible light of friendship, ad-venture, and content.
' "Almost too heavy."
'Jack grinned back.
' "Not for the two of us." '

But very soon the harsher sound of the Shell drowns the delight. It is clear that the making of rules may have as much to do with the desire to inflict punishment as the desire for order, for that, too, figures large in boyish games. The profound difference between the second assembly and the first is that the dark side of boys' psychology unmistakably makes its presence felt. The 'littlun' with the strawberry mark, describing his terrifying night-time vision of a 'snake-thing' or 'beastie', is voicing that part of the child's psyche that is beset with terror of the unknown in himself or his environment. That this is widespread among the children is shown by the intent eyes which fail to respond to Ralph's reassurances, and by the unexpectedly passionate reaction to his promise of rescue. There is nightmare as well as delight on this island. And finally, with the lighting of the fire, the note of irresponsibility in the Sound of the Shell reaches its full resonance.

We may feel impatient with Piggy's premature middle age: 'I bet it's gone tea-time. . . . What do they think they're going to do on that mountain'; and with the 'martyred expression of a parent who has to keep up with the senseless ebullience of the children'. But if we do, we soon learn the implications of acting 'like a crowd of kids'. We are made aware that innocence which consists largely of ignorance and irresponsibility may be far from harmless. Jack's arrogant chauvinism may find it easy to contrast English boys with savages, as Ballantyne complacently does. But as the fire spreads into the jungle because nobody looks further than keeping 'a clean flag of flame flying', we get a deeper insight.

'Small flames stirred at the bole of a tree and crawled away through leaves and brushwood, dividing and increasing. One patch touched a tree trunk and scrambled up like a bright squirrel. . . . The squirrel leapt on the wings of the wind and clung to another standing tree, eating downwards. Beneath the dark canopy of leaves and smoke the fire laid hold on the forest and began to gnaw. . . . The flames, as though they were a kind of wild life, crept as a jaguar creeps on his belly. . . . They flapped at the first of the trees, and the branches grew a brief foliage of fire. The heart of flame leapt nimbly across the gap between the trees and then went swinging and flaring along the whole row of them. Beneath the capering boys a quarter of a mile square of forest was savage with smoke and flame. The separate noises of the fire merged into a drum-roll that seemed to shake the mountain. . . . Startled, Ralph realized that the boys were falling still and silent, feeling the beginnings of awe at the power set free below them. The knowledge and the awe made him savage . . .'

Irresponsibility and ignorance liberate a power that is more and more 'savage', the 'squirrel' turns into a 'jaguar', and that power appeals to something 'savage' in the boys themselves. There were good reasons for bird and beast to be terrified by the harsh sound of the conch as it 'spread through the intricacies of the forest'. And not only bird and beast:

' "That little 'un—' gasped Piggy—'him with the mark on his face, I don't see him. Where is he now?"
'The crowd was as silent as death.
' "Him that talked about the snakes. He was down there—"
'A tree exploded in the fire like a bomb. Tall swathes of creepers rose for a moment into view, agonized, and went down again. The little boys screamed at them.
' "Snakes! Snakes! Look at the snakes!" '

'Like a bomb' isn't such a cliché now, nor is 'silent as death'. And if it is rather over-emphatic for Piggy to look 'into hell', since there is no real evil here, nevertheless we could say that if this was Eden, it has been destroyed; and there has been a 'snake-thing' manifest, not the creepers, but the children's own irresponsibility. The 'drum-roll' of the fire will remind us not only of savage tom-toms, but of the ceremony of execution. What the Sound of the Shell announced was also the coming of Death into the Garden.

As the second chapter focuses on the irresponsibility that had lurked largely undetected in the first, the third proceeds to explore the differences between the boys, present obliquely in the first expedition to the mountain:

'Here they paused and examined the bushes round them curiously.
   Simon spoke first.
   ' "Like candles. Candle bushes. Candle buds."

'The bushes were dark evergreen and aromatic and the many buds were waxen green and folded up against the light. Jack slashed at one with his knife and the scent spilled over them.

' "Candle buds."

' "You couldn't light them," said Ralph, "They just look like candles."

' "Green candles," said Jack contemptuously, "we can't eat them. Come on." '

Now however we begin to see below mere difference to division and antagonism. Ralph is trying desperately not only to build shelters, but a sense of 'home'; his instincts are to domesticate, to ward off terror by social community, to civilize, to provide against the littluns' nightmares the security of 'home'. Jack on the other hand rediscovers in himself the instincts and compulsions of the hunter that lie buried in every man. On all fours like an animal, he learns to flare his nostrils and assess the air, to cast across the ground for spoor. But the rediscovery is deeper than that, deeper even than 'the compulsion to track down and kill that was swallowing him up'. It is another dimension of awareness:

'The silence of the forest was more oppressive than the heat, and at this hour of the day there was not even the whine of insects. Only when Jack himself roused a gaudy bird from a primitive nest of sticks was the silence shattered and echoes set ringing by a harsh cry that seemed to come out of the abyss of ages. Jack himself shrank at this cry with a hiss of indrawn breath; and for a minute became less a hunter than a furtive thing, ape-like among the tangle of trees.'

In the very first paragraph of the book a bird had 'flashed upwards with a witch-like cry'. For Jack, as for human imaginations in all ages, the forest becomes not only a place to hunt in but also a place where one sometimes feels hunted; a place where the human being momentarily locates his intuitions of evil. Jack is in some ways 'reverting to savagery', so that the idea of rescue is hardly real to him any more and pigs matter more than a ship which might take him back to civilization; and so that his eyes sometimes have an 'opaque, mad look' from his compulsion to track and kill. But we are not simply to write this off as evil; he is also acquiring a kind of knowledge that Ralph singularly lacks and would be better for having. Jack understands the littluns and their nightmares, knows that it is not sufficient to proclaim that 'this is a good island'.

But as the difference between the experience of the two boys widens, so understanding becomes more difficult and antagonism mounts. They become 'two continents of experience and feeling, unable to communicate'; and in a later formulation, 'the brilliant world of hunting, tactics, fierce exhilaration, skill . . . the world of longing and baffled commonsense'.

Both of them are worlds apart from Simon, whom they consider faintly crazy. One can see easily enough what Golding meant by calling Simon a 'saint',* even a 'Christ-figure'. He acts as peace-maker between Jack and Piggy; he is to be seen suffering the little children to come to him, and getting them fruit where flower and fruit grow on the same tree. Afterwards, by himself in the heart of the forest, he has communion with nature or nature's God, in keeping with the poetic and mystical vein that contrasted so markedly, over the candlebuds, with the visions of the utilitarian and the hunter. What the communion is we do not know, but the place is like a church, as the darkness submerges 'the ways between the trees till they were dim and strange, as the bottom of the sea.'

'The candle-buds opened their wide white flowers glimmering under the light that pricked down from the first stars. Their scent spilled out into the air and took possession of the island.'

There is something saintly in Simon; but such labelling accomplishes far less than one might imagine. What brings Simon alive is not good works, or prayer, or faith, or a personal relationship with his creator, and a ten or eleven year old is a slender reed to bear the symbolic weight of saint, let alone of Saviour. This kind of reading will not stand up to examination. What does, demonstrably, bring Simon alive and make the passages where he is by himself among the finest things in the book, is the quality of the imagination that goes into creating his particular sensibility. He

* In an interview with F. Kermode, *Books and Bookmen,* 5 Oct. 1959.

is not so much a character, in the sense that the other boys are, as the most inclusive sensibility among the children at this stage.

The presentation of Simon in this chapter is not as symbolic as we think when it starts, and not symbolic at all as it goes on. Those littluns, if we look at them, are 'unintelligible' and 'inscrutable', not paradisal. The flowers and fruit raise the question of Eden, certainly, but they also come direct from *Coral Island*, and represent simple physical fact in the South Seas where many fruit trees bear all the year round. Moreover the enormous fecundity, 'the scent of ripeness and the booming of a million bees at pasture', will strike most readers as excessive for Eden.

This assertive fecundity sets the tone of the scene as it develops. What strikes us with considerable force, as Simon moves through the jungle, is that it is alien to man, and the way that its fecundity is rooted in dissolution. The pale flowers parasitic on the tall trunks are 'unexpected' by the civilized eye; the birds not only 'bright' but 'fantastic'. In the treetops life goes on 'clamorously'; the clearing below is an 'aromatic . . . bowl of heat and light'; the 'rapid' climber 'flaunted' red and yellow blossoms; the butterflies are 'gaudy', the colours 'riotous'. Underfoot the soil is markedly soft, and 'the creepers shivered throughout their lengths when he bumped them'. They are dropped 'like the rigging of foundered ships', and the climber is parasitic on a great tree that has fallen and died. This, clearly enough if we look, is no Eden and never was; there was no death in Eden, no riot or urgency, no creepiness.

Simon is the first child to know, to register fully, what the island and its jungle are like in themselves. The qualities that were present in Ralph's daydreaming at the finding of the conch, but have subsequently been overlaid by his need to think and lead, are fully realized in Simon. On the other hand, in solitary communion with nature, he taps Jack's sensitivity to the creepy as well as the beautiful. But he is outside the hunter mentality, the leader mentality, outside even himself. He exists in terms of his sensitivity to what is outside him. This allows him to know comprehensively. He not only registers the heat, the urgency, the riot, the dampness and decay; he also registers the cool and mysterious submergence of the forest in darkness, the pure beauty and fragrance of starlight and nightflower, the peace. Finally he not only registers both, but accepts them equally, as two parts of the same reality. It is these qualities of acceptance and inclusion that give us the 'Simon-ness' of Simon.

In his fourth chapter Golding turns from the 'biguns' to find out whether in the 'passionately emotional and corporate life of the littluns', when they are too small to have 'characters' or different 'points of view', there may be visible a basic showing-forth of the human, that will cast light on *all* the children. When Roger and Maurice romp through the 'castles' and 'interesting stones' and the 'complex of marks, tracks, walls, railway lines' of the littluns' domain, filling Percival's eye with sand, we are still in a recognizable moral landscape:

'. . . Percival began to whimper . . . and Maurice hurried away. In his other life Maurice had received chastisement for filling a younger eye with sand. Now, though there was no parent to let fall a heavy hand, Maurice still felt the unease of wrong-doing. At the back of his mind formed the uncertain outlines of an excuse.'

It is not very reassuring, however, because the suggestion is that 'morality' is a matter of conditioning and memory, not something innate; and if it depends on memory it may well fade as memory does. What about a child too young to have been conditioned, or to remember?

'Percival finished his whimper and went on playing, for the tears had washed the sand away. Johnny watched him with china-blue eyes; then began to fling up sand in a shower, and presently Percival was crying again.'

Johnny, almost the tiniest boy on the island, and the first to arrive to the summons of the Conch, was the only one whom the author then described as 'innocent'; but although his babyishness makes him morally innocent still, he is clearly not harmless: 'Johnny was well built, with fair hair and a natural belligerence.' The last words may be suggestive.

Meanwhile, rather older and bigger, Henry busies himself at the water's edge:

'The great Pacific tide was coming in and every few seconds the relatively still water of the lagoon heaved forwards an inch. There were creatures that lived in this last fling of the sea, tiny transparencies that came questing in with the water over the hot, dry sand. With impalpable organs of sense they examined this new field. Perhaps food had appeared where at the last incursion there had been none; bird droppings, insects perhaps, any of the strewn detritus of landward life. Like a myriad of tiny teeth in a saw, the transparencies came scavenging over the beach.

'This was fascinating to Henry. He poked about with a bit of stick, that itself was wave-worn and whitened and a vagrant, and tried to control the motions of the scavengers. He made little runnels that the tide filled and tried to crowd them with creatures. He became absorbed beyond mere happiness as he felt himself exercising control over living things. He talked to them, urging them, ordering them . . .'

There is a comment here both on the 'nature' of the 'myriad of tiny teeth'; and on the 'nature' of the human child whose activity goes beyond food and 'beyond happiness'. The chapter is revealed as a commentary on 'nature' and the 'natural man', Johnny's 'natural belligerence' and Henry's absorption in exercising control are basic elements of human nature.

With Roger these elements develop into something more serious. In him, what we noticed in Johnny and Henry becomes deliberately relished. As he throws stones at Henry he is both enjoying exercising power over him, and flirting pleasurably with the idea of hurting him. Roger is a sadist, that is why he is so forbidding. But his sadism is only an excessive development of what we have seen in Henry and Johnny, revealing itself openly because of the absence of grown-up sanctions. For the moment, he throws to miss:

'Here, invisible yet strong, was the taboo of the old life. Round the squatting child was the protection of parents and school and policemen and the law. Roger's arm was conditioned by a civilization that knew nothing of him and was in ruins.'

But that last sentence shows that the restraint is only a taboo, a social conditioning or superstition, not anything innate. The stone he throws, itself 'a token of preposterous time' which has 'lain on the sands of another shore', speaks of ages which dwarf the waxings and wanings of human civilizations. Moreover, Roger's civilization is in ruins itself because its morality was not sufficient to stop men throwing atom bombs at each other. While he remains conditioned, Roger's incipient sadism is shameful to him: 'a darker shadow crept beneath the swarthiness of his skin'. But we have been made vividly aware, in this chapter on 'The Natural Man', of Roger's connection with Johnny and Henry—who in turn link him with us—and also of the frailty of the conditioning which suppresses that element of basic human nature.

Soon we find out that it is not difficult to invent devices whereby the 'natural' man can be released from shame, and the boys can remember other facets of 'civilization besides its morality. Jack remembers the dazzle-paint with which ships hunting or hunted conceal themselves from their prey; his face-painting starts off as a reversion to civilization, not to savagery. But when it is done,

' He looked in astonishment, no longer at himself but at an awesome stranger . . . his sinewy body held up a mask which drew their eyes and appalled them. He began to dance and his laughter became a bloodthirsty snarling . . . the mask was a thing on its own, behind which Jack hid, liberated from shame and self-consciousness.'

Then the last crucial scene in this fourth chapter throws into relief the distance we have travelled. As a ship slowly passes on the horizon, Jack and his hunters let the fire go out while they kill their first pig. But once again there is no 'evil'. Jack is still 'conditioned'. The arm that failed to descend on the piglet before has descended now, but even the painted hunter still twitches at the memory of the blood; and he is still 'charitable in his happiness', wanting to include everyone.

Nevertheless his new knowledge, 'that they had outwitted a living thing, imposed their will on it, taken away its life like a long satisfying drink', provides a last link in the chain. We understand now why the compulsion to kill in Jack has meant so much more than the idea of rescue, and has only disguised itself in the need for meat. Moreover the leader, fresh from this total imposition of his will, cannot brook moral condemnation and humiliation at the hands of Ralph and Piggy. His violence and frustration finally erupt as he attacks Piggy and smashes a lens of his spectacles. Here, if we like, is the birth of evil, since irresponsibility has become viciousness; and a will imposed on an animal has now turned in destructive violence on a fellow human being. Yet we would be mistaken to read in these simple moralistic terms. For, as Ralph asserts his chieftainship, as the newly lit fire builds up like a barrier between him and Jack, as the link which bound him to Jack is broken and refastened to Piggy, we ought to remain aware of both sides. There is no defence of Jack's brutality, or his blindness to what it is that he and his hunters have done. Yet the whole chapter has, surely, given us a human understanding of Jack that Ralph and Piggy lack. If it is an emblematic detail that Piggy now only has one eye, it is also humanly fair. Golding's vision is scrupulous. As Jack throws to Piggy the meat that the fat boy is glad enough to eat, he cannot in his rage express his feelings about the dependence on his courage, his cunning and his self-dedication of those who presume to judge him. It is his fate to look round for understanding and find only respect.

III

We hear the sound of the Shell again, as Ralph summons a second meeting to try to clarify and set right what has gone wrong. Half way through the novel we get a measure of how far we have come; Ralph, discovering his dirt and realizing how much of his time he spends watching his feet to escape falling, 'smiles jeeringly' as he remembers 'that first enthusiastic exploration as though it were part of a brighter childhood'. He and we have grown up since the *Coral Island* stage. This assembly has to be not fun, but business. Ralph is having to realize what it means to be a leader, to take decisions in a hurry, to think things out step by step. This brings out a new scale of values, whereby he sees how little fatness, asthma, myopia and laziness weigh against Piggy's one great quality—his ability to think. But thinking is complicated by the fact that things look different in different lights, and from different points of view. 'If faces were different when lit from above or below—what was a face? What was anything?'

Ralph produces a workmanlike programme to put things straight: a plan for better sanitation, for keeping the fire going, for never cooking except on the mountain-top. But at a level deeper than any programme can reach, things are breaking up because the children are frightened. So the meeting becomes a testing-ground for Ralph's faith that what is wrong can be cured by talking things over reasonably, and coming to a democratic decision on fear itself, on whether or not there is a 'Beast'.

Jack's experience as hunter tells him that there is no fearsome animal on the island, but it also tells him why the littluns are frightened and have nightmares. They are frightened 'because you're like that'; because it is human nature to be frightened of the world and of life when it is dark and man is by himself. But for Jack, 'fear can't hurt you any more than a dream'. Fear can be lived with, and any Beast can be hunted and killed.

Piggy disagrees about fear. For him, everything can be explained and anything wrong, even in the mind, can be cured. Life is scientific. There is no Beast to fear, and there is no need to fear anything 'unless we get frightened of people'. This rationality, however, is greeted with scorn by those whose experience seems to tell them otherwise. Maurice wonders whether science has, in fact, explored the whole of existence and rendered everything explicable and known. The littlun who claims that the Beast comes from the water, and Maurice's memory of great squids only fleetingly glimpsed by man, are both pointers to a sea that may contain a great unknown.

The worst contempt of the meeting, however, is reserved for Simon, who thinks that there may be a Beast that is not any kind of animal: 'What I mean is . . . maybe it's only us.' He is trying to say that man may fear darkness and solitude because they rob him of the world he builds with his daylight mind, and force him to live with his own interior darkness. Perhaps there is something bestial, something absolutely dirty, not external to man but present deep in himself. But Simon is howled down even more than Piggy; and when the vote comes to be taken Ralph is forced to realize that fear cannot be dispelled by voting.

Worse, with the voicing of these internal fears and darknesses, the world of the Conch has been brought into question. Piggy is not only scorned, but attacked again by Jack; and this time Jack's rebellion against Ralph also comes out into the open, as well as his growing disrespect for Ralph's concept of order.

' "The rules!" shouted Ralph, "you're breaking the rules!"

' "Who cares?"

'Ralph summoned his wits.

' "Because the rules are the only thing we've got!"

'But Jack was shouting against him.

' "Bollocks to the rules! We're strong—we hunt! If there's a beast we'll hunt it down. We'll close in and beat and beat and beat—"

'He gave a wild whoop and leapt down to the pale sand. At once the platform was full of noise and excitement, scramblings, screams and laughter. The assembly shredded away. . . .'

Perhaps they only exchange one kind of 'play' for another. But we have a clear hint of what the other game is: what is happening is a re-enactment of the chant and mime of pig-killing that had fleetingly brought them together again on the mountain. But now, with Jack's 'beat and beat and beat', and littluns staggering away howling, it is taking on significance as an expression of their fear and an incantation against it, while the littluns' cries already foreshadow something worse.

Everywhere there is fear, even among the saner, more responsible ones. Ralph no longer dares to blow the Conch in case it should be disobeyed, and all pretence of order be lost in defiance. Piggy, in a telling gloss on what he had said at the meeting, admits to his inner, intuitive fear of Jack. Piggy has a rational mind, but we get a new insight into him; the asthma always appears when he is confronted by something beyond his control and understanding: 'I been in bed so much I done some thinking. I know about people. . . . If you're scared of someone you hate him but you can't stop thinking about him. You kid yourself he's all right really, an' then when you see him again; it's like asthma an' you can't breathe'. Piggy's asthma is an expression of fear, and hate, and how hate may grow from fear and alienation. His sickness tells Piggy truths of human motivation that his rational intelligence, and Ralph's health, are blind to. Jack hates Ralph and Piggy and would hurt both if he could, but Ralph is Piggy's one protection. Simon knows that this is true.'

There is fear. In their misery they call to mind the majesty and order of the grown-up world and long for 'a sign or something' from that world; some sort of message that would tell them how to sort things out. But instead:

'A thin wail out of the darkness chilled them and set them grabbing for each other. Then the wail rose, remote and unearthly, and turned to an inarticulate gibbering. Percival Wemys Madison, of the Vicarage, Harcourt St. Anthony, lying in the long grass, was living through circumstances in which the incantation of his address was powerless to help him.'

It may be that other grown-up addresses are as powerless as the vicarage, but the main thing is what has happened to the Sound of the Shell. Man-sound has become a cry of absolute fear —a child lost, alone, in an alien world of nightmare.

IV

The second half of the novel repeats the structure of the first; not however telling us new things, so much as showing the real depths of what we already know.

There is another battle in the night sky three miles above the island, another 'sudden bright explosion and a corkscrew trail'; but instead of the burning plane with the passenger tube, the body of a single parachutist, riddled with bullets, drifts down to lodge on the mountainside. This, with its immediate ironic response to the children's prayer for a sign from the grown-up world, is obviously the most contrived feature of the novel so far. Given the initial situation, the first five chapters have developed with a fatal inevitability, but this, splendid *coup de théâtre* though it be, betrays the novelist's sleight of hand. Yet is it perhaps no more than a fine flourish of rhetoric, to emphasize what we should already have realized.

This is not a novel about children, demonstrating Golding's belief that, without the discipline of grown-ups, children will degenerate into savages. We could think this only if we had forgotten what had brought the children to the island in the first place; and if we had forgotten, the first function of the parachutist is to remind us. The 'majesty of adult life' is a childish delusion. There is no essential difference between the island-world and the grown-up one. There too, order can be and has been overthrown; morality can be and has been inadequate to prevent wholesale destruction and savagery. The parachutist shows man's inhumanity to man, the record of what human beings have done to one another throughout human history. The children are revealing the same nature as the grown-ups, only perhaps more startlingly because of their age and their special situation. The child world is only a microcosm of the adult world.

But the children are already disposed to objectify their inner darkness and expect a Beast who will be other than themselves; so the parachutist becomes identified as the Beast, sitting on the mountain-top, preventing them from keeping the fire and the rescue-signals going. Only Simon cannot believe in 'a beast with claws that scratched, that sat on a mountain-top, that left no tracks and yet was not fast enough to catch Samneric. However Simon thought of the beast, there rose before his inward sight the picture of a human at once heroic and sick.' But Simon, the dreamer who bashes into a tree because he isn't looking where he's going, cannot be accepted uncritically.

The exploration to find the Beast's lair provides a continually ironic commentary on that first golden day and its *Coral Island* explorers. Instead of the peacock-blue of the calm lagoon, Ralph becomes aware for the first time of the other shore, where no reef offers protection against the endless rise and fall of the sea, those eroding tides that 'soon, in a matter of centuries . . . would make an island of the castle', and manifest a time as preposterous to man as Roger's stone:

'Now he saw the landsman's view of the swell and it seemed like the breathing of some stupendous creature. Slowly the waters sank among the rocks, revealing pink tables of granite, strange growths of coral, polyp, and weed. Down, down, the waters went, whispering like the wind among the heads of the forest. There was one flat rock there, spread like a table, and the waters sucking down on the four weedy sides made them seem like cliffs. Then the sleeping leviathan breathed out—the waters rose, the weed streamed, and the water boiled over the table rock with a roar. There was no sense of the passage of waves; only this minute-long fall and rise and fall.'

This, while it has the factuality of the conch and the weed, has no allure; its sinister quality is all the more powerful because it is so muted. It will not carry human meaning, the waters obliterate the table rock, it is utterly 'strange' to man. And if Ralph's mind gives it to him as the breathing of a gigantic beast, it is so inconceivable and alien that it is beyond terror.

Moments of resurgent glamour merely underline the irony. When Jack cries out excitedly 'What a place for a fort', or discovers a rock that could be rolled onto the causeway, there is a new sense of the need for protection against enemies that gives the excitement a more sinister undertone. It is with a sickening sense of their childishness that we watch through Ralph's eyes as the children roll a rock into the sea. Only, in the midst of his anger, we can detect the beginning of a diminished sense of civilization in Ralph himself:

' "Stop it! Stop it!"
 'His voice struck a silence among them.
' "Smoke."
 'A strange thing happened in his head. Something flittered there in front of his mind like a bat's wing, obscuring his idea.
' "Smoke."
 'At once the ideas were back, and the anger.
' "We want smoke. And you go wasting your time. You roll rocks." '

He can no longer convince them of the imperative need for rescue, and has to exert sheer authority against their mutinous grumblings.

If this is the ironic comment on the glamour of chapter one, chapter seven is even darker than chapter two. Ralph becomes vividly aware not only of how dirty and unkempt they have become, but how their standards have fallen so that they accept this situation as normal. Moreover what his eye had already taken in of this 'other side' of the island, now imprints a despair on the understanding:

'Here . . . the view was utterly different. The filmy enchantments of mirage could not endure the cold ocean water and the horizon was hard clipped blue. Ralph wandered down to the rocks. Down here, almost on a level with the sea, you could follow with your eye the ceaseless bulging passage of the deep sea waves. They were miles wide, apparently not breakers or the banked ridges of shallow water. They travelled the length of the island with an air of disregarding it and being set on other business; they were less a progress than a momentous rise and fall of the whole ocean. Now the sea would suck down, making cascades and waterfalls of retreating water, would sink past the rocks and plaster down the seaweed like shining hair: then, pausing, gather and rise with a roar, irresistibly swelling over point and outcrop, climbing the little cliff, sending at last an arm of surf up a gully to end a yard or so from him in fingers of spray.

'Wave after wave, Ralph followed the rise and fall until something of the remoteness of the sea numbed his brain. Then gradually the almost infinite size of this water forced itself on his attention. This was the divider, the barrier. On the other side of the island, swathed at midday with mirage, defended by the shield of the quiet lagoon, one might dream of rescue; but here, faced by the brute obtuseness of the ocean, the miles of division, one was clamped down, one was helpless, one was condemned, one was—'

Simon's quality of sheer faith—'*I just think you'll get back all right*'— brings a momentary lightening of despair. But the remembered cottage on the moors (where 'wildness' was ponies, or the snowy moor seen through a window past a copper kettle; and 'spectre', like the awful picture of the spider in the Magician book, was either not looked at at all, or else safely replaced between the *Boys' Book of Trains* and the *Boys' Book of Ships*) is utterly out of reach and unreal; a flimsy dream.

'Reality' is really wild nature; a charging tusker in the forest. But Ralph's first experience of the hunt is also a revelation of his own darker side; he discovers in himself the excitements, the 'fright and apprehension and pride' the others have known. Moreover, as the boys mime to one another again, their underlying tensions suddenly carry them away, including Ralph. They begin really to hurt Robert, who is acting the boar, and his cries of pain excite them still further. Ralph also feels the 'sudden thick excitement'; and as the chant rises ritually, as Robert screams and struggles, 'Ralph too was fighting to get near, to get a handful of that brown, vulnerable flesh. The desire to squeeze and hurt was over-mastering.' The 'game' is becoming dangerous; changing from an imitation of an action, to a ritual of release for fear, hatred, violence. It begins to need a victim to be wholly satisfactory.

Lastly, in this chapter of darker sides, Jack's hatred of Ralph emerges fully. As soon as he ceases to lead and control, Jack turns vicious; and he has clearly begun to hate the boy who bars his leadership. Any possibility of responsible and sane decision on this expedition is sabotaged as Jack insists on turning it into a personal challenge and duel. The next morning, seizing on Ralph's 'insult' to his hunters as excuse, Jack blows the conch and openly challenges Ralph's courage and leadership. When he fails to displace him, Jack splits away to form his own tribe.

What is most immediately remarkable however is the way that the language shows a reversion, not so much to savage, as to schoolboy: 'He isn't a prefect and we don't know anything about him. He just gives orders and expects people to obey for nothing. . . . All right then . . . I'm not going to play any longer. Not with you . . . I'm not going to be part of Ralph's lot—' Jack has never been able to make real to himself the 'democracy' of the conch, or the leadership of anyone else, or the need for responsible thought, or provision for rescue. All that makes sense to him is his own need to control others and impose himself, and hunting, because it is a kind of power assertion. The sudden humiliating tears, and the schoolboy language, affect us in very different ways. There is pathos in the realization that this bogey-figure is only a child. There is the equally sudden realization that power obsession is essentially childish when it is stripped of the disguises of the adult world.

What the coming of the 'Beast' has meant is an acceleration of the divisions among the children. Chapter eight corresponds with chapter three as an examination of the implications of the division. The hut-builders and home-seekers are now penned to the lagoon and the shoreline. They fear the forest and they no longer have either the view from the mountain or the view from the other side of the island; a limitation of consciousness as well as a limitation of area. Piggy's intellect conceives the daring idea of lighting the fire on the rocks instead of the mountain top; but they cannot disguise the fact that they want it as much for reassurance against the darkness as for rescue, the idea of which is getting steadily more remote. The fruit diet, the conch, and the platform are an insipid contrast to the life of the tribe. With the departure of Jack, Piggy can be fully recognized and given his rightful voice in affairs, but there remains a question mark over the range of his vision. Is it enough to regard Jack as the reason why everything is breaking up?

Jack, for his part, is 'brilliantly happy' now that his leadership is assured. Having renounced communal decision, and having no interest in rescue, the idea of a tribe becomes a satisfying way of life. There is the Beast, but they can keep out of its way and forget it; and if it is a hunter like themselves they can propitiate it with part of the kill. Since a tribe is a power-grouping in a world where strength counts, they believe 'passionately out of the depths of their tormented private lives' that they will dream less as they get nearer to the end of the island where the Fort is sited, and where they can barricade themselves. Hunting is no longer merely a question of getting meat, or even of exercising control or imposing oneself. As the hunters chase the sow through the oppressively hot afternoon, they become 'wedded to her in lust'; as they hurl themselves at her the violence has unmistakably sexual undertones; and finally the sow 'collapsed under them, and they were heavy and fulfilled upon her'. Roger's spear up the pig's anus only shows again a peculiar heightening of an impulse common to all. Having renounced the world of Piggy and Ralph, they begin to reveal what their world of hunting really is. It is only incredible if we think that 'bloodlust' is an empty word; for Golding, in opening out the 'thick excitement' we have already accepted, is vivifying what for him is not a cliché. There is an impulse both in lust and in killing, which seeks the obliteration of the 'other' as the most complete expression of the 'self'. The first killing satisfied Jack's bloodthirstiness 'like a long drink'; now his bloodlust is fulfilled in a killing-wedding.

Meanwhile Simon, as in chapter three, is in his place of contemplation, but this time not only watching the butterflies dance in the almost unbearable heat; he is watching also the place erupt with the squeals and the death-struggles, and watching the disembowelling, the decapitation, the offering of the head to the Beast. Into the quiet place have entered the buzzing flies, the spilled guts, the pool of dried blood, the vile thing on the sharpened stick. What Simon 'sees' is the Lord of the Flies, Baal-Zebub, the Devil. The title of the book tells us we have reached its heart.

Simon is tempted to pretend that nothing important has happened, that the offering was a 'joke', that he has made a 'mistake' in taking it seriously. The temptation is to avoid being thought 'batty' by Ralph and the others. He is then tempted to keep quiet for a different reason. To try to make the others see the truth about what has happened will be very dangerous. But these voices come from inside Simon's own head, and from the very first they only tell him what he already knows. In spite of hallucination, one thing he knows quite clearly is that what he sees is not the Beast, but 'Pig's head on a stick'. The worst temptation both for Simon and the reader is to see the encounter as a dialogue with the Devil. The difference is really the difference between Simon's view and Jack's:

' "Fancy thinking the Beast was something you could hunt and kill!" said the head. For a moment or two the forest and all the other dimly appreciated places echoed with the parody of laughter. "You knew, didn't you? I'm part of you? Close, close, close! I'm the reason why it's no go? Why things are what they are?" '

To imagine that the evil is in any way in the pig's head; or, more insidiously, that the pig's head symbolizes an evil external to the individual, is in fact to commit the error from which only Simon, in spite of his hallucination, is free. The pig's head is not a symbol of anything abstract or outside the boys, like a Devil; it is, like the parachutist, a solid object with a history that human beings have provided. The hallucination ends with Simon falling into the mouth: he faints into his own emergent consciousness of evil. What is wrong on the island is not Jack, as Ralph and Piggy think, or a Beast or Devil to be propitiated as Jack thinks. What is wrong is that man is inherently evil, as Simon has already maintained; the 'ancient, inescapable recognition' is of something in Ralph and Piggy, and Simon himself, as well as Jack and Roger. This being so, there is reason to fear. Simon has known already an assembly crying out 'savagely' as he tries to tell them of 'mankind's essential illness'. Now the inner voice foretells the cost of trying to tell the truth; warns him not to 'try it on . . . or else . . . we shall do you. See? Jack and Roger and Maurice and Robert and Bill and Piggy and Ralph. Do you. See?' The macabre echo of Ralph's initial promise that they would have 'fun' on the island gains point when we remember what we have already noticed the 'game' of the dance becoming.

At the same time it is important to realize how Golding's imagination guards him against the simple thesis on original sin he is generally credited with. For if there can be little doubt after reading the whole book that the author is inclined to share this view of Simon's, this is by no means necessarily the impression that the scene would leave on an unprepared reader. It carries both mystery and ambiguity. Golding has left it open to a humanist to call Simon's vision sick, or even morbid. Simon himself 'hears' the charge that he is an 'ignorant, silly little boy', a 'poor, misguided child' who thinks he can 'know better' than other people. It is true that he 'hears' these voices as cynical, or with the patronizing testiness of a schoolmaster; but with his point of view he would inevitably do so. This doesn't mean that they are necessarily to be discounted. They might be a wiser and truer valuation. Moreover his peculiarity has been insisted on ever since we first laid eyes on him as he pitched on his face in the sand. If the heat makes him delirious and causes him to faint—he may be a mild epileptic—then where does the delirium start? Only with the pig's head expanding like a balloon, or is that the climax? Or is it that his vision is so frightening that it brings on 'one of his times' as Piggy's fright brings on his asthma? How can we tell for certain what is true vision and what sick hallucination? or which is the product of what?

We cannot of course; any more than men have been sure in real life whether the 'prophets' and 'saints' were sick, or possessed, or crazy; or whether they were saner than everybody else, the only sane ones. What does it mean to say 'the fit of prophecy was upon him'? We may suspect what Golding's own view is—but if we read what is on the page the question is certainly posed. This is not because Golding is evading the issue; but because his primary concern is with the creation of an inclusive account. There are three explanations of what has gone wrong, not one; and they amount to three different readings of the universe.

Piggy and Ralph believe in the essential goodness of people and of the island. If things 'break up'—the implication is that they are naturally whole—then it is the fault of individuals, who deviate because there is something wrong with them. In the adult world Jack would be cured by a psychiatrist or restrained by greater power than his, which would also solve the Beast. Horror and wrong happen, but they are deviations which can be overcome by sanity and responsibility.

Jack thinks that evil and destruction are live forces. In a world of power there are powers at work that are stronger than man. But these powers (Beast, Devil, or God), can be propitiated by ritual, ceremony, sacrifice. And if this view strikes us as 'primitive', we ought to be aware at least that Jack has been open to some kinds of human experience that Ralph and Piggy have not; and moreover that it has not always been the least civilized cultures who have held such views.

Simon's view declares that blaming bad men, and the Devil, is both right and wrong, there is evil, but it is not either outside man or confined to certain men, it is in everyone.

Piggy has one eye; Jack is a savage; Simon is a queer little boy who has fits. There are question-marks over all three views. This is not a *roman à thèse*. We are likely to respond most to Ralph emotionally, since we see so much through his eyes, sharing his feelings and his troubles. What is at stake has however not yet been fully disclosed.

Golding's ninth chapter corresponds to the chapter on Natural Man in the first half: it is the test case for establishing a basic conviction. Both the 'View' and the 'Death' of its title are Simon's; the question is whether they endorse his 'explanation'. It is inevitable that Simon should climb the mountain—'what else is there to do?' He cannot believe in a Beast, but it is established as the Simon-ness of Simon to want to contemplate and understand everything. It is inevitable, too, that we should see behind his slow climb, an age-old symbolism that involves Ararat, Sinai, Calvary, and Parnassus:—

> *On a huge hill*
> *Cragged and steep, Truth stands, and hee that will*
> *Reach her, about must, and about must goe,*
> *And what the hill's suddennes resists, winne so.*

But once again, the truth is nothing abstract, and it may not be as simple as we think.

Simon contemplates the rotting corpse, the 'mechanics' of its 'parody' of animation, the 'white nasal bones, the teeth, the colours of corruption' and the foul smell, and he is violently sick. The flies in a dark cloud about the head remind us, accurately, of the pig's head; for both record what human beings have done. One is taken up into the other. But then, after the toil of the ascent, and the sickness that expresses and purges the horror of realization, Simon is able to bend down and release the figure from its tangle of lines. These have made it keep drawing attention to itself, in a parody not only of animation, but of death and resurrection again and again. It won't lie down. Simon, because he has understood, can break the pattern and stop the repetition. He can lay to rest the 'history' of man's inhumanity, can be free and can set free. He goes down to the others to tell them that what they have erected into the Beast is 'harmless and horrible'. On a deeper level he has shown that, by recognizing the truth of man's evil, as it is revealed in what men have done, and by purging oneself from it, one can be free to begin again.

The children, already conditioned to expect a Beast external to themselves, are in a state of hysteria. At the feast which Jack has staged to tempt as many as possible to join him, the sense of his own power has given him a newly sinister quality behind his paint. He has ceased to be Jack, he has become the Chief. Personality is overcome by power and he loses his name. He has begun to adopt ritual and oracular speech, he sits throned 'like an idol', waited on by acolytes, and 'power lay in the brown swell of his forearms: authority sat on his shoulder and chattered in his ear like an ape'. All day the heat has been building up static electricity in the atmosphere and the tension of the approaching thunderstorm is palpable. Now the human tension of an approaching showdown between Ralph and Jack stretches the nerves still more. As the lightning begins, and the first raindrops fall, so that 'home' and 'shelter' become meaningful again, it seems for a moment that the balance might swing in Ralph's favour. But Jack begins the dance, and we have seen very clearly how that has been turning into a protective ritual, whereby the children first externalize what they fear and hate, and then 'kill' it. As the lightning scars sky and eyes the hysteria mounts with it, in Ralph and Piggy too, until at its peak of intensity Simon staggers out of the forest into the circle, and is taken for the Beast, whose killing becomes no longer mime but reality. In frantic savagery, a 'desire, thick, urgent, blind' that grows out of the fear but is distinct from it, they 'do him in'. As Piggy and Ralph feared when things began to go wrong, they have become animals who 'leapt on to the beast, screamed, struck, bit, tore. There were no words, and no movements but the tearing of teeth and claws'. The squirrel, the jaguar, the ape, have taken human form.

Meanwhile in the high wind on the mountain-top the figure of the parachutist is lifted, and swept in a great arc across the beach to be carried out to sea, as the screaming boys flee into the darkness of the jungle. Again this is a magnificent *coup de théâtre*, a calculated artifice of rhetoric. But again it merely emphasises what we should already know. As the parachutist extended the meaning of the pig's head into a wider 'history' of man, so the parachutist has now been subsumed in Simon. The children have done what their fathers have done. The 'sign' is released, not because the children are free in Simon's terms, but because they have made a sign for themselves and need no other.

The death of Simon is the fact on which the whole novel turns and the evidence by which any theory of its significance must be judged. But the first condition it has to meet is whether it can convincingly happen. The answer must be sought in the resources of the novelist, and not in theology. How does Golding convince us that these boys could and would do this terrible thing?

V

The method of the novel is revelatory as we have seen: the uncovering of an unsuspected depth to something we have already accepted. A backward glance will reveal a cumulative process.

Far back, on the first golden day, Ralph learned Piggy's nickname (and immediately betrayed it, the first betrayal of the novel):

' "Piggy! Piggy!"
'Ralph danced out into the hot air of the beach and then returned as a fighter-plane, with wings swept back, and machinegunned Piggy.
' "Sch-aa-owl!"
'He dived into the sand at Piggy's feet and lay there laughing.'

It is a 'game', in 'fun'. Ralph would no more deliberately kill Piggy than Jack can kill the piglet caught in the creepers, though, when we remember how he comes to be here, we might see in Ralph a dangerous blindness to the realities the game imitates. But, looking back, that 'danced' has a reverberation of unease, as is the 'next time' with which Jack drives his knife into the tree when they have allowed the piglet to escape; for the next time will in fact see both the killing of a pig, and the invention of the chant and the dance which will eventually be the death of Simon. Is this a verbal trick, a 'plant'? Or can we accept that a game may be a game and still reflect attitudes that only want opportunity to fulfil themselves; that there is visible in the nickname itself a conversion of human into beast expressing animus towards a nature disliked and distrusted; and, in the mime of the killing, a putting of that animus into action, permissible and humorous simply because it is recognized as 'only a game'? Ralph has already been trying 'to get rid of Piggy'.

'Next time', the reluctance to kill anything with flesh and blood is overcome, though Jack still twitches. The mimed action of driving the knife, at least, can become real action. But while the kill has been taking place the fire has gone out and the ship has passed, so there is real tension between Ralph and Jack. The knife has just been shifted from Jack's right to his left hand, smudging blood across his forehead, when he 'stuck his fist into Piggy's stomach. Piggy sat down with a grunt — Jack stood over him. His voice was vicious with humiliation.' (We suddenly remember a less vicious voice, but still a fierce one: 'You should stick a pig . . .') And though Piggy doesn't bleed, he is half blinded. Does the animus of the nickname and the 'Sch-aa-ow!' look so far-fetched now, and is this a game?

Not long after this Maurice reduces the tension, and reunites everyone but Ralph, by miming what had actually happened in the killing of the pig. The others sing the chant they made up to keep step by as they carried it back, and to express their triumph:

'The twins, still sharing their identical grin, jumped up and ran round each other. Then the rest joined in, making pig-dying noises and shouting.
' "One for his nob!"
' "Give him a fourpenny one!"
'Then Maurice pretended to be a pig and ran squealing into the centre and the hunters, circling still, pretended to beat him. As they danced, they sang.
' "*Kill the pig. Cut her throat. Bash her in.*" '

Grin, pretence and dance show that this is still a game. But we have seen how in different, tense circumstances, game can turn into actual violence. The tension has only been reduced, it is still there, and what they are acting is already a reality. The line between game, pretence and reality is becoming much more difficult to draw.

After the assembly's discussion of the Beast, and the break-up in disorder (with Jack's 'If there's a beast we'll hunt it down! We'll close in and beat and beat and beat . . .'), there is dangerous tension again:

'The sound of mock hunting, hysterical laughter and real terror came from the beach . . .
' "If you don't blow, we'll soon be animals anyway. I can't see what they're doing, but I can hear."
'The dispersed figures had come together on the sand and were a dense black mass that revolved. They were chanting some-

thing and littluns that had had enough were staggering away howling.'

The dance is becoming a way of fencing off terror, or even of taking it out on a projection of its cause, not merely of reducing it. Although there is no necessary suggestion that the littluns have been beaten, there is ringing in one's ear, both the first suggestion of hysterical animality, and the first cries of terror. The black, revolving mass, like a miniature tornado, is a forbidding phenomenon.

Next time, Ralph is also involved in the experience of hunting, and is caught up into the heady excitement of the mime. The children had been frightened by the boar and, stronger than ever, there is the tension between Jack and Ralph. This time, in the ring, somebody really hurts Robert who is acting the pig; and his cries of pain and frenzied struggle to escape produce a 'sudden, thick excitement' which carries away Ralph too:

' "Kill him! Kill him." '

'All at once, Robert was screaming and struggling with the strength of frenzy. Jack had him by the hair and was brandishing his knife. Behind him was Roger, fighting to get close. The chant rose ritually, as at the last moment of a dance or a hunt.

' "*Kill the pig! Cut his throat! Kill the pig! Bash him in!*" '

'Ralph too was fighting to get near, to get a handful of that brown vulnerable flesh. The desire to squeeze and hurt was overmastering.

'Jack's arm came down; the heaving circle cheered and made pig-dying noises. Then they lay quiet, panting, listening to Robert's frightened snivels . . .

' "That was a good game." '

The borderline of game has however clearly been crossed, though in a way which often happens in games ('I got jolly badly hurt at rugger once'). This one has clearly revealed not only the riddance of tension and the acting out of fear and hatred, but the excitement of inflicting pain ('Behind him was Roger, fighting to get close'). And, for the first time, the actor has become the victim. The children feel that they are still not doing it properly, they need a drum, someone dressed up as a pig, no, more.

' "You need a real pig," said Robert, still caressing his rump, "because you've got to kill him."

' "Use a littlun," said Jack, and everybody laughed.'
It is said in fun, but we have become uncomfortably aware of the impossibility of positing a secure barrier between 'fun and games' and the darker passions. After this the hunters discover their bloodlust, and Roger the torturer is rewarded by a more satisfying scream than Robert's, but we are disturbingly reminded of Ralph as we see him 'prodding with his spear whenever pigflesh appeared'. We are not likely to be convinced when the 'voice' of the Lord of the Flies tells Simon: 'It was a joke really—why should you bother?'

Finally, in the lightning and thunder, this whole process of revelation reaches a climax. The boys are hysterical with fear of the lightning, with the tension of the 'static', with the conflict between Jack and Ralph at its highest. Clearly and unmistakably, dance and chant have wholly moved over from game or narrative, to a protective ritual: 'Piggy and Ralph, under the threat of the sky, found themselves eager to take a place in this demented, but partly secure society. They were glad to touch the brown backs of the fence that hemmed in the terror and made it governable'. The ritual enacts the hemming in, and then the killing, of their own terrors, all of which are projected into the Beast. So, now, the words of the chant have changed: '*Kill the beast! Cut his throat! Spill his blood!*' The individual loses himself in the mob; the chant 'began to beat like a steady pulse'. 'There was the throb and stamp of a single organism.' Then, out of the screams of terror, rises once again that other desire 'thick, urgent, blind', the desire to 'beat and beat and beat'.

We have learned how each of these scenes revealed something which contained the potentiality of the next. Though it is a terrible shock to inspect the end in one leap from the beginning, or vice versa, there is no leap in the whole progress. Each step is just the same measured advance on the last, and connected with the same inevitability to what went before and what is to come after. Can we point to any discontinuity? Can we, accepting all the other links, refuse our assent to the last? For the achievement has nothing to do with dogma, or the assertion of original sin. Golding does not tell us, he shows us, and that is what makes the book so terrifying, whatever our private beliefs may be. He shows us, at the end of his progress, how 'Roger ceased to be a pig and became a hunter, so that the centre of the ring *yawned emptily*'.

It is impossible not to feel the suspense and menace here; that last phrase crystallizes our whole experience and our own emotions of fear and waiting. We know we are on the brink of tragedy without being able precisely to locate it; we know that blind mouth must close—on something.

So, as chapter three linked Johnny and Henry and Maurice with Roger, and Roger with Jack's 'bloodthirsty snarling', we have now seen all the children as part of a process of becoming which has ended in a second, more terrible death. Whether Simon's view of man be just or not, the prophecy of what the fun and games would lead to has been fulfilled.

Simon's view, however, is not yet complete, even though he is dead, for it has not depended on him only as a character, but on a way of seeing. Golding appeals to no heaven to right the wrong of man and there is no God in his novel; but as the storm gives way to calm and the Pacific tide comes in, Simon's body is beautified, if not beatified, and his kind of vision operates once more, as we take in the fact of its disappearance.

The scene re-orchestrates the earlier one in which Simon's vision was first given to us. The riot and clamour then gave way to peace and beauty; they do so again. After the storm, after even the dripping and running water dies away, the world of tension and violence becomes 'cool, moist and clear'. The residue of the terror, Simon's body, still lies 'huddled' while 'the stains spread inch by inch'. But as night falls, there advances in the great on-ward flow of the tide, a line of phosphorescence in the 'clear water (which) mirrored the clear sky and the angular, bright constellations'. The essence of Simon's view, *acceptance*, becomes explicitly the mode of the writing.

'The line of phosphorescence bulged about the sand grains and little pebbles; it held them each in a dimple of tension, then sud-denly accepted them with an inaudible syllable and moved on.'

The broken detritus of man's barbarity is made into something beautiful, like a work of art: as a pebble is decorated with pearls, as the pitted sand is smoothed and inlaid with silver, so:

'The water rose further and dressed Simon's coarse hair with brightness. The line of his cheek silvered, and the turn of his shoulder became sculptured marble.'

But the beauty is not prettified, it co-exists with the alien, even the sinister and the ugly. The acceptance has to include the bubble of Simon's last breath escaping with a 'wet plop', an ugly, final sound. The beautifying creatures are 'strange, moonbeam-bodied ... with their fiery eyes and trailing vapours.' Indeed, a moment's reflection will tell us more: they are the same 'transparencies' that come in in the daylight scavenging for food like 'myriads of tiny teeth in a saw'.

It was the nature of Simon's view to see things inclusively in both their heroic and their sick aspects, to accept the daylight and the night-time mood. We have to see both tiny teeth and phosphorescent beautification; both the huddled figure, the stains, the wet plop, and the bright hair and sculptured marble; both the riot and clamour of 'day' and the calm, fragrant beauty of 'night'. In the endless processes of the universe, there is the reverse of the terror of the ocean on the 'other side': there is the 'Pacific':

'Somewhere over the darkened curve of the world the sun and moon were pulling; and the film of water on the earth planet was held, bulging slightly on one side while the solid core turned. The great wave of the tide moved further along the island and the water lifted. Softly, surrounded by a fringe of inquisitive bright creatures, itself a silver shape beneath the steadfast constellations, Simon's dead body moved out towards the open sea.'

The studiously scientific description intimates a sense of quiet order; a huge and universal perspective, which yet does not dwarf because it includes everything, accepts Simon as he had accepted it. In a sense we are asked to experience the fact that he has 'got back to where he belonged', to a vision big and inclusive enough to be 'steadfast', to accept and order all. To be true to Golding's book, we must remember the heroism as well as the

sickness: not only the Lord of the Flies, the corrupting flesh of the
Parachutist, the teeth and claws and huddled body; but also the
vision that is given the beautification of this sea-burial.

To the 'world of longing and baffled common-sense' what has
happened is shameful and obscene. Ralph struggles, trapped between shame and honesty. Piggy's shrill outrage marks his un-
willingness to admit what cannot be hidden. There is attempted
excuse: 'It was dark. There was that—that bloody dance. There
was thunder and lightning and rain. We were scared.' But Ralph
knows how much more was involved. Piggy's excited 'gesticulat-
ing, searching for a formula' is stopped short by a voice in which
'there was loathing, and at the same time a kind of feverish excitement' as well as a note 'low and stricken'. But Piggy will not
accept guilt:

'Ralph continued to rock to and fro.
  ' "It was an accident," said Piggy suddenly, "that's what it was.
An accident." His voice shrilled again. "Coming in the dark—he
hadn't no business crawling like that out of the dark. He was
batty. He asked for it." He gesticulated widely again. "It was an
accident."
  ' "You didn't see what they did—"
  ' "Look, Ralph. We got to forget this. We can't do no good
thinking about it, see?"
  ' "I'm frightened. Of us. I want to go home. O God I want to
go home."
  ' "It was an accident," said Piggy stubbornly, "and that's that."
  'He touched Ralph's bare shoulder and Ralph shuddered at the
human contact. "And look, Ralph," Piggy glanced round quickly,
then leaned close—"don't let on we was in that dance." '

It is clear on one level that this amounts to a severe criticism
of Piggy—'We never done nothing, we never seen nothing'—and
this attempt to deny their involvement, this last pathetic effort
to hang on to the simple view that evil is something done by
other people, compares ill with Simon's. But it is pathetic, because
no one is fooled: 'Memory of the dance that none of them
had attended shook all four boys convulsively.' They have got
'frightened of people' as Piggy had said they should not. All that

was complacent about Piggy's point of view in the assembly has been pinpointed. 'We can't do no good thinking about it' is not a statement that inspires.

This however is not a disposal of 'the humanistic view of man', nor, as was obvious after the first assembly, does Piggy merely represent a complacent Humanism. We would even be misreading if we thought that this episode was a weighted demonstration of the superiority of Simon's belief in original sin. For, while it is easy to dispose of what is complacent and narrow in Piggy's view, it is not at all easy to dispose of the view itself; nor is it meant to be. For Piggy has a challenging point. Simon's view, we must remember, was of 'mankind's *essential* illness'. What has happened has proved conclusively that there is evil in all human beings, even in those who try to be rational and civilized. But this does not amount to any proof that the illness is of the *essence* of man. May it not be an 'accident', as one might argue medical illnesses are, produced by special circumstances? That is precisely the question that Piggy poses, and it is a good question for Golding to ask so openly.

Had Simon any business crawling out of the dark like that? Wasn't he batty? From his own point of view even, isn't the 'saint' crazy to believe that people he sees as inherently evil can be so easily converted into the belief that the projection of their inner darkness is 'harmless and horrible'? Doesn't he, on any point of view, allow too little for fear of the dark that he doesn't share? We remember Ralph having to rebuke Simon for terrifying the littluns, in the corresponding chapter in the first section, by moving about in the dark outside the shelters, and he was surely right to do so. That early episode can now be seen to have cast a long shadow. This is a searching psychological question too. If the martyrdom is partly created by the martyr, can he not be truly said to have 'asked for it'? Lastly, if the tragedy happens because of the coming together, at some uniquely dangerous corner, of the special circumstances of hysteria and the special 'case' of the martyr, is it not only the simple truth to speak of accident rather than essence? One is not suggesting that the vision of Simon may not be the more convincing and conclusive; nor that we are not inclined to take the 'impaired vision' of Ralph and Piggy in deeper senses than the physical. But Simon's vision establishes itself, if it does so, by its own imaginative force and the opposing views are given no inconsiderable weight.

On the other hand, both 'longing' and 'common-sense' are clearly shown as more and more vulnerable to the darkness. The longing for rescue is more difficult to keep alive, the flapping curtain in Ralph's brain more pronounced, and the barricades of commonsense can operate only in daylight. Ralph's nightly game of 'supposing' fails to comfort, because the 'wildness' even of Dartmoor and the ponies is no longer securely attractive.

'His mind skated to a consideration of a tamed town where savagery could not set foot. What could be safer than the bus centre with its lamps and wheels?

'All at once, Ralph was dancing round a lamp standard. There was a bus crawling out of the bus station, a strange bus . . .'

The mind releases its secret knowledge that there is no safe barrier between civilization and wild nature. The Conch is becoming emptied of significance, seen as fragile: 'I got the conch' is spoken with hysterical irony by a Ralph who sees no future in what he still pathetically caresses.

For Jack's tribe, on the other hand, the death of Simon is a catalyst. They know the horrors of the island well enough; what they proceed to build up is the full tribal technique for coping with them. They barricade themselves in the Castle with the huge rock poised over the causeway and sentries posted. This is an extension into daily living of the 'ring'; and the 'stamp of a single organism' is preserved by the absolute authority of the Chief. They know well enough what they have done, but they overcome the knowledge, not by hiding it, but by extending their projection of evil into the Beast. They persuade themselves that the Devil can take different shapes, and be 'killed' in those, but 'How could we — kill — it?' So far they have realized Simon's truth ('Fancy thinking the beast was something you could hunt and kill'); but they still see the Beast as outside them, an evil capricious force that must be placated. The world has fully become a power situation of 'us' and 'not us'. The strong Beast must be propitiated; the tribe makes a surprise attack on 'Ralph's lot' to take what they want. The Chief finally secures his authority when he captures the means of fire in Piggy's glasses. But the 'vicious snarling', hitting, biting, scratching, are now deliberately, not accidentally, directed against their fellows.

In this chapter, called *The Shell and the Glasses*, we see that for the tribe the glasses have lost all connection with sight; it is nothing to them that Piggy will be virtually blind and the Conch has no meaning whatsoever, so that the raiders show no interest in it. The release of their inner darkness in the killing of Simon has meant an end of all that the Conch stood for. If the world is one of power, there is nothing for power to be responsible to. Jack does not have to give reasons for beating Wilfred; and this is a revelation to Roger, who receives 'as an illumination . . . the possibilities of irresponsible authority'. The death of Simon precipitates the worst element in the tribe: there is nothing now but power, war against 'outsiders', and a darker threat behind.

The stage is set for a final confrontation, recalling the assembly at the end of the first section. The Conch sounds again, 'the forest re-echoed; and birds lifted, crying, out of the tree-tops, as on that first morning ages ago'; but now 'both ways the beach was deserted'. If the savages will not come to the Conch however, Piggy is determined to take the Conch to them.

' "What can he do more than he has? I'll tell him what's what. You let me carry the conch, Ralph. I'll show him the one thing he hasn't got."

'Piggy paused for a moment and peered round at the dim figures. The shape of the old assembly, trodden in the grass, listened to him.

' "I'm going to him with this conch in my hands. I'm going to hold it out. Look, I'm goin' to say, you're stronger than I am and you haven't got asthma. You can see, I'm goin' to say, and with both eyes. But I don't ask for my glasses back, not as a favour. I don't ask you to be a sport, I'll say, not because you're strong, but because what's right's right. Give me my glasses, I'm going to say—you got to!"

'Piggy ended, flushed and trembling. He pushed the conch quickly into Ralph's hands as though in a hurry to be rid of it, and wiped the tears from his eyes. The green light was gentle about them, and the conch lay at Ralph's feet, fragile and white.

A single drop of water that had escaped Piggy's fingers now flashed on the delicate curve like a star.'

The words are brave, but the mode of their reception is already established in the irony of the different salt water that has become the element of the 'fragile' white shell. And, though Ralph dimly 'remembered something that Simon had said to him once, by the rocks', Simon's fate has hardly made his faith reassuring. Nevertheless Piggy is given real stature at this moment, the stature of tragedy.

On the causeway before the castle, we hear the Sound of the Shell for the last time as there is a final hopeless attempt to summon back into the painted savages the consciousness of the British schoolboy. But the language of reminder has lost its meaning, because the standards it appeals to are gone. The 'silvery, unreal laughter' from the height is an insuperable element, dissolving the appeal to civilized value before it can have any effect: ' "If he hasn't got them he can't see. You aren't playing the game—" The tribe of painted savages giggled and Ralph's mind faltered.' The idea of rescue has quite vanished, and the protest of the twins against their imprisonment only underlines the helplessness, the lack of language, of their cries 'out of the heart of civilization': 'Oh I say!'; '—honestly!'

There is only denunciation, and the language can only be ironic. When Ralph shouts 'You're a beast, and a swine, and a bloody bloody thief', it is only our ears that take in the literal meaning, and even to us it is clear that it is really only an invitation to battle, for moral values have no validity here.

Piggy stops the battle by holding up the Conch . . . for the last time we see the emblem at work: 'The booing sagged a little, then came up to strength. "I got the Conch".' But it is only a momentary memory, and when they do listen to Piggy, it is as a clown. While he speaks, there sounds through the air the faint 'Zup!' of the stones that Roger is dropping from the height, where his hand rests on the lever of the great rock, feeling how 'some source of power began to pulse' in his body. From his height the boys are not even human: 'Ralph was a shock of hair, and Piggy a bag of fat.' Then comes the final challenge:

' "I got this to say. You're acting like a crowd of kids."

'The booing rose and died again as Piggy lifted the white, magic shell.

' "Which is better—to be a pack of painted niggers like you are, or to be sensible like Ralph is?"

'A great clamour rose among the savages. Piggy shouted again.

' "Which is better—to have rules and agree, or to hunt and kill?"

'Again the clamour and again—"Zup!"

'Ralph shouted against the noise.

' "Which is better, law and rescue, or hunting and breaking things up?"

'Now Jack was yelling too and Ralph could no longer make himself heard. Jack had backed right up against the tribe and they were a solid mass of menace that bristled with spears. The intention of a charge was forming among them; they were working up to it and the neck would be swept clear. Ralph stood facing them, a little to one side, his spear ready. By him stood Piggy still holding out the talisman, the fragile, shining beauty of the shell. The storm of sound beat at them, an incantation of hatred. High overhead, Roger, with a sense of delirious abandonment, leaned all his weight on the lever . . .

' . . . The rock struck Piggy a glancing blow from chin to knee: the conch exploded into a thousand white fragments and ceased to exist. Piggy, saying nothing, with no time for even a grunt, travelled through the air sideways from the rock, turning over as he went. The rock bounded twice and was lost in the forest. Piggy fell forty feet and landed on his back across that square, red rock in the sea. His head opened and stuff came out and turned red. Piggy's arms and legs twitched a bit, like a pig's after it has been killed. Then the sea breathed again in a long, slow sigh, the water boiled white, and pink, over the rock; and when it went, sucking back again, the body of Piggy was gone.'

The boy has now literally been seen and killed like a pig; the implications of his nickname fully brought out; what they hated about him turned into 'red stuff' welling out of an 'opened' head. The 'table' Ralph saw has become a place of sacrifice. 'Viciously, with full intention', Jack hurls his spear at Ralph to kill, while 'anonymous devil faces swarmed across the neck', and another human Pig 'obeying an instinct he did not know he possessed' swerves in his flight, and goes crashing through foliage to be hidden in the forest. 'Something', the words echo from far back, 'squealed and ran in the undergrowth'. We hear a familiar sound, but this time it is human, and what the Sound of the Shell has become is 'a great noise as of sea-gulls': the harsh sound not of the conch, but of the hunters screaming hatred and bloodlust.

The hunt is called off, for the moment. But there advances on Sam and Eric, finally liberated from all control, almost brushing Jack aside because of the 'nameless, unmentionable authority' that surrounds the Executioner and Torturer, the figure of Roger: 'The yelling ceased, and Sam and Eric lay looking up in quiet terror.' There is silence, but we know, although we do not hear it yet, that we are listening for something. Gulls' scream and hunters' cry, and the high scream of a victim in pain, these are only postponed, suspended—for a moment.

VI

Alone and terrified, Ralph goes on trying to believe that 'they're not as bad as that. It was an accident'; but he knows better. There is no further reliance on their 'common sense, their daylight sanity'; and there is that 'undefinable connection between himself and Jack; who therefore will never let him alone; never'. Jack can never be free from the Ralph-in-him till Ralph is dead. There can be no end to this game. It is the nightmare of 'play' that must go on and on past nightfall, with no rules, no 'Sir' or Mummy or Daddy to call a halt.

'Might it not be possible to walk boldly into the fort, say—"I've got pax," laugh lightly and sleep among the others? Pretend they were still boys, schoolboys who had said "Sir, yes, Sir"—and worn caps? Daylight might have answered yes; but darkness and the horrors of death said no. Lying there in the darkness he knew he was an outcast.

' "'Cos I had some sense." '

But this echo of Piggy poses once more the question of whether the reason for what has happened does not lie a good deal deeper. Ralph suddenly finds himself in the clearing, where a 'pig's skull grinned at him from the top of a stick':

'He walked slowly into the middle of the clearing and looked steadily at the skull that gleamed as white as ever the conch had done and seemed to jeer at him cynically. An inquisitive ant was busy in one of the eye sockets but otherwise the thing was lifeless.

'Or was it?

'Little prickles of sensation ran up and down his back. He stood, the skull about on a level with his face, and held up his hair with two hands. The teeth grinned, the empty sockets seemed to hold his gaze masterfully and without effort.

'What was it?

'The skull regarded Ralph like one who knows all the answers and won't tell. A sick fear and rage swept him. Fiercely he hit out at the filthy thing in front of him that bobbed like a toy and came back, still grinning into his face, so that he lashed and cried out in loathing. Then he was licking his bruised knuckles and looking at the bare stick, while the skull lay in two pieces, its grin now six feet across. He wrenched the quivering stick from the crack and held it as a spear between him and the white pieces. Then he backed away, keeping his face to the skull that lay grinning at the sky.'

Again, Golding himself is silent. We are asked to measure and judge the contrast for ourselves; the skull doesn't, in fact, hold 'answers'. There is the white conch, and the white skull; Ralph's and Piggy's 'meaning', and Simon's. There is the view that accepts the evil and takes it to himself; there is the 'sick fear and rage', the hitting out that expresses the loathing and rejection of something utterly alien. 'What was it?' It is for us, finally, to say.

The next day the inevitable hunt begins. Great rocks, 'big as a car, a tank' are sent crashing down like bombs in a full-scale war. This is not game, not defence, not even the work of a single sadist, but military strategy. We notice again the familiar opening-out technique spreading from that first delighted dispatch of the 'enraged monster' into the jungle. The forest is set on fire again, but deliberately this time, the smoke is not for rescue, and the drum-roll heralds an execution quite literally. Worse, it heralds a propitiatory sacrifice to a new Lord, not Beelzebub, but Moloch; for though Ralph does not recognize the meaning of the stick sharpened at both ends, we do. Ralph's head will replace the pig's. And Ralph is becoming an animal, launching himself snarling, knowing the experience of being hunted, desperate, with no time to think, and dreading always the flapping curtain in the mind which might black out the sense of danger and make him mindless. Finally he does become Pig. His last thought of rescue, the hopeless memory of Simon's groundless faith, is replaced by a 'scream of fright and anger and desperation. His legs straightened, the screams became continuous and foaming. He shot forward, burst the thicket, was in the open, screaming, snarling, bloody.' There is the cry of the hunters, the roar of the fire, the 'desperate ululation' advancing 'like a jagged fringe of menace', the narrowing pig-run to the beach past the blazing shelters, then certain and horrible death:

'Then he was down, rolling over and over in the warm sand, crouching with arm up to ward off, trying to cry for mercy.

'He staggered to his feet, tensed for more terrors, and looked up at a huge peaked cap . . . He saw white drill, epaulettes, a revolver, a row of gilt buttons down the front of a uniform.

'A naval officer stood on the sand, looking down at Ralph . . .'

There is probably no remark about his work that Golding regrets more than referring to this ending as a 'gimmick'.* For though there is device, there is no suggestion of trickery. The murder of Ralph takes place in the imagination as surely as if Golding had written FINIS under the word 'mercy'. But what happens is like turning on the lights in the theatre before the curtains close, and then letting the cast suddenly step outside the action that had mesmerized us. We are forced to distance the completed experience, and measure how far we have travelled. For that measurement Golding needed Ralph's eyes.

The change of perspectives justifies itself as a challenge to us in the midst of shock. Suddenly we see 'a semicircle of little boys,

* Interview with Kermode, *Books and Bookmen*.

their bodies streaked with clay, sharp sticks in their hands'; some tiny tots 'brown, with the distended bellies of small savages'; a 'little scarecrow' who 'needed a bath, a haircut, a nose-wipe, and a good deal of ointment'; and another 'little boy who wore the remains of a black cap on his red hair and who carried the remains of a pair of spectacles at his waist'. Is that all?

There could have been no more dramatic way of bringing home to us how much more there is, than thus forcing us to measure the gap that separates what the officer sees from what we ourselves know, through seeing with the eyes of Ralph. To our horror, the officer's language reveals the kind of attitudes to children and coral islands that we might very well have started with; each word is filled with corrosive irony: 'Fun and games . . . Having a war or something? . . . I should have thought that a pack of British boys—you're all British aren't you—would have been able to put up a better show than that . . . Like the Coral Island.' We measure the implications of that 'pack' against the Jack who had voiced just such a confidence in the British at the second meeting. 'We've got to have rules and obey them. After all, we're not savages: We're English; and the English are best at every-thing. So we've got to do the right things.'

But the novel has gone beyond being a critique of *Coral Island*; and there is much more involved than our better knowledge of what children are like. For the measure of the officer's inadequacy is not only that he doesn't know what children are like, but that he doesn't know what adults are like. For as our eyes take in the uniform, the revolver and sub-machine gun, the 'trim cruiser' on which the eyes that are embarrassed by the children prefer to rest, we know the significance of uniforms and weapons as the officer does not. 'Having a war or something' . . . in thinking of himself as not only superior to, but even other than the children, it is the man that is the child.

It is Ralph who is 'grown-up', but he shows his adulthood by weeping. Golding needs him not only to see, but to register the proper response in pain and grief.

'Ralph looked at him dumbly. For a moment he had a fleeting picture of the strange glamour that had once invested the beaches. But the island was scorched up like dead wood—Simon was dead

—and Jack had . . . The tears began to flow and sobs shook him'
He gave himself up to them now for the first time on the island;
great, shuddering spasms of grief that seemed to wrench his
whole body. His voice rose under the black smoke before the
burning wreckage of the island; and infected by that emotion, the
other little boys began to shake and sob too. And in the middle
of them, with filthy body, matted hair, and unwiped nose, Ralph
wept for the end of innocence, the darkness of man's heart, and
the fall through the air of the true, wise friend called Piggy.'

This is the truest of all the sounds; in the sense that it shows the
human response to all the others that Golding wishes to leave in
our ears.

It is however a *response*, not an answer. What Ralph weeps for is
the failure of Piggy's idea of a rational world, Piggy's friendship,
Piggy's intelligence. We might ask whether there has not been a
truer 'innocence', a greater 'wisdom', a more loving 'kindness', a
better attitude to 'darkness' and the 'fall'. If Ralph weeps for
Piggy, may it be because he only knows one degree better than the
officer? Ought we to be weeping . . . for Simon? But, though we
may ask such questions, the novel will give us no dogmatic
answer. Golding's fiction has been too complex and many-sided
to be reducible to a thesis and a conclusion. *Lord of the Flies* is
imagined with a flexibility and depth which seem evidence of
finer art than the polish and clarity of its surface. Even in his first
novel, it is not explanation and conclusion, but imaginative impact which is finally memorable.

II

THE INHERITORS

(1955)

To come to *The Inheritors* fresh from *Lord of the Flies* is to be made quickly aware of opacity and puzzle not present in the earlier novel. We feel uncertain about both the direction of the narrative and the status of the characters, and it is often difficult to see, on the simplest level, what exactly is going on. It is only as we continue to read that we begin to place our difficulty. The style is simple enough, with a vivid sensuousness that carries us forward in spite of uncertainties. The difficulty lies in the point of view:

'As he watched, one of the farther rocks began to change shape. At one side a small bump elongated then disappeared quickly. The top of the rock swelled, the hump fined off at the base and elongated again then halved its height. Then it was gone.'

It is because we are placed behind a pair of eyes that only perceive, and cannot understand, that we may have no more idea than Lok what it is that he is watching. Perception is itself, no more; not what we normally expect it to be, a stepping stone to an idea rapidly transferred from the eye to the mind. We come to realize that Golding's Neanderthalers live through their senses. They can infer to a limited extent from their own experience but they cannot go beyond it because they cannot deduce or reason. What we watch is the moment when Neanderthal Man first confronts Homo Sapiens, but all we can be given is sharply focused visual detail of shape and movement. Lok cannot conceive a human creature with a nature wholly unlike his own; cannot deduce such a creature from the behaviour he sees; and consequently cannot understand that behaviour at all. We share his limitations as we use his eyes.

It is of course open to us to use our own reasoning powers on his experience. At several points before this one we could have deduced not only the existence of New Men but the difference in nature between them and Lok's People. They must have removed the communal bridge-log to make their own huge fire; it was their smoke that caused Lok to make his almost fatal mistake on the cliff; they must have been responsible for the disappearance of Ha.

As we watch the instinctive miming of Lok the tracker we can accurately deduce the differing natures of Men and People and hazard a shrewd guess at what must have happened to Ha; and once we have deduced Man's hostility, suspicion and fear, the opacity vanishes and Lok's vision sharpens for us. What he watches so uncomprehendingly is a Man treating him as though he were a predatory enemy, a man not 'another', as simple loving and fearless as himself, but peering stealthily round and above the rock he uses as cover, spying.

Any such process of understanding has however to take place outside the fiction itself. The only incitement to interpret, deduce, explain, comes from our own intellectual frustration at being confronted with the apparently unintelligible. This is not what concerns Golding. The response he seeks is essentially the imaginative one of knowing what it is like to look through eyes empty of thought and as innocent of judgement as of hatred, suspicion and fear. He had devoted all his resources to creating that experience, and Lok's incomprehension is a vital part of it. We cannot be prevented from analysing and judging, nor need we; but we would indeed 'murder to dissect' if we thought that analysis and judgement were supposed to be the object of the exercise. Imaginative exploration, through a vision quite unlike our own, comes first. Understanding will follow, but more slowly and mysteriously from a distillation of experience, and it may result in something far more complex than a black-and-white contrast between Men and People. If ever there was a book meant to be read through in one imaginative act, by which we seek to become, and to judge only when the experience is complete, it is *The Inheritors*.

Any account of the novel that does not centre on its qualities of imaginative exploration ought then to be highly suspect. It is easy to suggest apparently useful ways of looking at it, but it is more important to see just how they miss the mark. The epigraph suggests, for example, that Golding wishes to overturn H. G. Wells' account of the Neanderthaler (both in *The Outline of History* and his tale *The Grisly Folk*) as *Lord of the Flies* had subverted Ballantyne. So one could approach the novel as a fictional essay in prehistory, based on considerable knowledge of anthropology, and seeking to substitute a truer picture of Neanderthal Man for one distorted by faulty assumptions. The funeral of Mal, for instance, comes across vividly in just this archaeological and anthropological way.

Yet the novel is also a fictional *tour de force*, taking us to an otherworld and othertime that we enjoy for their own sake, irrespective of historical considerations. Isn't this science fiction if it is science at all: taking us backwards as space fiction takes us forwards, substituting Neanderthalers for Martians, but giving us the same pleasure in the exotic, or the familiar seen through strange eyes?

Yet again, the fiction seems to point to allegory. Golding's Neanderthalers are the true innocents, the harmless ones, not only without evil themselves but incapable of understanding it when it meets and destroys them. They run to meet their killers in love, and are quite incapable of preserving themselves by destroying their oppressors. The title reveals a bitter irony, for it is not the meek who inherit the earth but the killers of the meek. We can contrast every aspect of the 'fallen' life of the New Men with the 'unfallen' life of the People, and take home to ourselves the message that comes from realizing the nature of our ancestry. We may then reach the point when the novel seems no longer essentially about Neanderthal Man at all, but merely uses him as a way of analysing the nature of the Fall. Emblems now emerge: the dead tree from which Lok and Fa look down on the destruction of their Eden; the waterfall which marks the limit of innocence, but beyond which the sinful have to travel towards a line of darkness.

Each of these ways of looking seems momentarily convincing; each indeed contains an aspect of truth; but as soon as one turns back to the novel itself, all are manifestly unsatisfactory, suggesting something smaller and less valuable than what is actually there. For what they all leave out of account is the primary experience of reading: a reaching out through the imagination into the unknown. The mode of *The Inheritors* is one of discovery, not an exercise in literary archaeology, science fiction or a fable about the Fall. By committing himself so radically to the viewpoint of his People, by doing his utmost to ensure that he is kept out of his normal consciousness, Golding does contrive to see things new, not merely see new things. His imagination is at full stretch throughout because of the challenge of his basic form; it has to be, for the novel to be written at all. That is the real significance of the point of view.

It also drives his style to produce its finest effects. Simon's kind of perception through the senses dominates and does virtually all the work because the People have to be made to live convincingly through their senses. The style also has to persuade us that they are not merely defective, that their faculties of perception are so much richer than ours that the contrast can never be the simple one of 'better' and 'worse' so intrinsic to Wells.

' "I have a picture—"

'Then the people laughed too because this was Lok's picture, almost the only one he had, and they knew it as well as he did.

' "—a picture of finding the little Oa."

'Fantastically the old root was twisted and bulged and smoothed away by age into the likeness of a great-bellied woman.

' "—I am standing among the trees. I feel. With this foot I feel—"

'He mimed for them. His weight was on his left foot and his right was searching in the ground. "—I feel. What do I feel? A bulb? A stick? A bone?" His right foot seized something and passed it up to his left hand. He looked. 'It is the little Oa!" Triumphantly he sunned himself before them. 'And now where Liku is there is the little Oa.'

'The people applauded him, grinning, half at Lok, half at the story. Secure in their applause, Lok settled himself by the fire and the people were silent, gazing into the flames.

'The sun dropped into the river and light left the overhang. Now the fire was more than ever central, white ash, a spot of red and one flame wavering upwards. The old woman moved softly, pushing in more wood so that the red spot ate and the flame grew strong. The people watched, their faces seeming to quiver in the unsteady light. Their freckled skins were ruddy and the deep caverns beneath their brows were each inhabited by replicas of the fire and all their fires danced together. As they persuaded themselves of the warmth they relaxed limbs and drew the reek into their nostrils gratefully. They flexed their toes and stretched their arms, even leaning away from the fire. One of the deep silences fell on them, that seemed so much more natural than speech, a timeless silence in which there were at first many minds in the overhang; and then perhaps no mind at all. So fully discounted was the roar of the water that the soft touch of the wind on the rocks became audible. Their ears as if endowed with separate life sorted the tangle of tiny sounds and accepted them, the sound of breathing, the sound of wet clay flaking and ashes falling in.'

This is not one of the spectacularly beautiful passages that stud the novel, what it fairly represents is the overall sensuousness and accuracy of the style. Golding conveys the extraordinary experience of living through the feet as much as the hands, and having ears remarkably more sensitive than ours. The sensuous texture is a direct result of his challenge to himself to imagine what it is like to live through sense and instinct, not the mind, breaking the barrier of 'modern' consciousness. To turn from this to *The Grisly Folk* is to perceive that the significant difference is not the contrasting ideas of the moral nature of Neanderthal Man. It is that Golding has accepted the challenge to imagine himself into an alien mode of life, as Wells has not. Without imagination there is nothing between scientific data, obviously susceptible to opposite interpretations, and unsupported fantasy.

Yet his limited point of view presented Golding with a huge stylistic problem, for it involves not only intensification of the sensuous imagination beyond the normal, but also continuous and severe self-denial. He had to deprive himself of all analysis, by himself or his characters, and of most of the possibilities of dialogue, in order to create from within the consciousness of people who neither think nor communicate as we do. Yet he had also to make them credibly human; and create a style which would reach beyond them to us, communicating beyond the limits of their power. The solution is a brilliant one and the chosen discipline faithfully maintained.

In description, Golding allows himself one compromise. Once granted that the People have a vivid accuracy of sense-perception far exceeding ours, he allows himself 'modern' resources of language where these are exactly descriptive of what the People see, feel, hear, or touch, without themselves having words or images to express their activities. This is perfectly fair, their experience is wholly independent of language, and to pin it down to their linguistic resources would falsify totally; whereas to use the full resources of our language only conveys as accurate an equivalent as possible of something communicable in no other way. To take an obvious example from our passage, to speak of eye-caverns 'inhabited by replicas of the fire' merely states accurately what the people themselves see, though it requires a word totally beyond them. Indeed, they have no power of comparison; yet 'the likeness of a great-bellied woman' is the only exact way of conveying what the root looks like to us.

We probably hardly notice this licence, however, because the experience of living in the People's minds is so strong and so strange. There is a peculiar colouring in the style; they see anthropomorphically, investing their whole environment with humanity. The river sleeps or is awake, trees have ears, the island is a huge thigh, shin and foot, logs go away, everything is alive. So, here, the fire eats and dances, and the near-clichés suddenly reveal a freshness when we realize that we are in touch with a linguistic epoch, not only before metaphor has died, but before it has even begun to live as comparison. 'All their fires danced together' is said simply and literally. Metaphor is still the expression of identity. The light dancing in the eyes is not like fire, it is fire. The people see the root as Oa in little, the maternal fecundity incarnate in the wooden shape. There are ice-women, not simply ice-like women. The adventure of style escapes mere limitation and begins to carry us imaginatively into a strangeness of living.

In dialogue of course the losses are heavier and more obvious. Lok's words in the passage are little more than verbal accompaniment of mime and gesture, and though he is the simplest of the People, this is true of most of their speech. Words for them are only one stage beyond expressive noises, and we can see how simple the process of verbalization might be if we imagine the 'original' language that Golding translates into English. It might be rather like those first beginnings in a foreign language that the tourist experiences, where he can make do with names and action words, without grammar and inflection. Indeed, when Lok becomes excited, his 'words' become emotional noises with little or no meaning; he 'gibbers' or 'babbles happily in admiration, his head thrown back, words coming out at random'. Clearly the limitation for the novelist is a huge one.

Yet there is also a linguistic interest in the People's speech which is an interest in progress. In Ha, and Mal, and Fa, and in Lok too, when circumstances force him to develop from clown to leader, we can watch the People's language trying to transform itself and reach out to the incomprehensible and the incommunicable. On the opening pages Mal can only cope with the problem of the vanished log by calling on his experience and giving orders based on memory; but we watch the quickness of Ha to catch on. Again, we can see how from Mal's version of the myth of creation told in simple narrative, feelings and attitudes are distilled which require a moral or religious language. We watch the struggle of this more complex language to meet the challenges of necessity and change. Fa battles with language as she tries to invent cultivation and irrigation. Such actions cannot exist until they have been conceived. Lok struggles with words, trying to learn to reason, and to use the linguistic tool of comparison and analogy. We start off vividly aware of limitation, but there is also a linguistic experience of unique strangeness and excitement. In the book's dialogue we reach back through history to experience for ourselves how language must have developed in time. By the end we have been forced to make real to ourselves the dimensions, and the cost, of our linguistic inheritance.

The style also has to convey a kind of mental experience totally unknown to nearly all of us, for words are by far the smallest part of the People's resources of communication. They mainly communicate by telepathic picture. For Golding's purposes as a novelist, this is a fine invention, for it allows him, as soon as there is something communicable on a basis of past experience, to use among the People and for their own 'thoughts' something of the resources of language he can use descriptively, and with the same justification.

The pictures are of course visualizations, not conceptualizations. If they are part of the People's abnormally rich life of sense and instinct, they are also part of their incapacity for abstract thought. Here however we get not only the experience of growth towards our own consciousness; we get also the experience of a faculty that modern man has almost entirely lost. We can watch the People trying painfully to learn to put pictures together in a chain of thought. But we can also experience a fellow-feeling so intense that the People literally participate in one another when they share pictures, living not as individuals, but as part of a communal whole. Mime becomes far more than an attempt to compensate for linguistic insufficiency; it becomes a method of imaginative sympathy and a mark of natural, instinctive love. The People not only share Mal's mind with its cloud of pain and premonition, they share also his body, and their actions do not merely parody his, they are also a way of participating in his suffering. When, in that firelight scene, 'one of the deep silences fell on them, that seemed far more natural than speech, a timeless silence in which there were at first many minds in the overhang; and then perhaps no mind at all', that 'perhaps' should make us pause. The main point is not their insufficiency of language and the limitation of their minds when compared to ours. We are not looking at the mindlessness of animals; we are not indeed looking at mindlessness at all. What we glimpse is a kind of consciousness wholly without that individual separateness and loneliness which is the definition of human consciousness as we know it; a togetherness so complete (feeling 'one' without needing to feel one about anything), that in our terms it is 'perhaps no mind at all'—more than our language can cope with. We discover imaginatively what it is like to be not Men, a mere collective tag for a number of separate individuals, but People, a collective phenomenon. The style reaches out into the unknown, to bring it within our imaginative comprehension. It is an adventure, and we are the Inheritors; but the novel does not tell us, it makes us discover what that means.

II

Given the primacy of experience over analysis, we can nevertheless see that the effect of the first four chapters is to build up, through our detailed imaginative response to the behaviour of the People, a sense of their nature and way of life. We learn, without knowing that we are learning, how they think, how they govern themselves, how their traditions direct their attitude to their environment, how they have developed a religion, a morality, and a way of looking at life and death that are human, and yet challengingly different from our own.

This growing perception of what it means to be People rather than Men is indeed very nearly the whole fascination of these early chapters; for, in narrative terms, the life of the People has an intractable sameness. 'Today is like yesterday and tomorrow' is no ideal formula for a novel. The People's existence is essentially static: the cave by the sea in winter, the overhang by the waterfall in summer; the search for food and firewood; the endurance or the satisfaction of hunger and thirst; the experience of birth, sex, and death. In such a life there is little pattern or excitement, unless it be some natural disaster or external challenge. Indeed, if we look back on these chapters, we shall see that the Neanderthalers simply come home, find a doe, and suffer the death of Mal, and the interest is not in these particulars so much as in their revelation of what it is to live and die as People.

What narrative interest there is comes from the intrusion of the New Men: their removal of the bridge-log which indirectly hastens Mal's death, their smoke which causes Lok to fall on the cliff edge, the disappearance of Ha. It is Lok's fear of the alienation he experiences when tracking and seeing the Other that forces him to risk the sanctuary of the ice-women. The New Men provide the only opportunity for suspense. In addition to the difficulties of putting himself behind the People's eyes, the very nature of their life complicates the novelist's problems: not only will his chosen method make his early chapters obscure, but his chosen subject removes most of the possibilities of narrative excitement. It is hardly surprising that we should find *The Inheritors* more difficult to get into than the other novels. This is partly offset, however, by Golding's use of suspense in the gradual materialization of the New Men, so that curiosity is kept alive. For the rest, he manages to convey so vivid and detailed a sense of the People's life itself that we remain fascinated by its strangeness and caught up unawares by its challenge to our own consciousness.

Their existence is essentially communal. We have seen how they not only protect and warm Mal with their bodies, but also involve themselves, through mime and picture, in sharing his sickness and awareness of death physically, as well as imaginatively. We have seen, too, how the consciousness most natural to them is of so existing in one another that they become one mind. But there are more startling indications of the fact that it is the relationship among them that is central, and the relationships between them only secondary. Their sexuality is promiscuous in our terminology. They seem at first to live in couples, but when Mal touches a rock 'as Lok or Ha might touch Fa' the description turns out to be more pointed than it looks, for though Fa is in one sense Lok's mate, and Nil Ha's, Liku is Lok's daughter by Nil. Nil will dream, in a seriously reassuring way, of herself and Fa being slept with by both men. The sexuality that is as natural as hunger to them can clearly exist among the group as well as between the couples, and is only a part of their feeling for one another as a whole. It is 'animal', yet as Fa pats her hair when Lok touches her, it is recognizably human too. If we call it 'promiscuous' we simply reveal our different assumptions about relationship. Again, the depth of Lok's feeling for Ha is manifested in a sense of his 'Ha-ness' no less physical than his feelings for Fa; and we can make no useful distinction between the mourning of Fa and Nil for him, and the mourning that breaks from Lok's mouth. So when Lok the tracker feels that 'the other had tugged at the strings that bound him to Fa and Mal and Liku and the rest of the people, the strings were not the ornament of life but their substance. If they broke, a man would die . . .', we have to see that though Fa comes first on the list, it is the 'strings' as a whole that are the vital substance of living, and the particular relationships exist only within that feeling of oneness. The baby is not 'Nil's baby' but the New One for them all.

The group is directed both by the Old Man and by the Old Woman. She is the guardian of the Fire and the Hearth, the protective warmth at the heart of their society and their sense of Home; and she guards and uses fire with a sense of its preciousness and mystery. While she holds it she is set apart. She is also the priestess of their matriarchal religion: 'a woman for Oa', 'a man for smelling things out and having pictures'. This makes her numinous, and the other women share something of this; there can develop about them the same aura that makes Fa untouchable and awesome. Woman as mother is the vessel of the life force: 'As long as there was a woman, there was life.' The Old Man, on the other hand, is the governor. He commands every step of the way, he takes all decisions, and what he formally orders is obeyed without question. The others immediately realize that Mal in his weakness has made a mistake when he orders the young girl, and the nursing mother and her baby, to join in the hunt for food and firewood. There is tension and worry, but when 'it is spoken' it must be obeyed, and tension disappears in obedience. It never occurs to them to question Mal's decision to bring them into the mountains, though he has clearly brought them too early. The Old Man is the guardian of tradition too. As they settle into their summer quarters he formally reminds them of their Genesis and the continuity of their history, reckoning backwards through the record of each Old Man's name.

The matriarchal religion and the patriarchal government and tradition direct their whole attitude to life and death. We have noticed their animistic view of nature; how everything (with one exception we shall notice later) is instinct with life, reverenced, precious. The world 'belongs' to them in the sense that they feel completely at home in it and see it filled with the same life that pulses through themselves; but nothing 'belongs' to them as property or as of right. They fit the world and the world fits them. To come home to the overhang is to squat in an accustomed place and shuffle one's back until it 'fits', they do not build any sort of dwelling that belongs to them exclusively. It is to lay the hand on a rock which has a place for the thumb and around which the hand fits, with a useful edge for cutting. But such implements are found, not made, and are not carried around as property. Only the fire goes with them from place to place, and is laid on time-honoured hearths around which implements 'wait' to be used again, and nature waits to bring forth its abundance to sustain them.

Their deepest idea of life, including their own genesis, is as a continuous act of feminine creation: 'There was the great Oa. She brought forth the earth from her belly. She gave suck. The earth brought forth woman and the woman brought the first man out of her belly.' There is the memory of a paradisal state 'when it was summer all year round and the flowers and fruit hung on the same branch'; but though this has vanished, it was not through human sin, and there was and is no devil-serpent in the People's Garden. They recognize disaster; Mal remembers in his own life-time the terrible Fire that decimated the People to their present tiny group, but it was a purely natural disaster, and not, like Noah's Flood, a punishment for wickedness. Nature can and does

77

destroy, but it is ultimately creative and beneficent, and they treat all its manifestations with reverence. They revere the earth with its abundance that Oa annually brings forth for them, and the air with its riches of scent and information. They are uneasy with fire, but revere it also as their dearest treasure. They fear water as the element most foreign to them; but it is in the water and ice of the ice-women that Oa is most visibly manifested. Their sanctuary is both terrible, and astonishingly beautiful. It is numbing, deathly cold, with the horror of absolute winter. Yet the ice-women are linked together to the heavens like the People themselves. They are the culmination of ice-patterns that embody not only wintriness but the upward energy of growing trees and plants. From their terrible blue loins there issues water deadly cold, but the visible sign of the thaw and the spring. From the glittering ice, even in moonlight, there is reflected dazzling radiance and pure beauty. The description of the 'cathedral' is probably the most spectacularly beautiful thing in the novel; but its essence is the perception of the holiness of death-in-life and life-in-death, a vision that can see both steadily, and how they make each other significant. The religion of feminine creativity holds the terror of death in meaningful tension with the creative energy the People see pulsing through the living world. There is a place for Lok's sick fright, and a place also for his dances of joy and gratitude.

We can see the two strands again in Mal's death and burial. The death is tragic, even more so because it happens in the immediate aftermath of Ha's, and there is no doubting the depth of the People's love and grief. Yet the dominant note is acceptance, both by Mal and his mourners. As Lok digs the grave beside the dying man, the layers of hearth after hearth bear witness both to Time the destroyer, and to the continuity of life. The old bones are treated just like the earth and the stones, and Liku plays with them matter-of-factly before the dying man's face; there is no sense of the gruesome. The People are obviously accustomed to open the skulls and eat the brains of their honoured dead so that the qualities they honour will enter into them. Mal asks them not to, in his case, only because he fears to transmit his weakness. Yet there is nothing ghoulish. The baby plays in the grave, we see death and life in one focus; and the haunch of meat and the handfuls of water, indeterminate though their indication of life after death may be, speak a different language than the ashes and dust of a familiar ritual. As a last word: 'Oa has taken Mal into her belly'. The grave is the womb of nature. In the same way, when the ice-women fall it is summer, but the winter in which they will form again is the gestation of a new spring.

This natural religion contains no idea of crime or punishment, and, while it requires offering, it knows nothing of blood-sacrifice. The only idea of evil they have, in fact, is the destruction of life by violence. This comes out very strongly in the episode of the doe. For the first time we see both hostility and the conscious-ness of moral dilemma. The People are wholly non-violent; their thornbushes are walking-sticks and balancing rods, or when they are weapons at all they are purely defensive. But the hyenas are regarded with instinctive hatred, the only living things in these four chapters to call forth hostility, even aggression. The rock that Fa thumps into the bitch's ribs is a 'natural blade of stone', however, and the hatred clearly has a kind of moral basis: to the People's ears the hyenas are 'talking evilly'. The reason is of course that the hyenas belong to another 'nature', the world of the sabre-toothed tiger and the cave bear. The People only eat meat when it has been killed by some other agency and there is 'no blame' for shedding blood; moreover even this is only justifi-able on the same terms as their feeding on grubs or asparagus or fungi, the terms of human need.

But as Lok and Fa dismember the doe that a 'cat' has killed: 'The air between the rocks was forbidding with violence and sweat, with the rich smell of meat and wickedness.' To enter the world of cruel nature, even by proxy, is to be involved with an atmosphere and feelings unnatural to them. Their actions are described in a new, violent language. Fa tears fiercely, slashes with a splinter of bone, cries out in anger, splits the belly open; Lok pounds at the body 'breaking out the joints', his great 'hands tore and twisted and snapped the sinews', he 'beat in the skull . . . and levered open the mouth to wrench away the tongue'. When they finish, 'the limbs were smashed and bloodily jointed', the doe 'wrecked and scattered', leaving only 'torn hide, bones and hoofs' and a collection of 'torn and quivering fragments' with which they move away 'grunting and fierce'.

It is quite clear that they cannot simply be exonerated in their own eyes because they have not done the killing. The air may be 'forbidding' but it is also 'rich', Lok dribbles as he works, and Fa grunts with excitement as well as anger and effort. Yet their essential harmlessness is perhaps proved more by this episode than by any other, since it is here that their values are most consciously recognized and asserted through conflict. We see Lok acknowledging the 'darkness in the air under the watching birds', knowing that what they are doing is 'very bad' even when 'there is no blame'. His reverence for the female creature that Oa brought out of her belly is such that even the violent dismemberment of its dead body requires a penitent awareness, a definite justification: 'There is little food when the people come back from the sea. There are not yet berries nor fruit nor honey almost anything to eat. The people are thin with hunger'—we have seen, indeed, that they are famished—'and they must eat. They do not like the taste of meat but they must eat.' A little later he adds 'a brilliant thought, "The meat is for Mal who is sick." ' The whole rhythm of this is one of rationalization, yet it is the deep need Lok feels to justify what he does that really reveals his innocence. In the 'mixture of darkness and joy in his head' the joy is communal as well as personal or greedy; the darkness is known to be dark, and not to be complied with unless there is real justification. After this passage we know that the People are quite incapable of shedding blood themselves.

Perhaps the most astonishing thing is that Golding can convey so much by such limited means. Most of it, of course, comes welling out of description, where his linguistic resources are greatest; the experience distils its implications without needing either explicitness or analysis; we are largely unconscious of taking them in but find them in our minds when we have responded. Speech comes mainly in the narrative of Genesis, Numbers, and the Fire, and a few formulae of the kind that primitive people hand down orally. But in the deer passage the religion that can be conveyed through description begins to issue in a morality that must not only be enacted, but requires also to be brought into overt consciousness. This in turn demands a moral language: evil, wickedness, blame, bad. Objections might be made to this as inappropriate and imported, a breaking of the novelist's linguistic bargain; and the difficulty is real. Yet if it is credible that Neanderthalers should have a religious sense at all—and this must rest on unprovable assumption—such a sense must issue in moral attitudes and these must be communicable to us in moral language. 'Evil' or 'blame' are simply translations of noises which express distress, the desire to disassociate themselves from what is felt to be repugnant, feelings which any human not only feels but is conscious of feeling, as much as pleasure or pain.

By the end of these four chapters, then, Golding has not told us, nor analysed for us, but made us realize through imaginative experience, what it is like to be one of the People over the whole range of their lives. 'Today is like yesterday and tomorrow'; they move through a world which contains death, violence, and natural disaster, but their existence in it is stable, reverent, harmless, natural. Behind the fiction lie anthropology and archaeology, and centuries of speculation about the Natural Man, yet it would not be too much to claim that nowhere in our literature has either the primitive man or the Natural Man been realized more imaginatively.

Yet the richness of the imaginative discovery is such that we are also afforded a dim awareness even at this stage, though only the full sweep of the novel will confirm and elucidate it, that the People's life is poised more precariously than they know between the future and the past, in ways that are not confined to the advent of the New Men.

We can see clearly in retrospect, for example, that Nature is not constant but changing. The fact that they have arrived at the overhang too early is neither an accident nor merely the result of Mal's failing powers. In the Neanderthal world the ice-cap is shifting, and the seasons are changing with it. Today is not quite like yesterday, and tomorrow will be different again.

The People are changing too, even before the revolution that the New Men will bring about. On the opening pages, with the problem of the missing log, we see not only the limitations of their thinking but also the way that the most intelligent of them are beginning to push out their mental frontiers. Mal cannot communicate any 'idea' of what he wants by picture, because his picture comes only from his memory and has no counterpart in theirs. But as soon as his orders result in the finding of a new log and its placing in the water, Ha is very quick to learn the mechanics of getting it across and firmly in position. To do this he needs to be able to think by a logical process, and he proves capable, once given a start by Mal. Fa is even more brilliant in the People's terms. We are present at the moment when a human creature invents the idea of cultivation.* She is developing the power to connect one picture with another allowing action to be predicted, which could bring about a totally new situation. Asparagus grows here in earth, there is earth there, at the over-hang, therefore we could grow asparagus there. The last step eludes her powers of communication however, because there is no 'therefore' in a picture, and no word for 'therefore' in a language based wholly on experience and memory. She can only make 'bringing together' gestures with her hands. But her intelligence has begun to bridge the gap between inference from experience and deduction. She has begun to think in the new sense, of which Lok is still incapable when he sees the smoke of the New Men's fire a few pages further on. Later, she has another brilliant idea which could have developed into the invention of irrigation.† We see her struggling to separate out, from an inclusive snapshot memory of the sea-shore, the significant detail of Lok shaking salt water from a shell; and to extract from that the idea of holding water in a container. We then watch her trying to connect this with the significance of Liku carrying the little Oa through the forest. This time she manages to force the two pictures into some sort of combined picture; a picture *made*, not simply remembered, or seen. To Lok it is 'a meaningless jumble of shells and Liku and water, and the overhang', but the Old Woman understands. Only, her response is startling:

'. . . she swayed back, lifted both hands off the earth and poised on her skinny hams. Slowly, deliberately, her face changed to that face she would make suddenly if Liku strayed too near the flaunting colours of the poison berry. Fa shrank before her and put her hands up to her face. The old woman spoke.

' "That is a new thing." '

Past and future meet head-on in the present. There is beginning to stir in the People a new power of mind which could bring about a revolution in their existence, so that tomorrow will be utterly different from today. It confronts a hostile conservatism, for which all change is to the worse. With our modern consciousness we are of course on Fa's side, on the side of progress, but we have become sufficiently aware of the Old Woman's wisdom to pause. Are the People's happiness and security, perhaps even their innocence, dependent on the limitations of their consciousness? We can see how Lok's sunniness depends on his living in the present, incapable of predicting the future for good, but also for ill. Uncertainty, coming across the consciousness 'like a cold wind', is a 'knowledge . . . nearly like thinking'; in fact, a condition of thought. Moreover, thought is clearly beginning to give Fa the power to impose her will on the world and alter it to the shape of her mind. The inventions we see her making are 'good', but they are not the only ones such mental powers could make. The Old Woman may have a point, that the ability to choose to impose one's will is the beginning of evil, or at least the gateway; something attractively coloured but possibly poisonous. So, in a changing world, the opportunity to change for evil as well as good in the People themselves begins to raise questions about the stability of their innocence. We are only dimly aware of this, if at all, on a first reading; but it is a mark of the depth of the novelist's imagination that it should be there, waiting to be brought into our full consciousness later.

We should notice that an important change of perspective takes place as early as the second chapter, and in that chapter at its most beautiful: the account of Lok on watch. To have seen the People's homecoming is to have seen the natural man completely at home in the world. But now, as Lok's senses respond to the vastness of the night horizon, the stars pricking open, the expanse of country stretching out in darkness to the sea, we are taken imperceptibly beyond the poetry of sense, to a different aspect of the People's limitation. The bulk of the island, separated from him by terrible sliding water, is seen anthropomorphically as ever, in the shape of a giant's leg; but it is as remote as the moon 'so that it had no connection with life as he knew it'. Only a creature 'more agile and frightened' than Lok could reach it, and there is point to the juxtaposition of fear and agility. We are realizing that his consciousness does not operate on the whole world of human possibility, there is a bigger shape of man, requiring a different kind of consciousness to explore its darkness: a creature moved by fear to a daring inconceivable by innocence. Again, there is more than mere confusion in Lok's inability to grasp the relation between the world of his mind and the world out there. 'This part of the country with its confusion of rocks that seemed to be arrested at the most tempestuous moment of swirling' suddenly reveals itself as a whirlpool of 'becoming', not a safe and customary trail. He is given in the mist a further intimation of the Other, and seems 'for a moment on the brink of revelation', but 'he could not hold a new thought when there seemed no danger in it'. A challenge is coming from the darkness beyond the Neanderthal hearth, with a revelation of other human possibilities, but it comes to a consciousness unprepared and unpreparable. The world is bigger than Lok can realize, the shape of a human being more terrible, and also more extensive, than he can grasp. As he settles down to sleep we can see that he is not really fitted to the world, nor the world to him. He curls up *against* a night that is in some senses inimical. His posture cannot help reminding us of a foetus, but can a new life be born?

Hard to get into though they may be, these are four brilliant chapters. They start as Wells does from the scientific facts, but their superiority is not a matter of preferring the conclusions reached by different assumptions; it lies in the density and depth of the imaginative exploration. To imagine like this is to create a world which cannot be confined to categories. To respond to the experience fully is not only to respond to an 'innocence' more convincing than that of Milton's primal people, but to respond also with deep vibrations of unease.

III

We know that *The Inheritors* will reverse *The Grisly Folk*; but the more clearly we know it, the greater the danger of missing the value and power of Golding's fiction. We have continually to guard against moral certainties. Indeed, the value of some understanding of the implications of his chosen form, and some grasp of the complexity of his exploration of the People, is that these enable us to see with what care and artistry he sets out to frustrate any simple contrast.

It is significant that Lok rather than Fa should be the medium of our vision. Given the incomprehension of the People as a whole, faced with Otherness, to employ the simplest and most loving of them is to forestall our tendency to judge, and to force us for as long as possible to 'look without seeing', as Lok does. The basic mode of perception is affectionate and trusting long after it should have changed; and long after it has changed in Fa because of her greater intelligence. Being made to see familiar things as though we had never seen them before ensures that we respond with fascination, curiosity, even amusement, and certainly delight, before we become aware in darker ways. The uncomprehending eyes that see all things stripped of their implications guarantee at least an initial objectivity. Of course we come to the experience filled also with nascent horror and premonition, and the implications cannot be prevented from welling up in our minds; nor indeed should they. Yet the method can so restrain us that we become open to richer and more complex impressions than we are aware of or expect; and the richness and complexity become available to us because his method has made them available to the author, restraining his initial urge simply to tear Wells to shreds. He becomes Lok, 'there was too much to see and he became eyes again that registered and perhaps would later remember what now he was not aware of'.

It is remarkable, too, how long Golding manages to keep Lok away from a full confrontation with the New Men, so delaying his comprehension even further. In chapters 5 and 6 the tragic action happens largely offstage, and what we proceed to after the first four chapters is not, as we might have expected, an immediate marking of the opposite, but rather a continued exploration of new kinds of consciousness in the People. Chapter 5 starts us in their inner recesses; it begins in dream, and ends with nightmare coming to the surface in daylight. Then Chapter 6 takes us through Chapter 1 again, exploring revolutionary dimensions in the People before we are allowed really to see the New Men. This means that when we do confront them in Chapters 7–9 we no longer have a stability to judge them by. The points of view have suddenly multiplied. We see through Lok, but we are also aware of Fa, and of the chasm that has opened between their differing visions. Our own consciousness also begins to reach beyond them both, as they see things they cannot possibly understand, and which must remain radically obscure unless we use our own intelligence and powers of deduction. We begin also to be able to see from the point of view of the New Men, to see the People as they see them, and to understand why they behave as they do. No simple contrast emerges from all this. Finally, Golding puts Lok to sleep at the tragic climax of these chapters. We know from Fa's behaviour that something terrible has happened, and we can make certain guesses about it, but we do not and cannot know what it is, and we shall not until the end of the penultimate chapter. This is not wilful mystification, or cheating, but has a serious function. It is the firmest indication of Golding's determination to prevent us from judging until the full experience of both kinds of men is complete, until we know all that is needed for a fully compassionate judgement.

We start then in Chapter 5 with an exploration, not of the New Men, but of new 'deep waters' in the People's consciousness. The shocks they have already suffered, by the disappearance of Ha and the first experience of the Other by Lok and Nil, disturb not only their innocent foetal sleep, but also the stability of their daylight society. They dream, 'beset by a throng of phantoms from the other place', from a realm, which they still think of as Other to themselves, where violence, killing and alienation exist and must be encountered. Lok dreams of being hunted by the Other, but from the depths of his psyche in sleep, the shock he has experienced draws forth an answering strength of reassurance from his oneness with the People. 'Pulled by his desperate need' they come to him physically, 'they drove in until they were being joined to him, body to body. They shared a body as they shared a picture. Lok was safe.' But the strain is shown by the fact that only the fullest physical union can now bring the feeling of safety; and there is a sense of loss too: for in the dream the People are no longer at home in the universe. What was implicit in the foetal sleep is becoming explicit in the unconscious: 'They came in, closer and closer, not as they would come into the overhang, recognizing home and being free of the whole space.' Nil in her dream experiences the same psychological reassurance in a specifically sexual form, but this is no longer sex as natural as hunger, and she whimpers when she wakes. The People's communion with one another copes with the shock, the strings hold, but they have been badly strained.

With the daylight we realize the damage to government and leadership of the two empty spaces, for 'now there is Lok'. It is obvious how much his happy foolishness, his inability to join 'a picture to a picture so that the last of many came out of the first', fall short of the qualities of Mal and Ha; so that the Old Woman has to rescue him from his mistakes and put the right orders in his mouth. It is true that he begins to find words without pictures, to use a new tool of comparison, to conceive necessary actions, control his clowning, and develop responsibility; yet he will never make as good an Old Man as Ha would have done. The traditions remain, of course, and the best must be made of them. Stability must be reasserted. The Old Woman thinks she has the measure of the crisis: 'Now is like when the fire flew away and ate up all the trees'; when their life could continue in spite of decimation. Yet we wonder.

Indeed the significance of the chapter is that it dismantles the hope of continuity. Among the drifts of green buds, ironically proclaiming the Spring of new life, Lok dances in acrobatic friendliness as he greets the New: 'Hoe man', 'Hoe new people', excitedly expecting relationship. But the scene reorchestrates in darker tones the first sight of the Other. There is not only the same failure to respond; there is the sight of the huge logs the New Men use for their fires, at which Lok, though he cannot be said to understand, knows an unreasoning fear as deep as Mal's nightmare of a totally alien and destructive world. Twice the New Men have removed the log-bridges, with their social function of joining a trail for any traveller, to burn them up for themselves. When Lok hears their voices they make 'a picture in his head of interlacing shapes, thin, and complex, voluble and silly, not like the long curve of a hawk's cry, but tangled like line-weed on the beach after a storm, muddled as water'. They contain neither the simple assertion of destructive nature, nor the practical, communal order of the People. Yet we look less at what these things tell us about the New Men, than at what Lok's incomprehension implies.

There is the laughter of a child—or an idiot—at what he does not understand, and the reading of himself into what he hears so that the voices become 'laugh sound'. Though we continue to recognize the goodness of this innocence, we become more and more disturbed by its helpless inadequacy. The voices themselves herald deep waters of the mind; again cliché is becoming meaningful. There cuts across them the mindless screaming of Liku, caught in a world of panic and violence, moving 'away across the river'. The sea, the river; People cannot cross them, but they must.

When Lok sees the New Man's face it is totally unlike his own, with 'white bone things above his eyes and under his mouth so that his face was longer than a face should be'. But now delighted curiosity turns into horror for us, as the poisoned arrow thuds into the trunk at Lok's head while he remains wholly uncomprehending. 'A stick rose upright and there was a lump of bone in the middle . . . Suddenly Lok understood that the man was holding the stick out to him but neither he or Lok could reach across the river.' Innocence cannot hope for continuity; it must change, or be destroyed.

Finally, 'upside down over deep water', Lok experiences not merely the overturning of his world, but also, in daylight, the release of nightmare consciousness in the depth of his own mind. The vision of the Old Woman's body among the weeds of the river is one of those moments in Golding where he seems to write out of some deep psychological cavern,* with a disturbing power that reverberates well beyond what can be made rationally explicit. Not that it is difficult to produce explanations. The wisest of the People, who believed that the crisis confronting them was of the same kind as the Fire, has walked to meet Evil; she has been destroyed by the Fall. Her dead eyes ignore the mutilation of the human shape involved in this, as her living eyes had failed to conceive its possibility. Not death only, but murder has entered the garden. The priestess of Oa has encountered a phenomenon which calls the religion of beneficent creativity in question. The eyes and mouth which saw and voiced the unity of man and nature have no such message now; and in the otherworld of water, skinned over from the sky, death speaks only of deadness: 'the eyes shone

* See also our discussion, Ch. 6, pp. 249–250, and footnote.

as dully as the stones . . . her mouth was open, the tongue showing and the specks of dirt were circling in and out as though it had been nothing but a hole in a stone.' The world that knew dread but no fear has gone for ever, betrayed by its inadequate faith.

These are ways of putting it, and they express the upside-downness in a useful analytic way. But the real strength and significance of the passage lies elsewhere; not, again, in points that can be made about it, but in the activity of imaginative experience itself. What we have to respond to is primarily an eerie *rhythm*:

'The weed-tail was shortening. The green tip was withdrawing up river. There was a darkness that was consuming the other end. The darkness became a thing of complex shape, of sluggish and dreamlike movement. Like the specks of dirt, it turned over but not aimlessly. It was touching near the root of the weed-tail, bending the tail, turning over, rolling up the tail towards him. The arms moved a little and the eyes shone as dully as the stones. They revolved with the body, gazing at the surface, at the width of deep water and the hidden bottom with no trace of life or speculation. A skein of weed drew across the face and the eyes did not blink. The body turned with the same smooth and heavy motion as the river itself until its back was towards him rising along the weed-tail. The head turned towards him with dream-like slowness, rose in the water, came towards his face.'

The two references to dream are important, for the rhythm is that of nightmare. A formless thing disengages itself from the depths of the mind, becomes a dark spectre, rises with dreadful slowness, but 'not aimlessly', . . . and we are frozen, it is impossible to escape. It reveals sudden intimations of terror; hides them. Then, slowly, relentlessly, it turns towards us the full horror of its face. And as we respond to this we become aware of the sense in which it is happening in Lok, not merely to him. While he watches, the horrible world of water is the only world, whose dimensions the rolling body makes one take in as one follows its eyes: the surface, the bottom, the 'width of deep water'. Its rhythm is that of the river itself, and Lok is made to know it as a rhythm in his own mind. The chapter began with phantoms from another place, capable of being exorcised by inner psychic resources. At this moment there is no place but here, and no resources to meet the spectres. Innocence becomes aware of deep water, inside itself, inescapable.

Narrative now begins to confirm and explore what imagination has revealed. The sixth chapter is full of deliberate echoes of the first, but they mark ironically the nature of the new dimension. As Lok's feet unclench themselves from the bushes to slide down into water, we remember as part of a lost world the delighted onward rush of the clever feet leaping the puddles. As he shivers 'like Mal' the difference is plain to us: this is no natural disease of age. The game with the beech-branch becomes a hysterical release of unbearable grief and rage. In the clearing, there is another poisoned arrow to be plucked from the tree instead of the edible fungus for Liku. As Lok runs up the path to the overhang he sees not only the smoke he had smelt on the platform but one of the men who made it; and we have a sharp sense of what the people's inability to reason and predict has cost. He comes home to an empty overhang, a desecrated hearth, the traces of blood and milk which speak of the murder of the Old Woman and Nil. Fa remains, but the 'strings' have been cut, the links with the past and the future broken (we suddenly remember that Fa has been unable to bear children), the fire that was the centre of a whole warmth of community extinguished. The blood is terrible, but the milk, the abducted children, the dead embers are worse. The raiding party has set out not just to kill persons, but the People, and they have all but succeeded.

We have a fuller notation now of what the Old Woman's body prefigured, and Golding proceeds to explore the implications of both 'upside-downness' and 'deep water'.

The new situation is deeply tragic, and the more we took in of the nature of the People in the opening chapters, the greater will be our sense of loss. Yet the surest sign of a new dimension is that the sense of loss implies no longing to conserve. We know in our bones that any way out of the tragedy depends on Fa, and we become increasingly impatient with Lok as, even now, he cannot understand and continues to behave and feel as the People have always done. As he gallops to the overhang, or scratches himself uncomprehendingly under the chin, we suddenly become aware of his closeness to the ape as we have not been before. We may have mixed feelings as Fa fiercely compels him to accept her leadership, destroying their tradition, but we are in sympathy with her, knowing that revolutionary change is vital if they are to survive at all. As they watch the boat nosing along the bank it is her fear that offers the only way forward, and Lok's innocent incomprehension—'They have twigs'—can only be disastrous. It is not that Fa will learn to fight the New Men with their own weapons, indeed the outcome of her realization that the arrow is a weapon is the insistence that Lok 'give the twig back'. (It plunges into the water like a stooping hawk, but it is unnatural, and the People reject it.) Yet this does also involve the assertion of alienation from their side; if the action is 'good' because it rejects evil, it is 'difficult' because it involves a break with their nature and their natural vision.

We become still more sharply aware of how upside-downness is related to the deep water of the river and the fall. Far back in the novel, when Mal in his nightmare momentarily saw the world as essentially destructive, we had our first neutral and undramatic glimpse of a log going over the waterfall. There was no reason then to suspect any connection, but there is now. As Fa cries out 'Give the twig back', another trunk slides noiselessly over the lip. When the twig is thrown:

'The sun was right down in the gap and the river flamed so that the edge of the fall was burning bright as the ends of sticks in the fire. There were dark logs coming down river, black against the flaming water. There were whole trees, their roots behaving like strange creatures of the sea. One was turning towards the fall beneath them; roots and branches lifting, dragging, going down. It hung for a moment on the lip; the burning water made a great heap of light over the end and then the tree was going down the air to vanish as smoothly as the twig.

'Lok spoke over Fa's shoulder.

' "The old woman was in the water." '

To assert alienation, to realize the destructiveness abroad in the world in a vision which unites blazing fire and terrible water, is to begin to know the Fall; and even Lok recognizes the connection of this moment with his nightmare vision of deep water. The twig and the mutilated old woman fuse with the logs in a new connection of man and nature, destructive man adding his work to destructive nature. And the People cannot now be free, cannot simply dissociate themselves. The deep waters begin to exist permanently within them. Feeling rushes into Lok 'like a wave of the sea', it 'went through him and over him. It came from nowhere like the river, and like the river it would not be denied. Lok was a log in the river, a drowned animal that the waters treat as they will.' He knows not only the fall without but the tide within, and it never leaves him for long again. The essentially innocent Lok is going.

Then Chapter 6 gives us a last sardonic echo of Chapter 1 as Fa forces Lok to cross the deep water and thread the darkness of the giant's leg. They have become the creatures 'more agile and frightened' who alone would dare to do so; yet the agility is not only the product of fear, there is attraction too. 'The other people with their many pictures were like water that at once horrifies and at the same time dares and invites a man to go near it', and there is an obscure feeling that they are seeking not just the comfort of seeing Liku and taking her food, but also some 'remedy' that the New Men might afford for the misery they have caused. Now Lok and Fa *use* the logs and the river's pull towards the fall; they are made agile not only by fear but by the 'attraction without definition' of the darkness where the witchdoctor dances before the shelters and the huge fire. So, what the echoes of the first chapter measure is the gap between the new consciousness and the old. This new fierce Fa, with her daring ingenuity, her desperate terror, her clutching herself into the earth of the island after the terrible water, contrasts markedly with her former self. The new Lok has no impulse to clown, and the mighty jumper screams with wordless terror like Nil as he crosses the log. Reminders of their old selves occur when the clown's foolish luck achieves what Fa's intelligence is seeking, and when a loving Fa applauds his boasts of his cleverness, but even here there is difference. The boast is anxious, the applause indelibly ironic; and the foolishness of the old Lok of the People nearly destroys them both in the New Men's clearing.

The happiness, the security, the communal unity in the world of Oa, have gone for ever. When they get back to the overhang the hyenas have desecrated Mal's grave. Without the fire the past is as vulnerable as the present. They have only each other, but their sexuality in the new dimension is a 'new thing' too. 'The two pressed themselves against each other, they clung, searching for a centre, they fell, still clinging face to face. The fire of their bodies lit, and they strained towards it.' This is not the old natural hunger. Nor is it Nil's search for a centre in a sexuality essentially communal. The note is of strain, of a different kind of fire lit in the body to cure the sickness and fear of the soul, by two individuals isolated in a world unsuffused by the glow of a hearth. They don't lie, they fall together.

Only now, when the old stability of the People has modulated into the instability of Lok and Fa caught between two worlds, is Golding ready to give us a full look at the New Men. This can no longer involve any simple measurement of contrast; the points of view have multiplied and the experience must be complex. We have to measure Lok's fascination and objectivity against our sense of implication; measure his incomprehension against the hints in Fa's behaviour; measure both, against the point of view of the New Men and against our own fuller awareness; and finally recognize the limits of even our knowledge. Chapters 7–9 are amongst the most obscure and difficult in Golding's work, but the difficulty is functional and the rewards are great.

The fascination of seeing our savage ancestors through eyes which find them 'incomprehensibly strange' is fused with the upside-down discovery by Lok that they are utterly different from himself. The 'masks' of white bone are skin and there is no Neanderthal face hidden beneath them. The grey hairy skins are suddenly revealed as clothes out of which a naked body can step without pain. The hair-styles show that they are primarily individuals, developing and proclaiming their difference even from one another. The clothes show that they are creatures alien to their physical environment and needing to protect themselves from it. To eyes accustomed to the faces of the People, the New Men's eyes look little, dark and busy. Their nostrils are narrow slits between which the bone is drawn out to a point. Their ears are not pointed ar.d movable, but tiny and screwed tightly into the sides of their heads. These sense organs testify to the New Men's alienation from the People's life of the senses. Such eyes will not

see in the dark and will need fire for illumination as well as protection. Such noses will not perform 'miracles of perception'; the
New Men cannot track Lok to the tree, let alone inhibit their
scents as he can. Such ears have neither the power nor the fine
discrimination of Lok's. On a darker level of implication, the
teeth 'remember wolf'. (Even Wells notes that Neanderthal teeth
have no canines, but are big, even, grinders; though he doesn't
draw the conclusion that such teeth are primarily vegetarian.)
The eyebrows are thin, menacing, wasp-like; the scent is a 'sea-
smell, meat-smell, fearsome and exciting'; there are necklaces of
teeth and shells, the fangs of sabre-toothed tigers as earrings.
These are meat-eaters, hunters, killers. On the other hand, the
thin lips which 'putter' and 'flap' can speak with a quickness and
delicacy, a complexity of utterance beyond the People's power;
and they have no need of mime, whether 'communal' or to make
up for linguistic deficiency. Once again Golding's physical imagination authenticates the differences, while the multiple viewpoints
ensure that the contrast is not simple. Repulsion, attraction,
fascination hold us in eddying feelings as they hold Lok.

This is even clearer in the perception of the New Men's movement:

'They were balanced on top of their legs, their waists were so
wasp-thin that when they moved their bodies swayed backwards
and forwards. They did not look at the earth but straight ahead.
And they were not merely hungry. Lok knew famine when he
saw it. The new people were dying ... Their movements, though
they had in their bodies the bending grace of a young bough,
were dream-slow. They walked upright and they should be dead.
It was as though something that Lok could not see were support-
ing them, holding up their heads, thrusting them slowly and
irresistibly forward. Lok knew that if he were as thin as they, he
would be dead already.'

The perceptiveness and the limitations of Lok's viewpoint stand
side by side. The New Men are half-starved, but nowhere near
death; their slowness is largely a consequence of their carriage and
completely different physical structure. The evocation of a
creature that has evolved to walk upright through the eyes of one

that has not is beautifully exact and uncomprehending. Here the objectivity begins to bear fruit, so that we also take in the eyes that can look straight ahead because the figure is upright, the bending grace of a young bough, the sense of an evolutionary life-force driving them upwards and onwards at a higher level than Lok's.

The New Men build shelters against the world, fashion a defensive stockade behind which to feel safe, post armed guards, not merely look-outs. They manufacture implements, as against the natural blades of stone or bone that the People pick up and use. Both weapons and tools make implements of offence: we see Tuami making a bone knife that could stab a man through his rib-cage and watch him strike off a man's finger with a stone axe. Nil combs her curls with her fingers, Vivani has a bone comb; but Vivani is self-absorbed as well as better equipped. Greater technological efficiency is balanced against a different consciousness: these Men are individualists, killers, frightened, greedy, proud, as well as clever and inventive. The People play with gold and throw it away, the New Men use it in adornment. Tanakil's doll is a triumph of sculpture, wonderfully life-like to the People's eyes; but it hasn't the religious significance that makes the little Oa more than a doll. The New Men carry loads of property about. Their dugouts, with eyes also pointing forwards across the sea and up the river, are marvels of ingenuity, daring and skill, giving them the power to push out the human frontiers in exploration. But, as we watch the huge effort of humping them ashore, we become aware also of the new fear of theft, damage and loss that property brings, and of the cumbrous machinery of transport that it demands.

The differences grow deeper as we watch the New Men's relationships. There are moments when they share the People's togetherness. Watching Vivani suckle the New One, Tanakil and Liku playing and laughing together, Tuft and Chestnut-head sharing a burden and working in unison, brings the sunshine into Lok's head again. But, in the children, Tanakil's urge to dominate becomes cruelty when her will is thwarted, playing sharply against Liku's 'adoration' of her superior intellect. In Tanakil's mother we see again the Old Woman's poison-face, but there is not the only the misunderstanding and ignorance of natural good, but also violence, and readiness to see Liku as a hostile and treacherous creature. Yet there is penitence too, and the desire to atone, which Liku understands as little as the anger. There is no sense of community so basic that it controls all other relationships. Tuami the artist and highbrow considers himself apart from and above the others, and carries on a dangerous affair with Marlan's woman. Various kinds of dissension crackle beneath the surface. The society is wholly man-directed and the women are inferior, without the division of function that makes each sex equally precious. Their sexuality contains violence and exploitation. Tuami consumes Vivani and is consumed by her, sex contains fighting and eating so that there is blood on face and shoulder. They hunt pleasure like a wolf running down his prey or a fox playing with his victim, but 'there was no animal on the mountain and the plain, no lithe and able creature of the bushes or the forest, that had the subtlety and the imagination to invent games like these, nor the leisure and incessant wakefulness to play them.' When they walk back to the shelters, they do not walk together. Yet here we must be careful too. Tuami and Vivani are drunk, and they are drunk because they are frightened. Moreover, though Lok is bored by the play, he is absorbed and excited by the copulation itself. We ought to recognize the difference that instability has made to the apparently simple contrast. It is not just the natural hunger we have to compare this with, but the new sexuality born of fear that has brought Lok to the point where he can understand what he sees. (Later, we shall watch Lok and Fa when they are drunk.)

The New Men go beyond human need to indulgence, and beyond indulgence to excess. The People's hunger, thirst, and sexual desire are similar, and forgotten as soon as assuaged. Meat is shared and eaten to capacity, but there is nothing like Marlan's furtive wolfing while his people starve. The New Men have discovered wine and spirits; and drink has become a source of stimulus, and reassurance, and finally oblivion. There is drunkenness and the noise of vomiting in the darkness. Their fire becomes an inferno, going beyond their need for protection, warmth and light into an expression of frenzied revelry against the darkness; and in it blazes the log which 'killed' Mal. Firewood, meat, and water are too precious for the People to squander. Yet with the inventiveness Fa has groped for, the stone bottles and the wineskin, the transport of logs by water, there has arrived the possibility of excess. If we admired Fa, we can now see where her ideas could lead, and with what loss of the reverence born of scarcity and of natural religion.

The New Men's religion and government are one, and are based on fear and the politics of power. Marlan's authority as ruler-priest prevails only as long as the tribe fear him more than they resent him, and as long as his magic satisfies their needs. Behind failure lie mutiny and death. It is here that Lok's incomprehension is absolute, so that on a first reading it is very difficult to know what is happening, let alone take in its implications. Yet once again the description is so exact and vivid that our imagination and intelligence can reach beyond the powers of the People's understanding and see through the New Men's eyes as well.

Marlan is the witchdoctor of the totem cult of the Stag, and Tuami is the tribal artist. The tribe is half-starved, and terrified of the ogres who seem to block their path up-river. They leave the island because even there they prove not to be safe from Lok and Fa. In the clearing they build a stockade to keep the ogres out from landward while the river guards their backs. Tuami promises them that they will be able to make a sortie from this fortress to exterminate the last of the ogres, but to ensure success they need the help of their ritual magic. He begins to paint the image of the Stag. (To create an image of something brings it within one's power to influence.) The others begin a rhythmic incantation, chanting and clapping. As the witchdoctor in his stag-pelt dances in, they bow their heads to the ground in homage. He presides over the creation of the image while lots are drawn to determine who shall hunt and who provide the necessary sacrifice. This lot falls on Pine-tree, who allows a finger to be cut off in offering to the Stag, proving the seriousness of the crisis. The witchdoctor censes the chosen hunters and touches them with his fern-wand. They then ritually 'kill' the Stag in enactment of the power they believe the magic has given them. (The ritual imitation of an action helps to bring it about and gives one the strength to do it.) The tribe chants and abases itself again as the hunters leave the stockade. Tuami and Tuft close their eyes to avoid seeing the 'fey' ones who now contain the power of the god. Chestnut-head and

Bush are setting out for food, and to exterminate the last of the
People, to liberate the tribe from their terrible hunger and their
terrible fear.

The religion is a death-religion, which gives man the power to
impose his will on nature, at the cost of blood-sacrifice. It contains reverence, but born of fear not dread; and because its whole
business is with results, it must succeed or bring rebellion from
devotees who have sacrificed in vain.

Here the deepest significance of what Lok watches so uncomprehendingly ought to begin to dawn on us. For after the hunters
have left, the tribe still cluster round Marlan clamouring for food,
and are told by Tuami that they must trust to the Stag. Marlan
allows them a ration of wine to keep them quiet, but after drinking
on empty stomachs they bitterly resent being forced to get the
boats on dry land, and finally refuse to move the second one any
further despite Marlan's rage. They are drowsy and irritable.
Suddenly Pine-tree catches Marlan furtively wolfing the meat Lok
had thrown at his feet on the island, which he has hidden and
kept for himself. Irritation turns into dangerous anger, and pointing at the stag has lost its power to control them. They move on
Marlan shouting 'Meat, meat, meat!' Vivani rescues him by bringing the wineskin out again, but this time they refuse to be
rationed, a fight breaks out, and the wineskin is burst. Marlan
reasserts his authority, taking advantage of their sheepishness in
towering rage, and they are temporarily cowed. But quickly their
hunger becomes greater than their fear, and a furious woman dis-
plays the evidence of her empty belly and flattened breasts, while
she screams and spits at Marlan. Again he refers to the Stag ... but
at just this moment of crisis the hunters return empty-handed.
They have failed to find the ogres, they have failed to get meat, and
Chestnut-head has been wounded (by a stag, a bear, or a 'cat').
Marlan's magic has failed, and when the wounded man hears
about the hiding of the meat, there are the makings of a murderous
situation. He advances on Marlan with bow and arrow ready.

Now obscurity begins to thicken. Marlan tries to get hold of the
New One but Vivani bites his hand. The bow is bent, and the
crisis arrives. In utter silence Marlan faces Chestnut-head and
moves his arm round until his index finger points to one of the
shelters. Vivani laughs once, hysterically. 'The old man glanced

around the clearing, peered out to where the darkness was crowded under the trees, and then back at the people. None of them said anything.'

At this terrifying moment Lok falls asleep, bored with watching what he cannot understand, and tired out by the two terrible nights and the succession of shocks. Our source of information has gone. We know that something tragic must happen when hatred, fear and hunger have been raised to such a pitch. Having got this far we could even hazard some guess at the form it is taking. Marlan is trying to shift the blame onto the People, saving himself by converting them from 'ogres' into 'devils' who have thwarted the Stag-magic. Having failed to get hold of the New One, he points, it must be, to the shelter where Liku is. But that is the most we can even guess. Only the terrible face of Fa, who throughout has understood something of what she sees, reflects the horror of what is taking place, while like a mother she keeps Lok from seeing, and cradles him into a child's exhausted sleep. Her mouth opens, her breathing quickens, her face 'was like the face of a sleeper who wrestles with a terrible dream', 'her eyes, open, open for ever, watching'. When he wakes, she is streaming with sweat, but the crisis and its tragedy are over. The tribe are like a wolf-pack in cry, the fire has become a demented inferno, destructive 'like the fall, like a cat', the wild light makes everything leap up and down, the New Men are all roaring drunk on spirits. When they fall asleep Fa searches for the New One while Lok tries to track Liku down against her orders, but the sleepers awake in nightmare, and the two People are forced to leap the stockade, alone. Fa is wounded, and as Lok follows her trail it leads into the marsh, and ends.

Yet, however terrible the intimations of tragedy have become, it is clear that Golding has done everything in his power to prevent us from making a simple contrast, and to force us to defer judgement until the experience and our understanding of it are complete.

We respond still to Lok's lovingness, to the strength of the bond with Liku that will not let him submit to Fa's desire to run away and make a fresh start, in the hope that she will bear children after all. We can see that Fa's development has taken her further and further away from the consciousness of the People towards that of the New Men. But over and over again we are also aware that it is Lok's retention of the People's consciousness that makes him blind, and doomed, without Fa's intelligence and understanding. There is no simple choice, no obvious way to say that one path is 'better' than the other.

Moreover, more surely than ever before, we can see that Lok is changing too. There is not only the way that his experience has made him capable of understanding beings like Tuami and Vivani which the old Lok would have found wholly alien. There is the steady development of that new consciousness born of fear, whose beginnings we watched at an earlier stage. When he faced the crossing of deep water he became aware that 'there was outside of Lok and inside'. As he watches the stockade being built, Fa's fear begins to call forth in him too 'an agonized attention, a motionless and tensed awareness . . . Now, more clearly than ever before there were two Loks, outside and inside. The inner Lok could look for ever. But the outer that breathed and heard and smelt and was awake always, was insistent and tightening on him like another skin. It forced the knowledge of its fear, its sense of peril on him long before his brain could understand the picture.' The 'inside' of the man of the People plays against the 'outside' that knows in fear as the New Men do. But is this an 'advance', or a 'fall'? Is it an invitation to bitter contrast, as when 'Mal's voice of the summer land' blends in his sleepy confusion with the voice of Marlan below him? Is it some secure indication to us that, when the lottery takes place, 'Lok's head began to fill with the fall', and when the finger falls on the stag-image 'the fall sounded nearer'? Outside-Lok demonstrably makes him less spontaneous and affectionate. Yet it demonstrably also makes him more intelligent, more prudent, more responsible. Finally, after whatever tragedy takes place is over, Lok gets from Fa a dim premonition that links the new outside sense with the inner nightmare and the deep waters, and heralds a further inner growth:

'A kind of half-knowledge, terrible in its very formlessness, filtered into Lok as though he were sharing a picture with her but had no eyes inside his head and could not see it. The knowledge was something like that sense of extreme peril that outside-Lok had shared with her earlier; but this was for inside-Lok and he had no room for it. It pushed into him . . . He was possessed by it and did not know what it was.

'Fa turned her head sideways slowly. The eyes with their twin fires came round like the eyes of the old woman moving up through the water. A movement round her mouth—not a grimace or preparation for speech—set her lips fluttering like the lips of the new people; and then they were open again and still.

' "Oa did not bring them out of her belly." '

In the dead-tree, within earshot of the waterfall, Fa has experienced 'the knowledge of good and evil'. In that knowledge she becomes for Lok like the Old Woman, within the nightmare rising in the mind, summoning him to an awareness fully double, inside and out. It is still half-knowledge now, or premonition. He can only sense, not know it, yet it must come. Can we be sure, however, before it is completed in him and in us, of the calculus of gain and loss? If Fa has known the fallen consciousness, should we wish that Lok might be spared the disaster, as she does? Or is it, however terrible, also necessary to realize that the world is not ruled by Oa; and that a consciousness which cannot fall (or climb?) beyond People-feeling and Oa-religion may be an evolutionary and human failure? Is the speech of the New Men, which Fa has come within an ace of uttering, the terrible but necessary goal?

For, we remember, Lok has himself seen, beyond any easy contrast or calculus, the life-force pushing them forward, and eyes that can see ahead. At the first experience of the stag-ritual in the darkness of the island, his sensitivity has captured something we must not overlook. The belling of the Stag-Man is 'harsh and furious, full of pain and desire. It was the voice of the greatest of all stags and the world was not wide enough for him'. The eyes of the stag-pelt were 'looking up, past the new people, past Fa and Lok'. We should not lose the sense of desire and aspiration in our response of horror to the harshness, the fury and the pain. We should at least keep open the possibility that the world we look at is not yet wide enough, so that we too need to look past both kinds of men.

We must certainly begin to understand the New Men, and why they behave as they do. Their terror of the ogres who block their path upwards and onwards is bitterly ironic. But it ought not to be impossible to sense what was in the mind of that first Other when we saw the huge red hairy figures, and found Ha bounding up the cliff after him; what he felt when he heard Lok's bellowings at him across the river, and heard them again from the bushes on the island where he had felt so safe. We can see for ourselves how the People, appearing as if by magic from the dead tree and leaping the big stockade, must seem to the eyes of men just awakened from nightmare:

'The guard who had run after Fa was dancing in front of the new people. He crawled like a snake, he went to the wreck of the caves; he stood; he came back to the fire snapping like a wolf so that the people shrank from him. He pointed; he created a running, crouching thing, his arms flapped like the wings of a bird. He stopped by the thorn bushes, sketched a line in the air over them, a line up and up towards the trees till it ended in a gesture of ignorance.'

Of ignorance; it is not enough to see the error and the irony, or reflect that they come from the New Men's preconception about a world red in tooth and claw. For, in re-orchestrating the scene in which Lok had mimed the Other, this scene also has the effect of suggesting that *we* may have a vision of the New Men no less ignorant, because equally incomplete. We still need to know both the worst and the best about them. We need to know the full extent of the horrible thing they acted out in the clearing. We also need to know more about what thrusts them on up the river, the painful desire to widen the world, the force that got them onto their hind-legs and made them invent the boats that can explore and cross deep water, the eyes that see the way ahead.

The tragedy cannot be understood in the simple categories of better and worse, praise and blame.

IV

A new day begins with Lok hiding in the marshes, alone. What we watch is, however, more than pain, it is the way that Lok achieves through it, one by one, the steps by which the lost Fa had grown mentally beyond him. He clutches himself into the earth as she had done on the island:

'He writhed himself against the dead leaves and twigs, his head came up, turned, and his eyes swept round, astonished eyes over a mouth that was strained open. The sound of mourning burst out of his mouth, prolonged, harsh, pain-sound, man-sound . . . Far off, the stag blared again.'

This is different from the keening over Ha or Mal; and there is no reassurance in the earth after the terrible water. The leaves and twigs are, simply, dead. The sound is man-sound not people-sound; it has the mixture of harshness and pain of the stag's blare. Far back, we had begun to associate thinking with the chill wind of uncertainty, but Lok's new knowledge is coming from a level of suffering beyond the People's world. In our response, progress is fused with 'the pity of it'. Suddenly Lok finds that he can think, can deduce, from his memory of the dugouts being moved, what the noises the New Men are making must mean: 'This was an upheaval in the brain, and he felt proud and sad and like Mal . . . All at once it seemed to him that his head was new, as though a sheaf of pictures lay there to be sorted.' He can not only feel the solitary life-string binding him to Liku and the New One; but understand for the first time the 'terrified love' of outside and inside Lok for the New Men, and know now that they 'would kill him if they could'. It is with new clarity that he feels again the terrible inner tide of grief and loss swirling through him. Now, as he watches the dugouts being heaved through the forest, he becomes absorbed again, but is prudent in time to save himself. Unreasoning fear contains within it the perception of bloody illness: 'He was frightened of the new people, and sorry for them as for a woman who has the sickness.' But the illness is in him too; he instinctively reacts as animals or the People would, eating things that will make him vomit and purge the badness, but in vain:

'The new head knew that certain things were gone and done with like a wave of the sea. It knew that the misery must be embraced painfully as a man might hug thorns to him and it sought to comprehend the new people from whom all changes came.'

Finally, for that comprehension, 'in a convulsion of the understanding Lok found himself using likeness as a tool'. He has become capable of using analogy for deliberate analysis; and the comprehension it gives him is not only full but complex. The hunters are 'like a famished wolf'; but, remembering their moments of togetherness they are also 'like honey'. Tanakil's cleverness, her laughter, and her stick, are 'like honey in the round stones, the new honey that smells of dead things and fire', sweet, but rotten and burning. The Men are terrible, essentially destructive: 'They are like the river and the fall . . . nothing stands against them.' But lastly, most significant of all, they are creative too, 'they are like Oa', part of a life-force.

Shaped by grief and suffering, a new Lok stands before us; no longer a clown, but a rapidly maturing thinker who has begun at last to understand. He is 'like Mal', but also greater than Mal, knowing far more than Mal ever did because of what has happened to him. He has caught up with Fa; and we cannot but respond with admiration as well as pity.

All this time he has been unconsciously retracing his steps to the water where Fa's scent had ended . . . and suddenly, beyond hope, he catches it again and finds her coming towards him, wounded, but alive. They meet with an intensity of love unique in Golding's work and beautifully, tactfully rendered because we do not need to be told what the reunion means: the possibility of 'Peopleness' again, the intensity of shared feelings and pictures, seen at their most precious and exciting because they had seemed lost for ever.

Yet, as they commune, we become aware that Lok has not only caught up with Fa in consciousness, he has surpassed her. In the next few pages the 'point of view' of the novel becomes its hero in full stature. They are both unconsciously aware that 'the new people could not be left alone. Terrible they might be as the fire or the river, but they drew like honey or meat'; but only Lok has been able to bring the attractiveness of the New Men into conscious focus. All Fa's images are unremittingly hostile, full of the sad sense of destruction. While he is with her, he loses the sense of their 'Oa-ness'. Following the train of her thoughts leads only to the limited perception of Mal and the Old Woman, the terrible image, from memory now, that the situation is 'like when the fire flew away and ate up the trees.' But there has been more, and will be more again. Of course it is easy enough to explain why Fa sees as she does: every time Lok mentions Liku there is a reaction from Fa which reminds us that she has experienced something that Lok has not, and makes it steadily more certain that it was the murder of Liku. Yet the sense of Lok's new superiority remains, and finds physical expression too. As they move through the forest they walk abreast, but when they come to the clearing and see 'the pictures and the gifts', Lok takes the lead again while a frightened Fa slips in behind him.

The scene that follows is one of the most crucial in the novel because, while it brings them to (and, momentarily, over) the brink of fallen consciousness, it also begins to define that brink, and prove that they will never finally cross it because they remain People. Terror and pain have enabled them more and more to use their minds in ways that the New Men do. A new sense of the deep waters through which the New Men move has welled up tidally within them, they have known something of the consciousness of the river and the fall. But they have never acted like the New Men, and they have never entered the kind of being that is expressed in the stag-cult.

On the ground, Tuami has finished the new painting we saw him beginning as the guard mimed the ogres' escape. There is another stag-image, but superimposed on it and pinned to it by a driven stake is an image of the People as Tuami sees them, 'as though in the act of some frantic cruelty'. Swinging from the stake is a stag's haunch, and by the figure's head is an open stone bottle of honey-drink. Propitiatory offering and death-magic go together. Convinced by Marlan that the People are not just ogres but devils who have thwarted the stag-magic, the New Men have tried to tap the powers of, and exert control over, both God and Devil. The gifts are the propitiation born of fear, but the stake speaks of ritual killing.

The People see 'gifts'. But by eating the New Men's only 'comparatively bloodless' meat, and drinking their rotten honey, they do experience for the only time what it is to act like New Men. In a tragic novel this is a finely comic scene; unique in Golding. Yet knowing Lok and Fa as we do, we may find it also more and less than funny. In their drunkenness they discover excess, a reeling world, oblivion, ended by vomiting and a sick head and eyes. They become greedy, selfish, aggressive, sulky, furious, violent. Lok's voice comes out 'high and loud and savage'; Fa crawls round the ashes of the fire as the savage man had done 'like a moth with a burnt wing . . . talking to herself of hyaenas'. When Fa laughs drunkenly, 'kicking her legs in the air' we laugh too, but, as 'Lok and the honey fire responded to this invitation clumsily', they have taken another step towards Tuami and Vivani. Soon Lok belts her over the rump as Tanakil had beaten Liku, for not obeying his will, and Fa hits back devastatingly. Loving turns to fighting. Finally Lok 'discovered the power of the new people in him. He was one of them. There was nothing he could not do.' He feels himself imposing his will on the universe, he walks 'with what he thought was the slow swaying carriage of the new people', he lumbers round to tell Fa she must cut his finger off. 'The fall was roaring in the clearing, inside Lok's head.'

Yet the comedy remains secure. The fallen behaviour is purely the result of drunkenness, and when the People's stomachs vomit the rotten honey out they become themselves again. Our laughter has been a response to the extraordinary. When Fa strikes Lok she is immediately filled with tears as well as laughter, and the experience frightens them both. At the moment when he is closest to the New Men, claiming identity, we realize most emphatically that Lok will always be essentially different. He can think and be conscious in many of their ways, and for the duration of his drunkenness he can even act like them, but he can never *be* as they are. This is because, for Golding, it is the basic 'religious' attitude to the world that determines 'being', and only being can determine the kind of action that can define one's nature.* Lok can only think of the severed finger as some vague kind of initiation, he is quite incapable of the religious attitudes that lie behind blood-sacrifice and ritual killing. The alien behaviour he is trapped into, by what he sees as gifts, is founded on no basic self within and consequently disappears without trace. For a moment, in 'action', he crosses the boundary of the Fall, but there is no counterpart in his true 'being', and the effect of the experience is only to clarify our sense of how essentially unfallen that being is. Actions unfounded in being have no significance.

* See this developed in the 'theology' of *Free Fall*.

Fa, in her recovered self, teeters nearer the brink than Lok, as she has always done. In his hangover he allows her to take the lead again, and she proceeds to act in a way that for the first time looks like confronting the New Men on their own terms. She hurls stones at them as they shoot arrows at her. She conceives the idea of abducting Tanakil as they abducted Liku. Her teeth show, like Chestnut-head's as he comes at Lok. As a by-product of her strategy, one of the dugouts splits and smashes on the rocks, while for the first time a New Man takes the death-dive over the waterfall. Yet Fa's nearness to the borderline only emphasizes how impassable it is for her too. The rocks are only a distraction while Lok tries to rescue the New One, the abduction of Tanakil is conceived only for exchange, the death of Chestnut-head and the destruction of the dugout pure accident. Again the necessary basis in being is absent.

We realize this with finality when the differing 'religious' attitudes are juxtaposed in the overhang. Both Fa and Lok have become consciously aware of the terror of the New Men that lies behind their every movement, and their consent to the whip, as they frantically toil up the slope which leads above the waterfall to open waters, away from the devil-haunted forests. The awareness, now so explicit, comes from the new dimension of conscious knowledge; having experienced terror, not just dread, they can recognize it fully. But they think the New Men are baselessly terrified of the empty air, since there is nothing in the forest to fear; and this is because they can never, even for a moment, conceive of themselves as capable of harm. Without the willingness to impose the will at any cost; without the world-view that recognizes no more essential value than the preservation of the self and its imposition on the universe, if need be by destroying whatever is in the way, there can be no Fall. In their desperate extremity, the witch-doctor and the religious artist reveal the extent of the cost they are prepared to bear. Blood-offering, if necessary of part of oneself, turns into human sacrifice, as Beelzebub turned into Moloch in *Lord of the Flies*. There is no stag-image now, for the Devil has proved stronger than the God. The devil is 'savagely' drawn and far more terrible than before, with its pebble eyes supplemented by the tigers' teeth; and the stake has been driven through its heart with hysterical strength. They offer their young girl in propitiation for the death of Liku (no doubt warned by the 'anger' of Lok's cries of 'Liku'); but they give her also as a human offering for the devils to consume as they would consume the stag's haunch and the honey-drink, and the purpose is to acquire the power to kill.

Faced by the tethered Tanakil in her fit, 'Fa began to make noises. They were not words and they were not screams.' We are not told what they were, but Lok hears Tanakil's screaming as like Liku's crossing the water, and that was utter horror and revulsion. They work frantically to free her, and when they run to the terrace in a last despairing hope of the New One, they run without weapons and without any idea of using Tanakil as an exchange, since they immediately release her to her mother. On the terrace, by the waterfall, the Fallen finally confront the eternally Innocent; but with a last terrible irony, the death-magic works. A concussed Fa is carried over the Fall in a sunset river of blood. There can be no doubt which of the two natures is stronger, and must survive.

So, against the fiery water and the fall, there is the first of the final perspectives; a double one. On the one hand we have to set against Fa (the red squirrel running on all fours up the slope), the brilliant inventiveness, the scientific technology which has begun to understand the principles of the conveyor belt and the fulcrum and lever. On the other hand we have to set her essential innocence against the destructive fire and river, the terror, the whips, the blood-sacrifice and ritual killing, the murderous fallen nature. The harmless one, holding the blinding pain inflicted on a head which could conceive no evil, is trapped by a dead tree she can neither escape nor surmount, and swept by the bloody river over a fall she cannot survive. She is never a person of the fall, the river, the fire or the blood. Golding has taken her to the brink of the fall but she herself could never pass that brink. She is killed, carried back below, because she is the kind of being who cannot even begin to conceive of preserving herself by trying to destroy her enemy.

Before we can settle into any final horror of the Inheritors, however, we are made to look again. If the novel had ended here, where its action ends, our response would have been relatively clear-cut; the title a severe, but relatively simple irony. But it is always just where we expect Golding to end that the deepest insights begin.

The surprise ending of *Lord of the Flies* forced us, by a sudden change of perspective which 'distanced' the novel, to look at it again as a whole. This Golding contrives to do now, at the end of the penultimate chapter. Having made us live for ten and a half chapters within Lok's mind, Golding now becomes a distant, impersonal, and coldly objective narrator. This involves a different style, with a fully modern vocabulary, but there is a chilly scientific accuracy recording what it sees with no understanding or emotion. There is a 'red creature', and 'a dark hollow in the side of the cliff where there was evidence of occupation'. If we want a way of measuring the gap between the anthropologist and the imaginative novelist, we have it here.

These eyes can record only what Lok looks like, and the effect is as though we had never seen him before.

'It was a strange creature, smallish, and bowed. The legs and thighs were bent, and there was a whole thatch of curls on the outside of the legs and the arms. The back was high, and covered over the shoulders with curly hair. Its feet and hands were broad, and flat, the great toe projecting inwards to grip. The square hands swung down to the knees. The head was set slightly forward on the strong neck that seemed to lead straight on to the row of curls under the lip. The mouth was wide and soft and above the curls of the upper lip the great nostrils were flared like wings. There was no bridge to the nose and the moon-shadow of the jutting brow lay just above the tip. The shadows lay most darkly in the caverns above its cheeks, and the eyes were invisible in them. Above this again, the brow was a straight line fledged with hair; and above that there was nothing.'

The gap between this and our knowledge is like the gap between the Officer and Ralph; what is seen is accurate, and yet meaningless without the understanding that so manifestly does not accompany the vision. What we measure is the extent of what the novel has achieved for us by making us live behind Lok's eyes instead of looking at him with our own. We can, for the first time, appreciate the tactic of Golding's choice of point of view, because if this kind of vision had appeared in its logical place on the opening page, we could never have responded to such a figure as we have responded to Lok. We could never have been made to realize his true humanity, let alone his greater humanity, in some directions, than our own. Every detail here seems to speak of the innate superiority of *homo sapiens*, though no conclusions are drawn. The temptation must have been to regard such a creature complacently, with a readiness to draw inferences not only of difference, but of inferiority . . . as Wells did. Indeed that is exactly the point. These are the eyes of Wells, and to take in the difference is to take in the full measure of what Golding has done to *Thè Outline of History* and *The Grisly Folk*.

To watch Lok so coldly, while his eyes follow the tree that has killed Fa until he loses sight of it in the distance, is to make us uneasily aware of how blind we would have been even if some accident of time had placed us on the terrace at that moment. We watch while he retraces the whole circuit of the tragic action, so small-looking now; while he revisits one by one the stations of his agony, and the effect is like looking through the wrong end of a telescope so that everything is diminished. Yet the final effect is just the opposite, and the tactic reveals an unexpected stroke of genius. For there rises in us a passionate reaction against this vision, a sense of poignant pity and loss far more powerful through this excess of understatement than could have been achieved by any direct appeal to emotion. As the creature 'seized a great swinging beech-bough and lugged it back and forward until its breathing was fierce and uneven' the full emotional impact hits us of what has happened to that first happy onrush, and the delighted game between the sunny father and the laughing red-haired child.

Only now is the full horror revealed, moreover, as the creature digs from the churned earth and ashes of the fire 'a small, white bone':

'The creature stood and the splashes of moonlight stirred over it. The eye-hollows gazed not at the bone but at an invisible point towards the river. Now the right leg began to move. The creature's attention seemed to gather and focus in the leg and the foot began to pick and search in the earth like a hand. The big toe bored and gripped and the toes folded round an object that had been almost completely buried in the churned soil. The foot rose, the leg bent and presented an object to the lowered hand. The head came down a little, the gaze swept inward from that invisible point and regarded what was in the hand. It was a root, old and rotted, worn away at both ends but preserving the exaggerated contours of a female body.'

The old Lok's 'only picture' is transformed into a 'still' from a horror-film. Liku has not only been killed, she has been *eaten*. What Marlan did was not only to save himself by shifting the blame onto the devils, whose representative could be ritually slaughtered in vengeance; but also to offer her as meat to the famished tribe for a cannibalistic orgy. (This is Golding's bitterest rejoinder to Wells, whose Grisly Folk 'thought the little children of men fair game and pleasant eating'.) We are frozen with the same horror as Lok. The wrong end of the telescope seems unable to give us any reaction. Or does it?

'The creature looked again towards the water. Both hands were full, the bar of its brow glistened in the moonlight, over the great caverns where the eyes were hidden. There was light poured down over the cheek-bones and the wide lips and there was a twist of light caught like a white hair in every curl. But the caverns were dark as though already the whole head was nothing but a skull . . .

'There was light now in each cavern, lights faint as the starlight reflected in the crystals of a granite cliff. The lights increased, acquired definition, brightened, lay each sparkling at the lower edge of a cavern. Suddenly, noiselessly, the lights became thin crescents, went out, and streaks glistened on each cheek. The lights appeared again, caught among the silvered curls of the beard. They hung, elongated, dropped from curl to curl and gathered at the lowest tip. The streaks on the cheeks pulsed as the drops swam down them, a great drop swelled at the end of a hair of the beard, shivering and bright. It detached itself and fell in a silver flash, striking a withered leaf with a sharp pat.'

We realize that Lok is weeping without making the slightest

sound. The objective accuracy of the description not only protects the moment from any trace of sentimentality or exploitation, it also puts the experience into our minds before we know it is there, and the delayed-action response is all the more powerful. We watch what must be said, quite simply, to be one of the most tragic moments in contemporary fiction.

Nevertheless, though our knowledge and our response seem now so complete that we can hardly believe there can be more to come, Golding is not finished with us yet. For the sudden distancing proves to be more than a device to produce, without sentimentality, a welling up of horror, and grief, and love for innocence destroyed. It may be *necessary* to get to a distance, or we may still see and respond too simply.

'If the strings broke, a man would die', and Lok does. The cliché of 'a broken heart' receives its full meaning because there is not only nothing to live for, but no way of living. Lok tries to get into Mal's grave, but he is already too weak to move the stone. He curls up into a foetal position again, but now he seems 'to be growing into the earth, drawing the soft flesh of (his) body into a contact so close that the movements of pulse and breathing were inhibited'. The foetus does inhibit life, it is 'growing' only backwards into the womb; and with the little Oa before his face Lok can also not fail to make us think of a dead child, which has failed to develop into the full shape of a man.

Throughout these chapters we ought to have been aware, as an ironic undertone announcing itself more and more strongly, of the advance of spring into summer: the sun getting hotter, the leaves burgeoning, the wood-pigeons nesting. The fullness of the river speaks of the thaw in the mountains, and water cascades from the ice-woman sanctuary onto the rocks beyond the terrace. As the hyenas approach the body they know to be dead, 'a sudden tremendous noise' sends them 'shivering back'. It is the avalanche proclaiming the beginning of summer, and probably also the end of the ice-age. There is the irony that the abundance so eagerly awaited has come too late; but there ought also to be the sense that it is not enough to feel that Innocence has been wantonly destroyed. The People have failed to grow beyond the Spring of mankind, have failed to move beyond the waterfall, the full evolutionary march of man has necessarily left them behind. If we are filled with grief and pity at the extinction of Innocence, we should not fail also to take in its inability to surmount the Fall, and move forward into a life beyond.

So it becomes necessary to take in a final perspective; to enter for the first time the mind of a New Man, and discover what moving beyond the Fall entails. The language is immediately the nautical one of the seafarer. The tree-trunk that slips past the solitary boat with one root lifted 'like a mammoth's tusk' reminds us that the time is prehistoric, but the boat itself, the navigational calculations, the mind of the helmsman, point straight into the future, however slowly and hesitantly.

We find out their past, and the explanation of much we could not know before. We know their names, with the sense of personality that proper names give. In some directions the darkness of their history merely confirms impressions we already have. Marlan has stolen Vivani from her husband, and his followers are consequently not merely exploring, but flying from the vengeance of their tribe. Tuami wants Vivani too, and the ivory knife he is making is destined for Marlan's heart as, we remember from the scene in the clearing, Marlan himself has sensed. Vivani's statu-esque self-absorption and magnificent selfishness are reinforced; and so are our impressions of their malice, their lust, their deadli-ness. Yet, as we see them from inside, we see also that they are not quite what we thought. We take in also a confirmation of Lok's other impressions. Though the People could never have called anyone 'Master', or have snapped at each other with faces so twisted by grief and hate, these men and women can remind us of Peopleness too. As the New One sucks at Vivani's breast 'the people were grinning at her too, as if they felt the strange, tugging mouth'. Moreover their voyage has not simply begun in lust and rapaciousness and fear. There has been something else, 'whatever it was', that impelled them to voyage on. There is also a level of motivation unknowable to Lok. Vivani, like Fa, has lost her baby, and the New One was taken to ease the pain of her swollen breasts and console her for her loss; while Tuami spared Liku arbitrarily, 'for a joke'. It is not, perhaps, very much of a qualification, but it does mean that they are less deliberately and strategically destructive than we thought.

More important, however, is that hitherto we have unconsciously tended always to regard them statically, as determined. Now we begin to see that for them, as much as for the People they destroyed, the encounter has involved new dimensions of growth, and the waterfall has been a Rubicon. To Tuami 'it seemed as though the portage . . . from the forest to the top of the fall had taken them to a new level not only of land, but of experience and emotion'.

At first this new level is wholly appalling. Tuami feels 'haunted, bedevilled, full of strange irrational grief . . . the world with the boat moving so slowly at the centre was dark amid the light, was untidy, hopeless, dirty.' The world is defiled, in a way that cannot be remedied by squaring off the boat. In Tanakil's mad eyes he sees 'the night going on'; and the encounter with the People has made her 'a changeling'. It has made 'a new Tuami too'. We watch again, as we watched with Lok, the release of a new sense of the mind's deepest waters: 'I am like a pool, he thought, some tide has filled me, the sand is swirling, the waters are obscured and strange things are creeping out of the cracks and crannies in my mind.' There is nightmare again, as the red leg of the New One suddenly becomes part of a monstrous hairy spider creeping from a crevice, but the horror is in the mind behind the eyes, not in the harmless baby. If the world has become dirty and dark, and the brain filled with visions of nightmare, it is because of guilt. 'What else could we have done?' he cries. 'If we had not, we should have died.' The diagnosis, we know, is tragically wrong; but the feeling is not, and it is a wholly new human dimension beyond the capacity of the Innocent.

It is also beyond the Old Man in the boat. Marlan has not changed; he is still confined within his old self-justifying categories. The People were 'devils', the evil was within them, not himself, and he escapes any sense of its continuity by the assurance that the 'devils' will not cross water. Yet this can only be the birth of superstition; while the other is the birth of a new 'religious' sense of the world. Tanakil's terrible cry of 'Liku' is born of the horror of what they have done; it is not a devil's name which only she can speak because she is 'possessed' by an external evil. Tuami sees with utter clarity how much smaller and weaker Marlan has become in his sameness. He looks at the witchdoctor to find something to hold onto, but the new dawn reveals his inadequacy in a light as horrifying, in its way, as Lok's vision of the Old Woman below the fall: 'The sun was blazing on the red sail and Marlan was red. His arms and legs were contracted, his hair stood out and his beard, his teeth were wolf's teeth and his eyes like blind stones. The mouth was opening and shutting.' He is the relic of the old dead way, himself the embodiment of the blind, vicious, insensible evil he had read into the People, his hope of escaping the darkness by keeping to the waters and the plain a manifest stupidity. There is no way out, by flight, or by fight. Tuami's ivory blade is useless: 'What was the use of sharpening it against a man? Who would sharpen a point against the darkness of the world?' In the consciousness of guilt is the fear of the price to be paid: 'What sacrifice would they be forced to perform to a world of confusion? They were as different from the group of bold hunters and magicians who had sailed up the river towards the fall as a soaked feather is from a dry one.' They, as much as the People, have been immersed in deep water, from which there can be no escape.

Yet there is a thoroughfare. The people in the boat already respond to the New One with a 'well of feeling' which includes not only fear, but love. Suddenly the tremendous booming of the avalanche reverberates across the water with its intimation of a new season, and a new age. The baby scuttles into Vivani's furs as we have often seen him do with his mother, and in a sudden release of tension 'the people, released as if a lifted weapon had been lowered, turned their relief and laughter on the devil'. This is simple psychology; but for Tuami there is a revelation, and a cure, not a mere diversion: 'The sun shone on the head and the rump and quite suddenly everything was all right again and the sands had sunk back to the bottom of the pool.' Why?

The 'rump' of the old and the 'face' of the new have suddenly become a single shape, unified and harmonious; contrasted, but seen to fit:

'The rump and the head fitted each other and made a shape you could feel with your hands. They were waiting in the rough ivory of the knife-haft that was so much more important than the blade. They were an answer, the frightened angry love of the woman and the ridiculous, intimidating rump that was wagging at her head, they were a password. His hands felt for the ivory in the bilges and he could feel in his fingers how Vivani and her devil fitted it.'

The sculptor will change the death-weapon to a form of loving, even religious vision, an answer to guilt, a password to a new expedition of the spirit. This starts from the ability to love both the fallen and the unfallen nature, and to see the downward path of the innocent and the surmounting movement of the guilty as essentially related. The People's plunge to extinction by the fall is necessary to the progress of the New Men beyond it. The new vision and love are the product of sin and shame unknowable to innocence. Neither the People, nor Marlan with his mutterings about darkness and his Wellsian ogre-consciousness, can grow; the dead 'evil' and the dead 'good' are left behind. But the sculptor creates something one can see all round. He finds a way to voyage beyond the fall to a creative knowledge of good *through* evil, perceptible only to a consciousness newly aware of guilt, but offering a password to go forward. This is the vision 'past the new people, past Fa and Lok' which Lok glimpsed on the island but could never himself achieve. The ability to focus good and evil in essential relationship, and see lovable human shape in both, is a better vision than that of either the children of darkness or the children of light. This makes Golding's novel explicitly what it has always been implicitly, not a mere lament for lost innocence, but also a subdued testimony to the ability to know the worst and remain loving. Tuami cannot see to the end of the deep water, or 'if the line of darkness had an ending', but this is because he is blinded by the light the water reflects. Whatever the end, the new beginning is good. The artist has captured a new vision. It is for his people to inherit.

V

More accurately, the vision can neither be 'given' nor simply 'inherited'. It had to be discovered by its author, and has to be discovered by his readers, by imagination at full stretch, laying hold of a complex truth graspable in no other way. By comparison, although we have been anxious to point to ways in which it arrives at a vision richer than its apparent thesis, *Lord of the Flies* remains a smaller and simpler work. *The Inheritors* also began from a thesis —a quarrel, but it transforms and expands itself to a far greater extent. The manuscript version had no waterfall, no last chapter; it was wholly the tragedy of the People, with neither as complex an exploration of their consciousness, nor as full a perspective on its implications. The most symbolic elements came last of all. Golding's way of writing turns out to be more like Lawrence than Milton, in ways that can hardly be accounted for by treating him as fabulist and pattern-maker. After finishing a first version that is already a considerable achievement, he clearly felt he had only begun to see what his novel was about, and started again. The discovery implies an even bigger and more difficult adventure of the imagination. It is equally discovery, not pattern-making, that *The Inheritors* forces on its readers by the nature of Golding's art.

The triumph of technique hardly needs further emphasis, the novel appears in retrospect as a dazzling *tour de force*. Yet it is never pyrotechnic, but always functional, and the function is always to keep the imagination alert and flexible, so that there can be no stasis until the whole act of discovery is complete. The revelation technique of *Lord of the Flies* reappears as situations are reorchestrated to bring out ever richer levels of implication. This means that Golding can pack an extraordinary weight of meaning into a single sentence: 'Terrible they might be as the fire and the river, but they drew like honey or meat'; and can bring the entire novel behind the tragic plunge of Fa over the waterfall. But the purpose of writing like this is to force the imagination to hold all its knowledge in tension, so that in the final chapters the entire experience can be gathered together and re-viewed. The shifts of perspective ensure that we should be able to see all round what has been discovered. The basic choice of point of view ensures that we have experienced imaginatively before being allowed to analyse or judge; and ensures also that we will have experienced a growth of thought and a history of language.

In some ways the book gives a sense of perfection; of being one of those rare novels which seems to encompass the whole of its subject. In this respect it is perhaps the most perfect of Golding's works, but it is the kind of perfection which suggests its own limitations.

Partly these are inherent in archetypal myth with its constant drive towards the essential and its impatience with the contingent. In character, for example, the search is for the being of Man rather than the complexities of the individual. There is less concern with relationship as a complicated and mysterious flux between individuals, than with defining the essential nature of relationships. Oddly, the relationship between Lok and Fa is probably the most fully developed in Golding's work, yet he uses it always to explore through, to Peopleness, Deep Waters, the Brink of the Fall. Relationship itself is never the statue. It is the marble in which the statue has to be revealed by cutting away what is non-essential.

The subject of *The Inheritors* cannot but increase this selectivity, and hence the sense of limitation. It is obviously a great advantage to work on a subject which offers the least resistance to treating Man, rather than individuals in complex social relationships. Prehistory suits Golding's art better than an island and a group of boys. There is even less marble to cut away. But it then becomes inevitable that our powerful sense of the archetypal should be accompanied by a rather startled realization of just how much in human existence as we usually encounter it is rendered contingent by such vision. How deeply and richly significant from one point of view, how startlingly *naked* from another, Golding's statue turns out to be.

If however it is a valid idea of art to see the artist whittling away to find the shape of the basic human condition, then Tuami with his ivory images his author's achievements. Yet the stress in *The Inheritors* should be on the more inclusive image of the artist as voyager through deep waters. The art has grown deeper and more complex in the second novel, and the vision which concludes the book looks forward to an exploration of individual man in society. The next two novels will seek to extend Golding's range in different ways, until Tuami's vision of unified opposites can become the single vision of *The Spire*. *The Inheritors* reveals Golding as an explorer, and his art 'not still, but still moving'.

III

PINCHER MARTIN

(1956)

I

This is a book about a man alone on a rock in mid-Atlantic—which seems a bleak prospect; but the novel at its simplest is already a *tour de force*, the challenge met by a vivid realization of the castaway's predicament. We feel in their grandeur and terror the realities of rock, sky, and sea; the pressure on a man of a Nature crushingly alien to him; the struggle to stay alive and sane; the physical and mental deterioration; the madness that is convincing on a naturalistic level before it is anything else. Golding's first achievement, to borrow words from Philip Larkin, is that he can 'overwhelmingly persuade' that this is a real man on a real rock, 'in every sense empirically true'.

Yet 'realism' is a notoriously treacherous concept for the critic of the novel, and we need to remind ourselves that there are as many 'realities' as there are kinds of imaginative vision that can persuade. If we feel tempted to pinpoint Golding's achievement by contrast with, say, Defoe's, this cannot be a matter of praising him for greater fidelity to some supposed criterion of 'reality'. The usefulness of the comparison will be that it may help us to define the kind of imaginative vision we are dealing with, by contrast with another kind:

'. . . the Sea having hurried me along as before, landed me, or rather dash'd me against a Piece of Rock, and that with such Force, as it left me senseless, and indeed helpless, as to my own Deliverance; for the Blow taking my Side and Breast, beat the Breath as it were quite out of my Body; and had it returned again immediately, I must have been strangled in the Water; but I recover'd a little before the return of the Waves, and seeing I should be cover'd again with the Water, I resolv'd to hold fast by a Piece of the Rock, and so to hold my Breath, if possible, till the Wave went back; now as the Waves were not so high as at first, being nearer Land, I held my Hold till the Wave abated, and then fetch'd another Run, which brought me so near the Shore, that the next Wave, tho' it went over me, yet did not swallow me up as to carry me away, and the next Run I took, I got to the main Land, where, to my great Comfort, I clamber'd up the Clifts of the Shore,

and sat me down upon the Grass free from Danger, and quite out
of the Reach of the Water . . .

'. . . I walk'd about on the Shore, lifting up my Hands, and my
whole Being, as I may say, wrapt up in the Contemplation of my
Deliverance, making a Thousand Gestures and Motions which
I cannot describe, reflecting upon all my Comrades that were
drown'd, and that there should not be one Soul sav'd but my
self; for, as for them, I never saw them afterwards, or any sign of
them, except three of their Hats, one Cap, and two Shoes that
were not Fellows.'

Defoe keeps our attention fixed on the man, so that although the
sea threatens to overwhelm him, we never doubt that he is in
control. The verbs accumulate to establish our response; for a
short while they belong to the sea, but the loose syntax turns, the
object becomes the subject and the passive the active. 'I must have
been strangl'd in the Water; but I recover'd . . .', 'I resolv'd . . .',
'I held . . .', 'I clamber'd up . . . sat me down . . . quite out of the
Reach of the Water'. The things denoted by capitals are objects,
with no resonance, that the 'I' and the actions deal with. The
imaginative vision sees the world as one of objects for humans to
act on, objects dangerous, or useful, or not useful like the shoes
that are largely denuded of their pathos by the automatic
recording of their uselessness. It is clear that the 'reality' Defoe
seeks to convey has little to do with the experience of what it must
feel like nearly to drown and then be saved. His is the 'realism' of
pure record—this happened and then this. The very absence of
personal feeling testifies to the 'truth' of what is said, the 'facts' are
presented as they have to be in a law-court, stripped of imaginative
connotation with nothing between them and us. We are aware
not so much of an individual character, or even an individual
situation, as of a detached narrative voice neutrally recording
a crisis overcome.

Pincher Martin shows another man drowning and seeming to
strike shore:

'Then he was there, suddenly, enduring pain but in deep communion with the solidity that held up his body. He remembered
how eyes should be used and brought the two lines of sight together so that the patterns fused and made a distance.

'The pebbles were close to his face, pressing against his cheek and jaw. They were white quartz, dulled and rounded, a miscellany of potato-shapes. Their whiteness was qualified by yellow stains and flecks of darker material. There was a whiter thing beyond them. He examined it without curiosity, noting the bleached wrinkles, the blue roots of nails, the corrugations at the finger-tips. He did not move his head, but followed the line of the hand back to an oilskin sleeve, the beginnings of a shoulder. His eyes returned to the pebbles and watched them idly as if they were about to perform some operation for which he was waiting without much interest. The hand did not move.

'Water welled up among the pebbles. It stirred them slightly, paused, then sank away while the pebbles clicked and chirruped. It swilled down past his body and pulled gently at his stockinged feet. He watched the pebbles while the water came back and this time the last touch of the sea lopped into his open mouth. Without change of expression he began to shake, a deep shake that included the whole of his body. Inside his head it seemed that the pebbles were shaking because the movement of his white hand forward and back was matched by the movement of his body. Under the side of his face the pebbles nagged.'

Where Defoe's passage is dominated by the personal pronoun, in Golding it is not the beholder but what is beheld that takes all our attention. He works to make us experience as directly as possible what is being described; these are the sensations that might have been ours if we were skilful enough to catch and record them. Defoe's scene is framed within the will of his character, in Golding the scene itself is hypnotic, drawing the eye to note with increasing intensity whatever is placed before it. The pebbles are first felt, then seen: 'solidity . . . dulled and rounded . . . potato-shapes . . . whiteness . . . qualified by yellow stains and flecks of darker material'. Attention is gradually focused, we are made to see with the same kind of riveted attention as Pincher. Then, almost imperceptibly, out of sensation wells emotion. The passage seems to start even more disinterestedly than Defoe's, but the dulled objectivity is charged because we sense the suffering that has produced it. We are dimly aware that the obsessively detailed vision is somehow abnormal; as the body begins to shake there is released in us a veiled kind of horror, diffuse, undirected. We are never, as in Defoe, an audience for a narrator. We are inside a head, we are a pair of eyes, a consciousness aware of fear and pain.

The two kinds of 'realism' these passages aim at is an inseparable part of the imaginative vision, and hence the structure of the novels from which they come; we can detect in the organization of each a hint of an overall rhythm. Defoe's narrative stance and cataloguing tone have the immediate effect of distancing his story so that we feel it capable of swift onward movement. The novel will be a loose, widely ranging, rapid account of actions which gradually impose a man's organization on the world. Golding, on the contrary, will do everything to cut down distance, to maximize detail, to build up the narrative in the detail itself. The novel will be hypnotic, densely textured, a growth not of action but of consciousness. It will seem at first that the awareness is mainly, even obsessively, physical; an experience through the senses of a man's subjection to his environment. But in fact where the 'realism' is taking us is inside his head. We might not be able to predict the full outcome, but it will eventually reveal a fearful imaginative logic. The rock, whose 'realism' is itself so considerable an achievement, will disappear; the inside of the head will remain the only 'reality' that exists.

Realism in *Pincher Martin*, then, turns out to be increasingly ironic. Yet we must begin with the convincing rendering of rock and sea and sky, for these are the primary imaginative experience, it is their hypnotism that rivets us, and it is only in and through them that Golding can hope to capture the full resonance of his myth:

'He worked across the rock and back from trench to trench. He came on the mouldering bones of fish and a dead gull, its up-turned breast-bone like the keel of a derelict boat. He found patches of grey and yellow lichen, traces even of earth, a button of moss. There were the empty shells of crabs, pieces of dead weed, and the claws of a lobster.'

'He lowered himself carefully and inspected the cliff. Under water the harvest of food was even thicker for the mussels were bigger down there and water snails were crawling over them. And among the limpets, the mussels, the snails and barnacles, dotted like sucked sweets, were the red blobs of jelly, the anemones. Under water they opened their mouths in a circle of petals, but up by his face, waiting for the increase of the tide they were pursed up and slumped like breasts when the milk has been drawn from them.'

'There was something peculiar about the sound that came out of his mouth . . . He held his nose with his right hand and tried to blow through it until the pressure rounded his cheeks. Nothing cracked in his ears . . . He stood up, facing a whole amphitheatre of water and sang a scale . . . The sound ended at his mouth . . . He closed his lips, lowered his hand slowly. The blue, igloo-roof over the rock went away to a vast distance, the visible world expanded with a leap. The water lopped round a tiny rock in the middle of the Atlantic. The strain tautened his face.'

The man's physical predicament is vividly there. Food is nauseous, water perilous, the body blotched with bruises and urticaria, the mind and senses swept by waves of fever through exposure. We are made to experience the bruising rock, the crushing weight of air, the idiot depth of water, the suffering body, and the agonized mind trying to keep an ever more precarious hold on identity and sanity.

Moreover, it is against this experience that the stature of the man's struggle to survive becomes measurable. The terrible food underlines the indomitable will that forces him to eat; the tasteless water held in so precariously by furry red silt heightens our appreciation of the intelligence which creates the 'Claudian aqueduct'. The way we get to know the rock ourselves in all its bleak inhospitability, allows us the measure of the 'naming of parts', the attempt of frightened and solitary man to tame his environment by netting it down with names. The creation of 'man-shape'—the 'dwarf' with the silver-paper face, the line of seaweed as a man-mark visible from the air—has a heroic as well as a pathetic side. On the one hand the rock cuts man-shape down to size. The dwarf enacts the diminishing, and how in the absence of other faces the 'face' merely reflects an alien, inhuman environment. The seaweed measures the puniness of unaccommodated man whose intelligence sees so much, but whose frame can accomplish so very little. Man is seen unromantically, clinically, for what he is in himself: Pharaoh without the ant-hordes who built the pyramids, the officer without the great machinery of his century. Yet for all this, man is not simply diminished: his qualities of endurance, courage, resourcefulness are also thrown into sharp relief.

So we spend an entire novel on a tiny rock, fascinated, convinced, and imaginatively extended by a deeper understanding of the pressures of sea, sky, and rock on unaccommodated man, and involved with what is in some sense an epic of human endurance, whatever else it may turn into. The man is an Atlas holding up an alien world that threatens to crush him; but the scene is not facile because we can feel the strain on the physical muscles. He is a Prometheus tortured on a rock; but when pain, delirium, and madness arrive, they are very far from notional or 'poetic'. There is about his predicament, and his response to it, the stature of Man against the Elements. Is Man no more than this, this bare fork'd animal? Perhaps, but he is certainly no less.

On the level we have been discussing so far, *Pincher Martin* has in common with *Robinson Crusoe* a lack of concern with individual character; we find it easy in both cases to talk about 'the man', or even Man. Nothing we have said so far depends upon what the particular man was like in society, what he had done, the nature of his personality and relationships. But a substantial part of *Pincher Martin* is very much concerned—in a special way—with the character indicated by its title, and his past. Here, necessarily, a very different imaginative vision is at work.

We are left in no doubt about the nature of that character. He was an actor, and the part he played most successfully in life, summarized in his nickname, is sufficiently indicated when the producer of a morality play introduces him to the masks of the seven deadly sins:

' "What's it supposed to be, old man?"
 ' "Darling, it's simply *you!* Don't you think, George?"
 ' "Definitely, old man, definitely."

‘ "Chris—Greed. Greed—Chris. Know each other."

‘ "Anything to please you, Pete."

‘ "Let me make you two better acquainted. This painted bastard here takes anything he can lay his hands on. Not food, Chris, that's far too simple. He takes the best part, the best seat, the most money, the best notice, the best woman. He was born with his mouth and his flies open and both hands out to grab. He's a cosmic case of the bugger who gets his penny and someone else's bun. Isn't that right, George?" ’

‘Chris—Greed. Greed—Chris'—the identification is documented in the manner of a dossier throughout the novel. The record is almost altogether black, the elements stark and unqualified. There is remorseless self-assertion: the young Pincher on a new bike manoeuvring a rival into a crash rather than be beaten; the resisting girl given the choice of walking home from a parked car or being maimed in a speeding one. There is sex for power and sex for advancement, sex with men and sex with a boy. There is theft plain and simple, a rifled cash-box and a conscience at ease: 'What are you going to do about it? There was nothing written down.' At strategic moments there are elaborate images which serve as choric commentary on these episodes. One of the most dominant is a carefully set scene between Martin and the producer he has betrayed, in which, with overtones borrowed from *Hamlet*, we get both moral anatomy and prophecy:

‘ "I love you, Chris. Father and mother is one flesh. And so my uncle. My prophetic uncle. Shall I elect you to my club?"

‘ "How about toddling home now, Pete?"

‘ "Call it the Dirty Maggot Club . . . We maggots are there all the week. Y'see when the Chinese want to prepare a very rare dish they bury a fish in a tin box. Presently all the lil' maggots peep out and start to eat. Presently no fish. Only maggots. It's no bloody joke being a maggot . . . It's a lousy job crawling round the inside of a tin box and Denmark's one of the worst. Well, when they've finished the fish, Chris, they start on each other."

‘ "Cheerful thought, old man."

‘ "The little ones eat the tiny ones. The middle-sized ones eat the little ones. The big ones eat the middle-sized ones. Then the big ones eat each other. Then there are two, and then one, and where there was a fish there is now one huge, successful maggot. Rare dish . . . 'N when there's only one maggot left the Chinese dig it up— . . . Have you ever heard a spade knocking on the side of a tin box, Chris? Boom! Boom! Just like thunder. You a member?"

As the flashbacks to the past accumulate the world they reveal was 'eat or be eaten', and in that world the man on the rock, Pincher Martin, was, for the moment, king.

In the course of the flashback record, however, two characters stand out in total contrast: Martin's great friend Nathaniel Walterson and the girl Nat marries, Mary Lovell. Mary is a first version of the girl who was to become Beatrice in *Free Fall*. For Martin she is a maddening contradiction: an anthology of petit-bourgeois convention, 'gloved and hatted for church, the Mary who ate with such maddening refinement . . . the pursed up mouth, the too high forehead, the mousey hair'; but also 'a treasure of demoniac and musky attractiveness that was all the more terrible because she was almost unconscious of it'. She calls his whole view of life in question: 'set there in the road to power and success, unbreakable yet tormenting with the need to conquer and break'. His feeling for her is not lust so much as a kind of hate, his 'nights of imagined copulation' go not with sensation or satisfaction but with the rhythm of 'take that, and that'. She eats into his existence like acid. Understanding nothing of the values which give her life its quality (the unity of Mary and Lovewell), he can only seek to break her will; he fails to do so in the desperate car journey in which he threatens that she will be 'burst and bitched', and earns only her contempt and loathing.

Nathaniel is a more elaborated figure. He is the 'saint' of the novel—wholly unworldly and innocent, genuine, humble, unselfish, loving. He is, it is true, presented as peculiar and even ludicrous—the extraordinary spidery lankiness, the language of 'meditation', the theories of soul-migration and astrology, the spiritual lecturing, the total lack of humour. But this is no more than a familiar technique whereby one tries to win acceptance and credit for 'goodness' by making it slightly comic. There is little doubt that 'sheer niceness' is meant to be our predominant and final impression. He marries Mary, asking Chris to be best man.

In the darkest hour Chris knows before he hits the water: in Oxford, when, hearing the communal summoning of the bells, he recognizes in himself a complete blackness of solitude and exclusion—'Because of what I did I am an outsider and alone'—it is Nathaniel who arrives as Comforter, with a warning, but also with the warmth of companionship and love, and a promise about dying into heaven. He is entrusted on this occasion with the novel's central 'ideas'. And he produces in Chris the only unselfish moment that the whole kaleidoscope of memory reveals: a moment when he is driven to give warning against himself, before calculation and jealous hatred take over again. He cannot help loving Nat 'unwillingly . . . for the face that was always rearranged from within, for the serious attention, for love given without thought'; but he also hates him 'quiveringly . . . as though he were the only enemy'. This of course is what he is. The face whose expressions come from genuine movements of feeling and relationship within, is a continual reproach to the actor's manipulation of a mask that conceals the true features of Greed; the serious attention and love a standing index to the loveless egotism. The affection for Nat is the only feeling he has apart from that of self; but the goodness is hateful and must be destroyed because it threatens the autonomy of the selfish ego. It is far more than jealousy over Mary; Nat stands in the way of his whole existence. So, as with Mary, he plots to destroy him. At the moment when the torpedo strikes the destroyer, Chris had shouted the order 'Hard a-starboard, for Christ's sake', which would have been the right order for avoiding the torpedo if it had been given a few seconds earlier. But in fact the order was attempted murder; for Nat, swaying unsteadily against the rail with eyes closed and hands before his face in prayer, is vulnerable to a sudden change in direction and a sea taken over the starboard bow. The final motive however is not rage, or jealousy, or hatred. Martin is searching for 'a kind of peace'—and only the destruction of Nat (or the destruction of himself) could give it to him.

From the drift of the flashbacks and the treatment of Nathaniel and Mary it can easily be seen that Golding is aiming at a very different kind of reality from that on the rock. There everything was excessively concentrated, densely particularized; here everything is distanced and type-cast, the web of circumstance calculatedly removed. We do not in fact find 'character' in the sense we tend to expect from fiction; we are confronted with moral figures in the past where we had been confronted with archetypal Man in the present. So there exist in constant and even violent juxtaposition a world of dense, non-individualistic sensation, and a world of morality-play or illustrated catalogue for the confessional.

One's first reaction is probably to see these contrasted realities in succinct terms of imaginative success and failure: to insist that the morality play is a rhetoric of statement rather than imaginative creation; that its attitudes are damagingly oversimplified to the point, often, of crudity; that it is frequently artificial and unconvincing as a portrait of credible people in credible situations; that its language tends both to the unimaginatively coarse and the imaginatively over-elaborated; that, in a word, the worst and the best of Golding lie side by side. Moreover, is there not a curious gap in causality between the two worlds? We hardly needed Golding to tell us* that he set out to make his protagonist as unpleasant as he possibly could, but why? Rock, sea, and sky, are great levellers; it hardly seems to matter, when we are cast away with Martin, what kind of a man he is. He could not, it is true, be gutless or stupid, but do we really need to assume so monstrous a character to explain his will, courage, endurance or resourcefulness? Are the novelist's left and right hands not only doing different, but essentially unrelated things?

Yet we had better pause again. For the effect of the flashbacks is obviously calculated; and if there is a failure it must lie in the conception rather than the realization. Indeed the cliché term flashback is itself more accurate than usual, for Pincher makes continual photographic and cinematic reference to his memories as 'pictures', 'glossy and illuminated scenes', 'snapshots', 'film trailers'. Golding clearly wants the memories to have only the same relation to real life as photography has: they must seem framed all round, artificially lit and polished, stills rather than motion pictures aiming at the illusion of reality, and, if they do move, giving the sense of being deliberately selected from a bigger film in order to provide an artificially heightened sense of the nature of the whole. He has deliberately chosen to emphasise the

* Interview with Kermode, *Books and Bookmen*.

artificiality by making Pincher's past an actor's world and its language a theatrical argot. Above all, the technique is designed to enforce the sense of the past as utterly over, completed, with that quality of a vanished world that old films and photographs possess.

There will be reasons for this—but for the moment it may be useful to notice a new sense of the peculiarity of the novel's conception: for behind the superficially violent contrast of the 'real' world of the rock and the glossy pictures with their moral configuration, there can now be seen to lie a more significant resemblance. Both are essentially static, outside time. Both are already determined, incapable of change. This is immediately obvious in the flashbacks; but it will not take us long to perceive that the 'life' on the rock, too, can only be further revealed for what it already is. The man may become more aware of his situation, or fulfil it, but he cannot change it. He may die, but he is already dying.

In fact, of course, the last page of the novel notoriously reveals that its hero is dead, and has been dead since the second page:

'But the man lay suspended behind the whole commotion, detached from his jerking body. The luminous pictures that were shuffled before him were drenched in light but he paid no attention to them. Could he have controlled the nerves of his face, or could a face have been fashioned to fit the attitude of his consciousness where it lay suspended between life and death that face would have worn a snarl. But the real jaw was contorted down and distant, the mouth was slopped full. The green tracer that flew from the centre began to spin into a disc. The throat at such a distance from the snarling man vomited water and drew it in again. The hard lumps of water no longer hurt. There was a kind of truce, observation of the body. There was no face but there was a snarl.'

Seconds later, 'his distant body stilled itself and relaxed.' This is the moment of Pincher's death: 'the real jaw was contorted . . . the mouth slopped full'; yet 'there was no face but there was a snarl'. The disparity between reality and moral figure, and the resemblance, are exposed in two sentences. The novel is static: it exists out of time, where a lifetime can be expressed in a moment, the moment of death. Both kinds of rhetoric are ways of expressing a stasis. On the one hand Golding sets up his obsessional rhythms of sensation so that we are caught and held in an overwhelming now (this is what it is like to drown). On the other, the now reveals just as starkly and statically the eternal figure of the man (a mask of Greed, snarling). There remains only the question of the connection between the present and the past, the face and the snarl: but that is what the novel is going to be about. What is absolutely and necessarily missing is the future.

Where then does the dynamism of the novel come from, our immediate sense that there is a future as we read, that the situation can change? It comes from what can now be seen to be the novel's most cardinal fact: it can only exist if its protagonist is the kind of man who is totally incapable of accepting his own extinction and who must refuse to die, to the point where the greatest conceivable leap of the novelist's imagination will fail to follow him into the unknown. That is why the protagonist had to be, not Everyman, but a particular kind of man pursued to the limit of his figure: the Christ-bearer become Pincher.

What will a Pincher do at the moment of death?—the moment when there is either no time or eternity? He *invents* a world in which the ego he will not relinquish can continue to exist. And it is his invention of a future that gives the novel its dynamism and its meaning. This is where we shall find the energy of the fiction and its conflict; yet increasingly we are also made aware that it is all illusory, that we exist in a moment blown up like a bubble to the point at which it will and must burst . . . A 'present' that overwhelms the senses, a 'past' so remote that it is like 'a show of trailers of old films', both of them determined—the novel is the record of the unique moment when these two are precariously brought together through a wholly invented 'reality'. It is this invention which gives the novel both its subject and its form. Neither 'a real man on a real rock' nor 'a morality play' are the 'real world' of the novel . . . it has no real world outside the moment of death on which it begins and ends. But we have to learn to see that moment for what it is. The novel is like one of those tapestries that show different pictures when one stands on one side of the room or the other; but we only look from the right angle when we can see a third perspective coming magically into focus, containing and explaining the others.

II

In the split second of death, Pincher Martin conceives an image which gives him a world of consciousness into which he can try desperately to escape.

'The jam jar was standing on a table, brightly lit from O.P. It might have been a huge jar in the centre of a stage or a small one almost touching the face, but it was interesting because one could see into a little world there which was quite separate but which one could control. The jar was nearly full of clear water and a tiny glass figure floated upright in it. The top of the jar was covered with a thin membrane—white rubber. He watched the jar without moving or thinking while his distant body stilled itself and re-laxed. The pleasure of the jar lay in the fact that the little glass figure was so delicately balanced between opposing forces. Lay a finger on the membrane and you would compress the air below it which in turn would press more strongly on the water. Then the water would force itself farther up the little tube in the figure, and it would begin to sink. By varying the pressure on the membrane you could do anything you liked with the glass figure which was wholly in your power. You could mutter,—sink now! And down it would go, down, down; you could steady it and relent. You could let it struggle towards the surface, give it almost a bit of air then send it steadily, slowly, remorselessly down and down.

'The delicate balance of the glass figure related itself to his body. In a moment of wordless realisation he saw himself touching the surface of the sea with just such a dangerous stability, poised between floating and going down. The snarl thought words to itself. They were not articulate, but they were there in a luminous way as a realisation.

'Of course. My lifebelt . . . Suddenly he knew who he was and where he was. He was lying suspended in the water like the glass figure; he was not struggling but limp. A swell was washing regularly over his head.'

And so the body of the sailor lifts its head, pulls off its seaboots, inflates its life-belt, and 'lives'. Refusing to accept extinction he plays God to himself, raising the pressure on his own rubber membrane so that the figure of Pincher Martin rises to the surface of a world he himself creates. But if the novel wrily illustrates Nat's lecture-topic, 'the sort of heaven we invent for ourselves after death, if we aren't ready for the real one'; the essence of the experience is the knowledge that existence is only possible by a kind of temporary permission, a rope paid out, an inscrutable game going on below the surface. The jar and the glass figure, the little world 'quite separate, but which one could control', in fact only give the appearance of control. The operator thinks in his Pincherish way that he is the power-wielder exercising his will. But 'the pleasure of the jar lay in the fact that the little glass figure was so delicately balanced between opposing forces'; and these are not under the finger's control, though they may allow it to operate while they remain constant. There are physical forces like water and the body, but there is a controlling factor above all: the pressure of the real heavens outside the little world of the jar, of God if He exists, or of the blank immensity of empty space if He does not.

Consequently when one re-reads the book with its last sentence still in one's ear—'He didn't even have time to kick off his sea-boots'—the experience of the first reading is radically altered. The world which one had hailed for its dense and detailed 'reality', now reveals for page after page the terrifying strain of maintaining it, indeed, of making it up. What the experience *is* is that of surface tension, of inflating the bubble with infinite care and precision because it has to keep out absolute nothingness; or of teetering along a tightrope over an infinite chasm, never knowing, not only when one's own foot might slip, but when some cosmic hand might decide to give the rope a sudden twitch. And the mind must never allow itself consciously to know what it is doing; or the whole of existence will be annihilated. Pincher must invent his whole world by a kind of deliberate dreaming which must always obey every law of being awake so that he never finds out it is a dream. And there is a wry game going on all the time which can never be admitted either; there is a secret Antagonist.

Now his wars on God begin,
At stroke of midnight God shall win.

God, or utter nothingness.

There plays across the narrative chapters, in fact, another structure altogether: a kind of parody of the Divine Week of Creation, but ending at the beginning of the Seventh Day when the work of human hands must be set aside.

On the first Day the Will creates sea and sky around itself, creates day and night, creates the rock. A convulsion of will moves the body into buoyancy, but the move leaves him 'no better off than I was' because the Antagonist counters with the necessity, if the dream is not to be revealed as dream, of experiencing numbing cold, terrible depth of water, absolute blackness, of facing (though alive) 'an eternity inseparable from pain'. He creates dawn, but pictures in his mind like the one of a jam jar try to tell him the truth and get between him and the urgency of his movement towards the dim light—yet the will sees them in a way that robs them of significance. All the same the cold seeps in, and the hopelessness. But the will summons him to another effort. 'Think. My last chance. Think what can be done'—and the imagination summons up a shape. A ship? No, too complicated; a not-ship, a rock, that in its own way is no less terrible than the water, but promises a kind of safety.

As he lies slumped in exhaustion on the pebbles, there is still danger. The pictures in the mind and the pebbles under the face are perilously interchangeable, as though one were as real, or as unreal, as the other. The mind still treacherously threatens to give the game away by remembering sailor and jam jar; as the will recovers its sense of identity the abyss can always open without notice, at any moment. To think of the rock as 'one tooth set in the ancient jaw of a sunken world, projecting through the inconceivable vastness of the whole ocean' can, for a reason still obscure, produce a 'deep and generalized terror (which) set him clawing at the rock with his blunt fingers . . . "Think, you bloody fool, think." ' Hastily he 'remembers' a captain pointing to a rock on a chart whose real name cannot, had better not, be remembered. (Rockall is too near a miss to an obscenity whose meaning would be disastrous.)

He is still 'no better off than I was', though 'the consciousness was moving and poking about among the pictures and revelations ... like an animal ceaselessly examining its cage', and finding some reassurance in the knowledge of its own intelligence. But, suddenly, the Adversary moves again. If this is a real sea and rock there must be tides—the cleft cannot be safety—it must be a sea-trap. He must climb. But though he imagines an initial foothold, an opening shaped like an ashtray, suspiciously facile, there is something in the mind which knows the real nature of the imagined surface and knows that it would be too smooth, like ivory. So the panicking consciousness traps itself, stuck 'like a dead man'. The snarl returns. But the mind makes another desperate convulsion: *not* like a dead man, 'like a limpet'—and in a panic-shot blind leap of imagination the body fantastically climbs through the funnel, on top of the rock, by using two limpets like mountaineering wedges. The Adversary has won the first round on points. The Will has survived, the thing was not absolutely impossible, but the bounds of credibility have had to be stretched to breaking-point.

Immediately, in near collapse, the Will makes what will turn out to be a serious error. There is a painful consciousness trying to get in through the 'eye', a needle continually probing the brain through the visual imagination. The Will tries to explain it, and so get rid of it. Remembering real rocks, and knowing at the back of the mind that the nature of this 'rock' requires the presence of whitish matter, the Will brilliantly invents guano, and then goes on triumphantly to explain the eye-pain as the effect of a solution of guano and water smeared across the eye when the body fell across the trench. But success is only partial: salt water will not wash the pain out. 'The idea that he must ignore pain came and it in the centre of his darkness where he could not avoid it.' Hopelessness returns:

'The chill and the exhaustion spoke to him clearly. Give up, they said, lie still. Give up the thought of return, the thought of living. Break up, leave go ... An hour on this rock is a lifetime. What have you to lose? There is nothing here but torture...

'His body began to crawl again ... There was at the centre of all the pictures and pains and voices a fact like a bar of steel, a thing—that which was so nakedly the centre of everything that it could not even examine itself. In the darkness of the skull, it existed, a darker dark, self-existent and indestructible.

' "Shelter. Must have shelter." '

So the first 'Day' ends with the body crawling into a crevice like a lobster. In the 'Night' the consciousness that wishes to rest, but cannot, edges around a realization of his predicament. There is a kind of being in which he floats, in the dark side of a kind of globe, 'like a waterlogged body':

'He knew as an axiom of existence that he must be content with the smallest of all small mercies as he floated there . . . If he could hit some particular mode of inactive being, some subtlety of interior balance, he might be allowed . . . to float, still and painless in the centre of the globe.'

But always the needle jabs the eye, forcing him to go on making the physical situation real and justifying its reality. So a new Day of creation must begin.

He imagines a gull clucking to wake him; but the second Day (pp. 56–72) starts with what will turn out to be another serious mistake. He 'sees' the gulls wrong, not as smooth-outlined birds but as 'flying reptiles'—but mistakes don't matter unless they are realized. The work of the Second Day is the food and water he needs to 'live'; but with horrible irony the 'rules' set limits within which he has to operate, and the cry of 'Bloody Hell' voices his horror at the 'oval brown foot' of the limpet and the 'blobs of red jelly'. What he is inventing, *pace* Nathaniel, is no Heaven. His invention of a water-supply is also an image of the perilous nature of his situation: the tasteless necessity only just held in by the furry silt mirrors his own predicament, 'held back so delicately that the merest touch would set his life irrevocably flowing—He backed away with staring eyes and breath that came quick. "Forget it!" ' But he cannot. The imagination also shows a submerged but perceptible hint of what the true reality of tiny cavity and red slimy rim might be; as does the language which describes the sea, 'the constant gurgling and sucking that ranged from a stony smack to a ruminative swallow. There were sounds that seemed every moment to be on the point of articulation but lapsed into a liquid slapping like appetite'. This also applies to a strangeness about the other great creation of the Second Day, the man-shape of the dwarf. On one of the jagged rocks that he has lugged from its place and manhandled across the trenches there is an unexplained trace of blood. The mind stirs treacherously again beneath the carefully maintained surface, always hinting at what it dare not express: exactly what the 'rock' is, and how he came to imagine *that* in his moment of need.

In the Night of the Second Day the Will, while ever more nearly admitting its predicament, nevertheless asserts itself more strongly than ever, in spite of everything. He remembers, dangerously, Nathaniel's words. 'You could say that I know it is important for you personally to understand about heaven—about dying—because in only a few years . . .' On the rock, as in the room at Oxford, stinging pain whips into the 'globe' as the consciousness anticipates the words that must not be spoken—'you will be dead'. The Will immediately 'wakes' itself from this dangerous corner, which nevertheless can safely be thought of as a 'dream' of the past. The response however is intense: 'I'll be damned if I'll die.' We can see clearly enough that it isn't a case of inventing one's own 'heaven' because one isn't ready for the real one. Pincher asserts himself *in spite of* 'everything'. There is the shout, a burst of jeering laughter, a 'hosing gesture' of urination at the horizon.

The morning of the Third Day (pp. 72–96) has begun. This is the zenith of Pincher's creative achievement: he makes his body real to himself, battered, but all the more convincing; he imagines in reassuring detail what there is in his pockets; above all, he remembers his identity disc and summons its objective statements before his eyes:

' "Christopher Hadley Martin. Martin. Chris. I am what I always was!"

'All at once it seemed to him that he came out of his curious isolation inside the globe of his head and was extended normally through his limbs. He lived again on the surface of his eyes, he was out in the air . . . The solid rock was coherent as an object, with layered guano, with fresh water and shell fish. It was a position in a finite sea at the intersection of two lines, there were real ships passing under the horizon.'

He assures the quiet sea that with health and education and intelligence he will win; but he knows that he is 'really' talking to himself. For him now, as for Robinson Crusoe, the island has become an 'estate', which can be 'inspected not only with the eyes but with the understanding'. It has a rational geological history which can incorporate without strain the image of how 'a tooth bursts out of the fleshy jaw'. Even when this becomes a mental picture of the line of rocks as like teeth gradually being worn away, there is irritation rather than fright, for the suggestiveness is buried in millennia of geological time. 'The process is so slow, it has no relevance to——'

But the sentence never gets finished, for the Antagonist moves again; the words spoken aloud seem to fall dead at the lips. For the situation which the wearing process is too slow to be relevant to is dependent on the pressure of an atmosphere; and if the rock is to be a real one, its isolation in enormous space without resonance must act thus on the human voice. Involuntarily he cries out 'My God!', clutches the Dwarf in his horror—and its head falls off. The moment that there is no faith in the ability of the human head to control reality, manshape is broken; but in a fury of willed activity he builds the Dwarf up again, bigger than before. 'Out of this nettle danger—' he has managed to pluck this flower safety, for the moment.

He preaches a sermon to himself, a practical one like Ralph's, about a rescue, about survival, about what must be done to keep the body going and 'the thread of life unbroken' in spite of sickness and suffering—but there is more obviously now a Spectre to be feared for him as well as Ralph. He starts to admit that he has already had 'hallucinations'; and though he cannot carry the admission through, he warns himself against insanity stealing up and taking him by surprise. For he has been shaken, in broad 'daylight', and his consciousness cannot settle its grip. He has stopped living on the surface of his eyes, and finds himself seeing through a window with three lights—eye, nose, eye—and a window-box of moustache; but the vision sometimes suddenly reverses itself so that 'reality' is outside him looking in: 'The window was surrounded by inscrutable darkness which extended throughout his body.' He tries to persuade himself that this 'is the ordinary experience of living'. He insists in imposing himself on the rock, refusing to adapt himself to its ways, netting it down and taming it with names. But the peak of achievement is past, and as the Third Day ends in Night the tiring brain drops its guard once more.

'This rock.
' "I shall call those three rocks out there the Teeth."
'All at once he was gripping the lifebelt with both hands and tensing his muscles to defeat the deep shudders that were sweeping through him.
' "No! Not the Teeth!"
'The teeth were here, inside his mouth. He felt them with his tongue, the double barrier of bone, each known and individual except the gaps—and there they persisted as a memory if one troubled to think. But to lie on a row of teeth in the middle of the sea—
'He began to think desperately about sleep.'

But he is afraid to sleep, afraid to let 'the carefully hoarded and enjoyed personality, our only treasure and at the same time our only defence . . . die into the ultimate truth of things, the black lightning that splits and destroys all, the positive, unquestionable nothingness'.

In extremity the material and the immaterial become confused again. A series of sharply distinct snapshot memories, whose meaning remains obscure because the mind will not explore them, is succeeded by one terribly focused because it speaks of the present as well as the past and is horribly meaningful:

'This was a bright patch, sometimes like a figure eight lying on its side and sometimes a circle. The circle was filled with blue sea where gulls were wheeling and settling and loving to eat and fight. He felt the swing of the ship under him, sensed the bleak stillness and silence that settled on the bridge as the destroyer slid by the thing floating in the water—a thing, humble and abused and still among the fighting beaks, an instrument of pleasure.

'He struggled out into the sun, stood up and cried flatly in the great air.

' "I am awake!" '

With a convulsion of his whole being, he creates a new Day.

The Fourth Day (pp. 96–122), the 'thinking day' he had promised himself, turns out to be one in which his imagination overtaxes itself. Existence becomes purposeful with the brilliant idea of supplementing the Dwarf's assertion to the sea with the line of seaweed asserting himself to the air. He is able to commit himself to the water again to gather weed, and he works hard—so hard that his concentrating mind makes another mistake about a lobster, which goes completely unnoticed, but will turn out to be disastrous. And what he has conceived is too huge to be done in reality; half of his mind is assailing him with hopelessness. The other half tries to distract him—there's a plop in the sea, is it a fish?—but not for long. He oscillates between assertion and despair:

'I may never get away from this rock at all.

'Speech is identity.

' "You are all a machine. I know you, wetness, hardness, movement. You have no mercy but you have no intelligence. I can outwit you. All I have to do is to endure. I breathe this air into my own furnace. I kill and eat. There is nothing to—"

'He paused for a moment and watched the gull drifting nearer; but not so near that the reptile under the white was visible.

' "There is nothing to fear." '

This has a dying fall. And after a day of empty waiting and endurance there is a night when the thoughts and pictures always contain an obscure threat, and the 'fires' in his aching body become 'a luminous landscape . . . a universe, and he oscillated between moments of hanging in space, observing them, and of being extended to every excruciating corner'. What he has constructed is hell.

This time he does not 'wake', which is itself significant. He is forced to admit that he has never been asleep at all. On the Fifth Day (pp. 122–67) day and night lose their maintained distinction, time begins to have its stop, and the laboriously constructed world begins to lose conviction. The High Street looks like 'a picture. He shut his eyes and then opened them again, but the rock and the sea seemed no more real.' Looking into a crack in the rock no wider than an eighth of an inch he looks into 'a terrible darkness'. His mind begins 'envisaging the whole rock as a thing in the water . . . familiar . . . remembered . . . imagined as a shape one's fingers can feel in the air'. Only another loud plop from the warning side of his mind manages to turn the dangerously freewheeling consciousness aside. He is becoming aware 'outside' of more and more weight, a 'ponderous squeezing. Agoraphobia or anyway the opposite of claustrophobia. A pressure'—the vast pressure of the heavens on the glass sailor. 'Inside', the mind is becoming more and more difficult to control. ' "I must have a beard pretty well. Bristles anyway. Strange that bristles go on growing even when the rest of you is—" He went quickly to Prospect Cliff and got a load of weed.' He plans the Claudian aqueduct and begins to work on it, 'imposing purpose on the senseless rock', but: 'There is something venomous about the hardness of this rock. It is harder than rock should be. And— familiar.' In the very act of self-congratulation there lurks the abyss, ever nearer: 'Anyway I'll hand it to you Chris. I don't think many people would—' Would what? Would have been able to keep it up this long? The confident talk is replaced by agonized cries . . . 'Christopher' . . . 'Oh, my God'. Two arms reaching out to grab a vanishing identity before the eyes in a gesture that pre-figures the last that Pincher will ever make.

The Will goes on asserting but it is clearly losing its grip. He mistakes his hand for a lobster, and this tells us something about the colour of the one he saw before, as well as pointing to the state of his consciousness now. He cries out against his lessening sense of identity now that there are no other people to define him for himself in their love or hate. The pools on the rock will not reflect a definite image of his face because he cannot remember it accurately enough. And fantasy begins to proclaim itself as such: a seal suddenly becomes capable of being ridden to the Hebrides before the imagination can stop itself. It is like the waking nightmares of childhood, when the mind is uncontrollable:

'. . . those nights when I was a kid, lying awake thinking the darkness would go on for ever. And I couldn't go back to sleep because of the dream of the whatever it was in the cellar coming out of the corner. I'd lie in the hot, rumpled bed, hot burning hot, trying to shut myself away and know that there were three eternities before the dawn . . . And I'd think of anything because if I didn't go on thinking I'd remember whatever it was in the cellar down there, and my mind would go walking away from my body and go down three stories defenceless, down the dark stairs past the tall, haunted clock, through the whining door, down the terrible steps to where the coffin ends were crushed in the walls of the cellar*—and I'd be held helpless on the stone floor, trying to run back, run away, climb up——" '

The child's horror is the man's; it exactly expresses (while veiling itself, if only just, as 'memory') the way he is being forced to confront what is there in the inmost darkness of his mind. He may try to assert that he and the child have nothing in common, but there is something crushing him, something terrible just ahead, a part of the play he doesn't know about.

Cleverly, he seeks a new sanctuary in delirium; for in fever one can let go for a while and still come out again. So he lapses into a state which can 'realize' without committing itself to acceptance. In delirium all the faces from his past are stone, hung in rows in a corridor leading away from the 'theatre' of daily life. At the far end is the

'other room, to be avoided, because there the gods sat behind their terrible knees and feet of black stone, but here the stone faces wept and had wept. Their stone cheeks were furrowed, they were blurred and only recognizeable by some indefinite mode of identity. Their tears made a pool on the stone floor so that his feet were burned to the ankles. He scrabbled to climb up the wall and the scalding stuff welled up his ankles to his calves, his knees. He was struggling, half-swimming, half-climbing. The wall was

* This has a source in Golding's childhood. See 'The Ladder and the Tree', *The Hot Gates*, pp. 166–7, for the cellar and the graveyard, and the whole essay for a gloss on the 'two worlds without a bridge' of *Free Fall*. The mysterious experience in *Free Fall*, p. 154, is also apparently a childhood memory.

turning over, curving like the wall of a tunnel in the underground. The tears were no longer running down the stone to join the burning sea. They were falling freely, dropping on him. One came a dot, a pearl, a ball, a globe, that moved on him, spread. He began to scream. He was inside the ball of water that was burning him to the bone and past. It consumed him utterly. He was dissolved and spread throughout the tear an extension of sheer, disembodied pain.

'He burst the surface and grabbed a stone wall. There was hardly any light but he knew better than to waste time because of what was coming. There were projections in the wall of the tunnel so that though it was more nearly a well than a tunnel, he could still climb. He laid hold, pulled himself up, projection after projection. The light was bright enough to show him the projections. They were faces, like the ones in the endless corridor. They were not weeping but they were trodden. They appeared to be made of some chalky material for when he put his weight on them they would break away so that only by constant movement upward was he able to keep up at all. He could hear his voice shouting in the well.

' "I am! I am! I am!" '

The talking voice, drooling away with its 'explanation' that this is all Freudian stuff, tunnels and wells and water, just sexual and familiar, known, cannot fool him, let alone us. This, and the insight of the cellar, are the 'truest' things to have happened since the opening pages, more essential than the manufactured present, or the snapshotted past which now merely glosses the insights which bring it into focus.

Now 'the pressure of the sky and air was right inside his head. A thought was forming like a piece of sculpture behind the eyes but in front of the unexamined centre . . . But he knew the thought was an enemy and so although he saw it he did not consent or allow it to become attached to him in realization.' What he sees through his 'window' has become only a pattern of colour, not exterior, but 'like a lighted picture on the wall', 'the only visible thing in a dark room'. Inexorably, the 'thought' rises like a Kraken from the depths:

' "There is a pattern emerging. I do not know what the pattern is but even my dim guess at it makes my reason falter."

'The lower half of his face moved round the mouth till the teeth were bare.

' "Weapons. I have things that I can use."

'Intelligence. Will like a last ditch. Will like a monolith. Survival . . .'

Almost for the last time the snarl rallies: 'Why drag in good and evil when the serpent lies coiled in my own body?' The Will makes a last effort to localize the poison that threatens its existence in a place where it can be purged; the administration of the enema curiously, but necessarily, mingles the heroic, the pathetic and the comic-grotesque. For a moment it seems to work. He has the sense that life has begun anew. Until, inevitably, real disaster strikes through apparent triumph.

On a real island, rocks seem to move when the tide is running strongly. The Antagonist feints, but Pincher is not fooled. He knows it is an optical illusion. But he is shaken—and as he looks sharply down at his feet to see that the rock is steady, the gesture brings back what he had seen the last time he made it, gathering weed. Now the appalled mind takes in what it 'saw' then: ' "Whoever saw a lobster like that swimming in the sea? A red lobster?" ' As we ought to have deduced from the mistake about his hands, he had forgotten that lobsters are only red when they are cooked. When he 'saw' the lobster, 'as if his eye had created it . . . among the weed, different in dragon shape, different in colour', he over-reached himself. Now the irony of the language comes home. In one shattering second, truth appears: 'Something was taken away. For an instant he felt himself falling; and then there came a gap of darkness in which there was no one.' The five-day-creation vanishes. Time stops. The abyss opens:

'Something was coming up to the surface. It was uncertain of its identity because it had forgotten its name. It was disorganized in pieces. It struggled to get these pieces together because then it would know what it was. There was a rhythmical noise and disconnection. The pieces came shakily together . . . There was a separation between now, whenever now was, and the instant of terror . The separation enabled him to forget what had caused that terror. The darkness of separation was deeper than that of sleep. It was deeper than any living darkness because time had stopped or come to an end. It was a gap of not-being, a well opening out of the world and now the effort of mere being was so exhausting that he could only lie sideways and live.

'Presently he thought.

' "Then I was dead. That was death. I have been frightened to death. Now the pieces of me have come together and I am just alive." '

It is only possible for Pincher to exist at all because the eye does play tricks in real life, and the Will can seize on one optical illusion it has just experienced, as a subconscious theory to explain another, provided it can forget what happened. But existence is utterly precarious now, depending on total lapse of memory and bound to fail. The 'reality' of the rock cannot be recaptured: 'This side of the gap is different from the other. It's like when you have finished a lights rehearsal and they cut. Then where there was bright, solid scenery is now only painted stuff, grey under the pilot light. It's like chess. You've got an exultant attack moving but overlooked a check and now the game is a fight. And you're tied down.'

Though there is a Sixth Day, it is no longer under Pincher's control. Lightning flickers, and 'some deep seat of rationality' in him sees, indeed creates for the last time, the promised rain from the lambent threat. Yet, as it pours torrentially, flooding him out of his crevice, we may remember another rain that fell and destroyed a false world, and we can certainly see that Pincher neither controls it, nor does it bring him the expected satisfaction. He tries to rebuild his precarious sanity, but while his mouth lectures uneasily about the uncertain borders between sanity and mania or neurosis, the 'centre' 'was moving and flinching from isolated outcrops of knowledge. It averted attention from one only to discover another.' It cannot last. Only too soon, on this Rock which is also the Cellar to which all the paths of his life have led, and where the Spectre he most feared must be faced, knowledge cannot be avoided any longer. Not only has he seen a red lobster which might be an optical illusion; he has also forgotten that guano is insoluble. To be sane is to be forced to admit what he has done; what cannot be explained away once it has been explained:

'His tongue felt along the barrier of his teeth—round to the side where the big ones were and the gap . . . His tongue was remembering. It pried into the gap between the teeth and re-created the old, aching shape. It touched the rough edge of the cliff, traced the slope down, trench after aching trench, down towards the smooth surface where the Red Lion was, just above the gum— understood what was so hauntingly familiar and painful about an isolated and decaying rock in the middle of the sea.'

One could draw Pincher's 'rock' only too easily now—that decaying and creviced molar set between the canine of Safety Rock before the Gap he came through, and the three other eroding grinders of Oxford Circus, Piccadilly, and Leicester Square. This is the foundation on which he has built his unreal heaven, his temporary hell, his escape from death.

'Now there was nothing to do but protect normality.' Knowing what he does, he will still not accept its implications. He goes on performing meaningless actions like eating, while his voice quacks away: 'I was always two things, mind and body. Nothing has altered. Only I did not realize it before so clearly.' Meanwhile 'the centre thought of the next move . . . The will could resist.' But the Spectres from the Cellar cannot be locked away now. In one moment of terror he sees in the Dwarf the Old Woman who lived in the darkest corner of childhood's cellar. He flinches away: 'That is not the next move.' But the moves are no longer in his hands. A piece of rock in the shape of a book has fallen from one of the trenches, engraved, not like that other Tablet of stone, with words 'which would have killed him immediately', but with a pattern that the eye can follow, a signature repeated, in the recess from which the stone has split, by the Engraver:

'It was like a tree upside down and growing down from the old edge where the leaves were weathered by wind and rain. The trunk was a deep, perpendicular groove with flaky edges. Lower down, the trunk divided into three branches and these again into a complication of twigs like the ramifications of bookworm. The trunk and the branches and the twigs were terrible black. Round the twigs was an apple blossom of grey and silver stain. As he watched, drops of water dulled the stain and lay in the branches like tasteless fruit.

'His mouth quacked.

' "Lightning!'

'But the dark centre was shrunk and dreadful and knowing. The knowing was so dreadful that the centre made the mouth work deliberately.

' "Black lightning." '

The formulation is Nat's, in that conversation which has kept making its way into Pincher's mind: 'Take us as we are and heaven would be sheer negation. Without form and void. You see? a sort of black lightning destroying everything that we call life.' On this view, because we are wholly egotistic, the Heaven that we could reach if we were only prepared to die to ourselves must seem totally destructive of all we hold most precious; what the saint knows as perfect love, compassion, peace, is a black destroyer to the sinner. The Creator who formed him with the choice of enduring death for heaven, and the Love which watched over him, must appear as the spectres of the Executioner and the Executioner's Wife whom the child pictured in the cellar under the graveyard. So, having seen and flinched from the Old Woman, Pincher recognizes the signature of her Husband. The 'tree' is the appletree of Eden as seen through evil eyes: a tree terribly black, its blossom bleached of colour to grey and silver, the fruit of the knowledge and love of God dull, watery, tasteless, the whole a signpost to destruction.

One last escape remains to be tried: 'There was still a part that could be played—there was the Bedlamite, Poor Tom, protected from knowledge of the sign of the black lightning.' Where sanity is hopeless, madness may be a hiding-place. So the brain begins to spiral as he beseeches the Old Woman-Helen, the Producer's Wife, for comfort and reassurance. Confusing past and present he relives the child's waking nightmare as he is compelled to the cellar: that ordinary coal-cellar transfigured into the 'death door' through which one meets 'the master'. But he keeps insisting that he must be mad, must have been mad to see the red lobster, the soluble guano, the flying lizards; or the 'kindling from coffins' and the axe 'not worn for firewood but by executions'.

' "Seals aren't inimical and a madman wouldn't sleep properly. He would feel the rock was too hard, too real; he would superimpose a reality especially if he had too much imagination. He would be capable of seeing the engraving as a split into the whole nature of things—wouldn't he?"

'And then fettered in the darkness by the feet, trying to lift one and finding a glue, finding a weakness where there should be strength now needed because by nature there was nothing to do but scream and try to escape. Darkness in the corner doubly dark, thing looming, feet tied, near, an unknown looming, an opening darkness, the heart and being of all imaginable terror. Pattern repeated from the beginning of time, approach of the unknown thing, a dark centre that turned its back on the thing that created it and struggled to escape.

' "Wouldn't he? Say he would!" '

Perhaps one could know that one's nightmare is an insanity, as the child knows, and such an 'explanation' behind the horror might reassure even Poor Tom? But no:

'There is no centre of sanity in madness. Nothing like this "I" sitting in here, staving off the time that must come. The last repeat of the pattern. Then the black lightning.

'The centre cried out.

' "I'm so alone! Christ! I'm so alone!" '

The mind cannot but recognize what it is and why it is as it is. Finally the whole flashback world resolves itself into two pictured scenes hung side by side. There is, once more, that scene with Nat which now reveals how much he loved him, and how much the goodness meant, that came to comfort him in the moment of blackness and exclusion that prefigured this one. Beside it is the scene which tells how he tried to murder that love and goodness. The 'centre' experiences again all the grief: 'Because of what I did I am an outsider and alone . . . Now there is no

hope. There is nothing ... If I could only be part of something ...'
But it also experiences the rage at the explosion which was an
opportunity to become part of God by the death of Pincher—the
rage of the eater eaten. Nothing is changed. He *will* not die.

So the madness increases in the mouth while the centre goes
on trying to pretend in the physical rock. The mouth shouts high
in self-pity, rage or defiance, trying to drown the 'other noise'
behind the storm; playing part after part—Prometheus defying
the Thunderer, the drummer-boy whose Emperor is taken, the
adulterer moving into the love-nest and threatening to leave
it. Explanation follows explanation—running together fact and
fantasy—trying to escape the noise of the spade against the box:

' "Mad," said the mouth, "raving mad. I can account for everything, lobsters, maggots, hardness, brilliant reality, the laws of
nature, film-trailers, snapshots of sight and sound, flying lizards,
enmity—how should a man not be mad?" '

'Mouth' and 'centre' become one, shouting against the storm and
the lightning: 'You bloody great bully.'
The body acts its part of naked madman. It hunts the Old Woman/
Nat/Mary/Actress across the rock and slashes her to pieces with
its knife for being the spectre which has been at his back, calling
his identity in question, all his life. But he is not mad: 'He and his
voice were one. They knew that the blood was sea-water and the
cold, crumpling flesh that was ripped and torn, nothing but an
oilskin.'

Finally there appears, as the terrified voice had predicted, what
is either the Truth itself, or Madness indeed; either the last figment
of Pincher's crazy imagination, or that great Mind of which
Pincher is only a projection, the producer of the whole drama. It
is a figure exactly like Pincher Martin in every particular but one:
'On the sixth day he created God. Therefore I permit you to use
nothing but my own vocabulary. In his own image created he
Him.' But the figure is wearing seaboots. If it is 'Martin', it is a
Martin who died and was united with God; if it is not madness, it
speaks with the voice of God insofar as Pincher can hear; and
the 'seaboots, good and shiny and wet and solid ... made the
rock behind them seem like cardboard, like a painted flat'. It is

an opportunity for Pincher to face what he could be, the 'self' he
he has rejected, to choose again:

   ' "Have you had enough, Christopher?". . .
   ' "Enough of what?"
   ' "Surviving. Hanging on.". . .
   ' "I hadn't considered."
   ' "Consider now.". . .
   ' "I won't. I can't."
   ' "What do you believe in?"
'Down to the black boot, coal black, darkness of the cellar, but
now down to a forced answer.
   ' "The thread of my life."
   ' "At all costs."
'Repeat after me:
   ' "At all costs."
   ' "So you survived.". . .
'He snarled. "I have a right to live if I can!"
   ' "Where is that written?"
   ' "Then nothing is written."
   ' "Consider."
'He raged on the cardboard rock before the immovable, black
feet.
   ' "I will not consider! I have created you and I can create my
own heaven."
   ' "You have created it."
'He glanced sideways along the twitching water, down at his
skeleton legs and knees, felt the rain and spray and the savage
cold on his flesh.
'He began to mutter.
   ' "I prefer it. You gave me the power to choose and all my life you
led me carefully to this suffering because my choice was my own.
Oh yes! I understand the pattern. All my life, whatever I had done,
I should have found myself in the end on that same bridge, at
that same time, giving that same order—the right order, the wrong
order. Yet, suppose I climbed away from the cellar over the bodies
of used and defeated people, broke them to make steps on the
road away from you, why should you torture me? If I ate them,
who gave me a mouth?'

' "There is no answer in your vocabulary."

'He squatted back and glared up at the face. He shouted.

' "I have considered. I prefer it, pain and all."

' "To what?"

'He began to rage weakly and strike out at the boots.

' "To the black lightning! Go back! Go back!" '

He prefers madness on his rock to sanity, heaven, with loss of himself. He chooses to reject what he will not even bring himself to admit may be the Love of God. He insists on black lightning, so black lightning it is. He finally does go mad, riding the rock like a horse into the storm, holding out his identity disc, and shouting what is at last a recognition: 'I spit on your compassion!' As the spade thunder is heard, and the first tendrils of black lightning lie across the western sky, the 'centre' tries to prove its madness by destroying the water-supply it needs to 'live'. But, as the voice above the seaboots has said so quietly, even madness is only another crevice that will crumble.

In two brilliant pages, the whole physical universe whose 'reality' seemed so persuasive, is dismantled with equal conviction, chillingly:

'There were branches of the black lightning over the sky, there were noises. One branch ran down into the sea, through the great waves, petered out. It remained there.

'The sea stopped moving, froze, became paper, painted paper that was torn by a black line. The rock was painted on the same paper. The whole of the painted sea was tilted but nothing ran downhill into the black crack which had opened in it. The crack was utter, was absolute, was three times real.'

The 'lightning' is only the fissure of dark nothingness that opens up as the paper world is torn apart. There is no noise. Then there is no mouth.

'Still the centre resisted. It made the lightning do its work according to the laws of this heaven. It perceived in some mode of sight without eyes that pieces of the sky between the branches of black lightning were replaced by pits of nothing. This made the fear of the centre, the rage of the centre vomit in a mode that required no mouth. It screamed into the pit of nothing voicelessly, wordlessly.

' "I shit on your heaven!" '

At any moment, if Nat is right, the black lightning can be converted into the everlasting arms of the real heaven, and the pit of nothing into the face of the Living God. But as sea and sky and Safety Rock vanish, the 'centre' that is still Pincher clutches the rock like the claws of a lobster:

'The lines of absolute blackness felt forward into the rock and it was proved to be as insubstantial as the painted water. Pieces went and there was no more than an island of papery stuff round the claws and everywhere else there was the mode that the centre knew as nothing.

'The rock between the claws was solid. It was square and there was an engraving on the surface. The black lines sank in, went through and joined.

'The rock between the claws was gone.

'There was nothing but the centre and the claws. They were huge and strong and enflamed to red. They closed on each other. They contracted. They were outlined like a night sign against the absolute nothingness and they gripped their whole strength into each other. The serrations of the claws broke. They were lambent and real and locked.

'The lightning crept in. The centre was unaware of anything but the claws and the threat. It focused its awareness on the crumbled serrations and the blazing red. The lightning came forward. Some of the lines pointed to the centre, waiting for the moment when they could pierce it. Others lay against the claws, playing over them, prying for a weakness, wearing them away in a compassion that was timeless and without mercy.'

In a sense the situation on page three of the novel has simply been revealed for what it then really was, as the six-days'-long pretence that masked it is ripped away. As the seventh (God's day?) opens, the Divine Love that can only appear as merciless waits to take Martin to itself by destroying Pincher. Or, from the other point of view, black nothingness waits to engulf him utterly, finally.

III

There *are* different ways of looking.

The final chapter, as in Golding's first two novels, is itself a device to get the author and his readers outside the consciousness in which we have lived, and to make us take stock of it. So when the corpse-disposal officer arrives at the Hebridean island to remove what is left of Christopher Martin, the episode has on a first reading the shock-value of the ending of *Lord of the Flies*. Indeed, where that invited us to judge our experience by taking in how much our consciousness had been changed, this challenges us with the disclosure that a whole relatively new experience and consciousness still lie ahead if we will read the book again. But when we understand what the full experience is, the significant resemblance is to the end of *The Inheritors*: the unsettling of any moral and emotional certainties the tale may have seemed to encourage.

The tone of the scene is delicately set. In the wintry sunset there is a strange, sad beauty—black drifter, leaden water, 'valley of red and rose and black', as the last of the sun lies across the sea in the drifter's path. Silence and soft voices contrast strongly with the overheated, frenzied consciousness we have been living in. But, if the sadness of death comes across for the first time in the novel, it does so quite without sentimentality; for the horror is present too, in the alliance of the body with lineweed and flotsam, the drinking that alone makes Davidson able to face his job, the paraffin poured for an obvious reason over the corrupting flesh, the effect of the body on Campbell's dreams. There has been an inevitable tendency in the novel to make death dramatic. Now the sadness, the gruesome pathos of dereliction are gently but firmly established.

Within this setting the questions, the large questions, seem right and even inevitable. Campbell has been looking at the lean-to while the naval man inspects the body inside; the broken-down building gives him a language to ask in:

'Broken, defiled. Returning to the earth, the rafters rotted, the roof fallen in—a wreck. Would you believe that anything ever lived there? . . .

'The harvest. The sad harvest. You know nothing of my—shall I say—official beliefs, Mr Davidson; but living for all these days next to that poor derelict—Mr Davidson. Would you say that there was any—surviving? Or is that all? Like the lean-to?'

The new 'distance' is new also for Golding, pushing aside the manuscript in which he has been living all this time; and whatever we think his official views may be, there can be no doubt that his imaginative voyage in the novel has not made him assertive. The tentative, gently posed question has a proper tact.

Davidson cannot understand, and converts it into a simpler question of whether the dead man had time to suffer. But even this can be filled with significance by Campbell's quiet voice. For the greatest 'suffering' might not be physical at all; it might lie precisely in there being no Time. It might be just to go down like the sun 'seemingly for ever', leaving 'nothing for a reminder but clouds like smoke'—or an identity disc in a stranger's pocket that no longer refers to anybody. It might be . . .

The emphasis is on suffering, wonder, mystery. One official view of Golding's we do know about is the belief that novels should try to tell the truth. But how to tell the truth about death? No matter what any of us believes officially about surviving, in our minds there obstinately lurks the opposite spectre. Only saints (religious or pagan) and simpletons escape the sense that the 'other side' might just be right after all. The pressure that allows the finger to work on the jar's membrane could be nothing but empty space. The seabooted figure, the force against which Pincher shouts defiance, could be figments of his mad imagination. The terrible final experience may be terrible precisely because it is a hopeless battle against Nothing and Nobody.

Again, there is real imaginative ambivalence about our attitude to the 'poor derelict'. The treatment of his past makes us see the struggle on the rock as emblematic of a life of ferocious self-concern, the ravening ego refusing the selfless act of dying. But his 'present' cannot escape, as an imaginative experience, a sense of the heroic. The 'selfless act of dying' is felt to be only a sub-mission to an overwhelmingly greater power, and this, whether God or Void, is felt to be destructive. If, in Nat's terms, the black lightning destroys 'everything we call life', everything may well seem too high a price, and to shout 'You bloody great bully' or 'I shit on your heaven' can seem either heroic or a damnable folly. Where 'heaven', 'love', 'mercy' are in fact absent (necessarily of course, for the character), the effect of the experience may be to push a deliberately violent contradiction like 'a compassion that was . . . without mercy' beyond the frontiers of imaginative realization. And this is all deliberately there, there are a large number of allusions that are both ironic and heroic. One imaginative eye sees Paradise Lost, the other sees a human hero fighting destruction and terror. It may be that the 'religious' view prevails, but the other has real imaginative resonance. An atheist setting out to rewrite the book would only have to change the lighting, the myth itself would still hold true. And at the end, deliberately pointing up the uncertainty, Golding is content to give a phrase like 'the harvest' a summarizing prominence, the novelist's metaphors fading into the ambivalence and euphemism of ordinary speech. Answers give way to questions.

Yet again, there are different ways of looking at the nature of the fiction. On one view it is the most myth-like of all Golding's fictions. If myth selects from multitudinous complexity an archetypal situation, there could be nothing more rigidly exclusive than the man on the rock, and nothing more archetypal than the vision which insists that even that might be stripped away to leave man facing God or Void, nakedly. It would be impossible to imagine anything more universal, timeless, basic . . . the ultimate situation, the final recognition. Seen in this way it is tremendous—and a complete dead end. What development could there possibly be beyond this point? On the other hand, though we have seen that *Pincher Martin* denies assumptions about 'character' and 'relationships' which we may tend to think of as central and axiomatic for the novel, we have only to compare it with Golding's previous novels to make an opposite point. For there is here, demonstrably, the beginning of *some* new kind of concern with character. This is the first Golding novel to bear for its title the name of an individual, the first to be told from a point of view within an individual consciousness, the first to have an adult, contemporary protagonist, drawn at length, and concerned (at whatever level) with sexual and social relationships in a modern world. The choice of point of view, moreover, has significant implications for style. Here for the first time the protagonist creates the fictional world. In the previous myths, which were purely archetypal, Golding used the full range of the concrete poetic style which is so uniquely his. (There were limitations in *The Inheritors*, but they tended if anything to maximize the effect of what Golding does best.) But in *Pincher Martin* the style must express an imperfect human being with an imperfect vision—for the first time in Golding we meet vulgarity, insensitivity, ugliness, banality, fitted to the consciousness we have to live in. There is a voice with a snarl, a voice different from Golding's own.

So, for the critic too, answers must give way to questions. Is this peculiar book dualistic, an unresolved conflict of warring opposites; or is it a unified whole, whose apparent dualism only comes from our failing to look at it from the right angle?

Any attempt at an answer must surely begin by trying to define the peculiarity of Golding's basic conception of character. We have argued that *all* the novel's 'worlds' (the past, the apparent present, and the real present) are essentially determined and static. Pincher is revealed as he has always been; his situation is revealed as it always essentially was. What are the implications of this for character?

The first essential implication is that the choice of protagonist absolutely and necessarily excludes complexity of character. The novel could not have been written if its protagonist were not a Pincher incapable of dying; and if he is Pincher he cannot be complex. Macbeth is a complex man who becomes a monster, Pincher is always a monster. Indeed we can now go on to see that despite the many references to Shakespeare, the basic concept is Sophoclean.

This is because Golding is essentially concerned with *Being*, not *Becoming*; and consequently his concept of character is static, not dynamic. Oedipus too might have cried that whatever he had done in life, whatever his relationships might have been like, he would still have found himself in the same position, giving 'the same order, the right order, the wrong order'. Oedipus also carries within himself a central darkness, determined and unchangeable; he too journeys through a world which looks like the ethical world in which a man acts, directing his own course and that of others; but the journey is an illusory progress through unrealities, and the false 'time' of his humanly constructed world has to give way to the eternal moment of the revelation of his Being, in which he is acted upon.

The Greek drama also helps us to see how the emphasis in a novel like this is on recognition. What there is to be seen has always been there, but men have tried to escape seeing it. The function of the art is to get the protagonist stripped of false seemings and get the audience looking from the right angle, so that knowledge of reality can no longer be escaped. And, only now is there choice. Neither Oedipus's nor Pincher Martin's is a moral tragedy, for neither can be said strictly to have chosen his Being. At the very end they choose, but what they choose is whether or not to accept the Being that they are, and always have been.

We can see this more clearly in *Pincher Martin* if we ask a question which Golding clearly, and very significantly, never thought it necessary or relevant to ask: How did Christopher Martin become Pincher? For as soon as we ask it, we see that it is a 'becoming' question that lies right outside the scope of Golding's conception, as it lies outside Sophocles'. The centrepiece of all Pincher's memories is the child and the cellar; 'psychologically' this seems to lie at the heart of the book. The man in the tunnel trying to escape the gods and the annihilating tears by trampling the faces, the drowning sailor constructing his world to escape into, the madman slashing the oilskin, all simply reorchestrate the child's horrified rejection of the cellar and the darkness. The cellar connects with the tunnel of Pincher's life, the tunnel with the rock, and the rock leads back to the cellar. But there is no chain of *causality* here at all, as we can see immediately by the absurdity of positing one. Golding is not saying that the moral character of Pincher is caused by the child's trauma. He is not concerned with cause and effect at all. He is interested in the Being of Pincher and its implications; and the child, the man, the madman are all simply and equally revelations of that Being. Indeed all the flashbacks, all the illusory Six Days' Creation, and the final terror, are pictures of the same thing, whose essence is a pair of claws locked against black lightning. It looks like a novel in which one thing leads to another: it is in fact a maze in which all paths lead back to the centre, and the centre is a single, simple image of a Being reacting to Non-Being.

We can see now why Golding wanted his flashbacks to be what they are; not what we expect in the cinema—glimpses of a past which explains how the present came to be—but a series of stills which focus more clearly the single image building up behind the apparent dynamism of the rock. On a naturalistic level we could say that the past must seem artificial and static at the moment of death; another country; a distant stage on which actors strut and fret. Or again, at one's last moment, the 'whole life' that is supposed to flash before the eyes might very well seem less like a travel-film, dense with complex detail, than a map starkly outlining the essential pattern. But the most basic reason is that the novelist of Being *sees* the past like that, as essentially static anyway; and sees artifice as the way of extracting from the cluttering complexities of ordinary life the essential signature of Being, by making use of the one perspective which is outside all possibility of time and change: the moment at which all the stills are on file together and the clearest ones, most definitely exposed in black and white, can be most tellingly mounted, juxtaposed.

Yet we may find ourselves still stubbornly objecting, finding it hard to accept that human beings, their relationships, their actions, can be validly treated in such simply reductive terms. Aren't the flashbacks too like posters in excessively flat primary colours, too diagrammatic? Taking this a step further: is it not too easy for the author to blacken a tooth or block in some disfigurement, since the mode is one of statement incapable of the kind of imaginative verification we demand from a Casaubon or an Osmond? Does not working in such swift and shallow sketches mean that Golding is never involved and imaginatively stretched beyond his existing vision? One step further: where the basic insights are already dangerously simple, does not the deliberately imperfect style tend to vulgarize and crudify even further until we find difficulty in adjusting the man who saw and spoke like *that*, with the man using the full range of his author's imagination and language on the rock?

We are however in difficulties if we want to voice such criticisms, for we are bound to become uneasily aware of how dependent they are on a basic objection to the mode of vision itself, a philosophic rather than a literary objection. A novel of pure Being may offend both against expectations based on more than two and a half centuries of novels, and against unspoken assumptions about 'real life and real people'. What we see as fiction lacking necessary complexity, Golding sees as going to the heart of the matter undistracted by what, for all their fascinating unevennesses of surface, are irrelevances—like the rock which must be cut away to get at the pure form of the statue. He might have been more tactful, but he is a man much given to facing the consequences without disguise. We can state our criticisms in such a way that they will seem to be literary ones; but as soon as we begin to ask why and how they come about, they lead us back to the concept behind the novel and reveal themselves as extensions of a basic objection to that concept. Questions of style are dependent on stance and treatment; questions of stance and treatment dependent on the basic nature of the informing vision. Moreover we cannot even distinguish, basically, the flashback world and the world of the rock, for the underlying vision is common to both. If we do not feel the same objections to the latter, it is surely only because the situation is so radically peculiar and other-worldly that it never challenges expectations based on 'ordinary life', and never reveals its awkward implications until we come to reflect afterwards.

Perhaps we might say that the whole myth is both too specific and too general—too specific to be really archetypal, for Pincher is a highly special case; too general because we find ourselves asking questions about this particular man that the fiction cannot or will not answer. But still we reveal ourselves as wedded to concepts of becoming, with a right to ask how a man becomes his being. How does the child in the cellar become the man on the rock? How, if a man carries within him so determined a signature of Being, can he be said to choose? Childhood is too early, is not manhood too late? Still what we are criticizing is the basic concept itself. Once we look from his angle, we see as the author saw . . . yet have we explained our criticisms away?

The fiction however is certainly wholly consistent and not dualistic at all. It may be ambiguous in the sense that we are made aware that there are two ways of reacting to it (according to whether God exists or not), but not in the sense that both views are right. We cannot expect Golding to know the answer to that problem; and it is a positive strength that he has created an image of man that will respond to either view. The image in all its aspects reflects a single vision of human life: an essential confrontation of Being with non-Being.

Yet it is not irrelevant to question the validity of that kind of vision, for this is precisely what Golding himself proceeded to do. The writing of *Pincher Martin* brought him up against questions strictly outside the scope of the fiction, but obviously vital for a novelist committed to seeking the truth. The questions we formulate are exactly those he poses to himself in *Free Fall*, and the need to answer them is the turning-point in his development so far. This marks an end and a beginning: the end of a set of novels in which the state of man is explored as a finite concept; the beginning of a set in which complex, searching, philosophically difficult questions begin to be asked about how one should look at man. These are necessarily more difficult, obscure and tortured for both author and reader, for they are significantly about authorship and ways of reading. The protagonist becomes himself an artist, asking not just 'what am I?', but also 'how did I become what I am?', and 'how do I find a way of looking at my being and becoming that will reconcile the contradictions I see?' The first three novels are visions, the next two seek a path through irreconcilable kinds of vision. They try to discover not what, but how, to see.

IV

FREE FALL

(1959)

I

If *Free Fall* seems the most elusive and difficult of Golding's novels, it is because Golding is now questioning the nature of understanding itself. Our first impression is likely to recall E. M. Forster's reaction to Conrad: 'Is there not a central obscurity—something noble, heroic, beautiful . . . but obscure, obscure? While reading one doesn't or shouldn't ask such a question, but it occurs not improperly, when the author professes to be personal and take us into his confidence.' Yet we can do a great deal to understand the nature of the obscurity if we come to the novel with *Pincher Martin* in mind, for *Free Fall* is profoundly illuminated by its predecessor.

We are immediately aware of both similarities and differences. We recognize familiar portraits: Mary has become Beatrice; Sammy is a subtilized Pincher; the love-affair that was only one set of stills among many is now the central tragedy which challenges the understanding. The flashback world has, as it were, increased in scope and complexity so as to become the main picture.

There is, however, a major difference immediately evident: the tragedy now has a before and after, we are led to examine what led up to it and what necessarily followed. In *Pincher Martin* the past merely focused the present to give sharper definition to the same picture: the static, determined Being of the protagonist. His Being was co-terminous with his life, and the activity of the book was one of recognition. Now we hear Sammy Mountjoy asking the kind of questions the earlier novel neither asked nor could answer, seeking to discover how he became what he is, seeking to explain how his childhood innocence came to be destroyed by the consciously choosing will, deliberately and self-consciously exploring his past in search of a pattern of Becoming governed by choice. Revelation and recognition of Being, then, gives way to exploration, explanation, discovery of Becoming. Consequently the new novel is concerned with moral analysis, and is inevitably about character, in exactly the way that *Pincher Martin* was not. So for the first time Golding seems wholly to abandon his isolated and isolating settings and give us the social scene. The novel takes place in the Britain of the last forty-five years and is in some ways a representative experience. It is also the portrait of the artist as a

young man: the slum childhood, the tough schooldays, the growing ability to paint, the college of art, first and overwhelming love.
It looks like a novel of character and environment, shadows of
Dickens, Wells, Joyce Cary fall across the pages. Such a novel
would seem to have its centre of gravity in notions of responsibility; and so we find Sammy Mountjoy asking an explicit question: 'What am I looking for? I am looking for the beginning of
responsibility . . .' The question takes us inevitably into the world
of Becoming, motive, choice, behaviour; it seeks a moral explanation of the story.

Yet this will not explain the form of the novel, or satisfy us as
even a shorthand account of the nature of the experience. For
Golding has not decided that the mode of vision of *Pincher Martin*
was wrong and so changed to a better one, and the new novel is
by no means as different from its predecessor as it looks. Both
novels reveal life 'islanded in pictures', there is still a careful
composition, a deliberate framing. There is, once more, a series
of crucial moments which are 'a split into the whole nature of
things'. And Sammy asks not only about the beginning of responsibility, but about its end. 'How did I lose my freedom? I must go
back and tell the story . . .' This is a story which seems to have
little to do with moral analysis, resting on free choice—this is a
story about determinism. Sammy in search of responsibility en-
quires into behaviour, clue yielding to clue in a process of detec-
tion, a motion-film; Sammy in search of lost freedom comments
on Being, on a series of stills, all of which tell the same story. We
are back in the world of Pincher,

'as I remembered . . . I could find no moment when I was free to do
as I would. In all that lamentable story of seduction I could not
remember one moment when being what I was I could do other
than I did.'

Here 'moral' questions—What ought I to have done?—or 'becoming' questions—How did I get to Be like this?—seem irrelevant and meaningless; the world of responsibility and the possibility of change gives way to another in which wisdom resides
in the humble recognition of what we unalterably are.

Neither of these patterns will cover the novel because both are inescapably there. Indeed, the form of the novel can now be seen to be the deliberate posing of one against the other, and its subject, the contradictions that result. Obscurity is inevitable when the experience is of looking at a human life through a pair of eyes, each of which sees in a different way and consequently sees different things. The novel is the result of Golding's need to explore the tensions between Being and Becoming which *Pincher Martin* had raised for him, but which he could not deal with in that form. How does a man become what he is? How can he be said to choose? If he is first free, then locked in Being, where is freedom lost? In childhood? Is that not too early? In manhood? Is that not too late? Golding has written three novels using one mode of vision, and felt it to be true; but he had come to realize how peculiar it was, and how different from another, more 'ordinary' mode of vision which could also command his imaginative consent, how many problems it raised. As a myth-maker he is committed to trying to tell the truth about human beings, but how if the truth is Janus-faced and one finds oneself imaginatively committed to both faces? So the pattern-finder is obliged to question the validity of patterns. The tentativeness which had grown over the three novels now occupies the centre. In *Free Fall* Myth becomes no longer a form designed to enforce the recognition of truths deeper than the surface of ordinary life; but a form designed to explore the nature of looking for truth. In one novel two different kinds of novel are allowed to fight it out, and this accounts for the elusiveness of the book. Of necessity, clarity gives way to opacity, revelation to agonized search, assured poetry to a violent opposition of styles and voices. Everywhere contradictions mount: a voyage of discovery into what is already known; paintings that reveal truths opposed to those of experience; vivid characters in commonplace situations and brilliant apocalyptic situations peopled by archetypes; the need to explain countered by the knowledge that explanation is futile.

The opening of the novel plunges us immediately into these contradictions; yet it also presents us with an opportunity to tune the opposed voices so that the distinction between them is clarified and they do not simply jam each other. The apocalyptic, fixed, is set at once against the world of becoming:

'I have walked by stalls in the market-place where books, dog-eared and faded from their purple, have burst with a white hosanna. I have seen people crowned with a double crown, holding in either hand the crook and flail, the power and the glory. I have understood how the scar becomes a star, I have felt the flake of fire fall, miraculous and pentecostal . . . I live on Paradise Hill, ten minutes from the station, thirty seconds from the shops and the local.'

Sammy in this mode needs no exploration; what there is to know has already been revealed to him and can be expressed in an old symbolism of revelation. This paragraph metaphorically summarizes all the facts of Being that the novel but for its final page will expand and annotate. The ordinary world of market-place, shops and local and the better-class suburb is seen to contain the eternal verities of the Spirit. Sammy has seen Lent and Easter revealed in ordinary life, has seen man's soul, having decayed from the Imperial, burst into pure resurrection through repentance. He has seen how ordinary people can reveal a glorious martyrdom, where the punishments of justice are counterbalanced by the love which lifts the fallen from the pit. He has himself experienced suffering that turns into glorification; has known in his own being the transfiguration through pentecostal fire. So the old symbolism is a true reflection of what happens to a man when he is touched by the world of the spirit. Yet Sammy is no Christian. 'My yesterdays walk with me. They keep step, they are grey faces that peer over my shoulder.' Sammy has known no Grace or forgiveness; to have been touched by the power and the glory is only to be the more violently 'self-condemned', to experience a sharper sense of the spectres of his guilty past. The Being revealed to him is irreconcilably split: the ordinary transfigured, but the evil simultaneously underlined. Yet in this mode of awareness a whole human life can be summarized in a paragraph. The symbols may need to be translated into the facts whose patterns they reveal before we can understand them fully, but when we do understand we shall merely recognize what we already know. In this sense *Free Fall* is just as static as *Pincher Martin*. On its last page we shall simply return to the first page with fuller comprehension; the pattern will have been fulfilled, not changed.

Here however the coherent pattern, the expert knowledge, do not satisfy: 'Yet I am a burning amateur, torn by the irrational and incoherent, violently searching and self-condemned. When did I lose my freedom? For once, I was free. I had power to choose.' Sammy cannot accept any determinism in which causes lead to effects by unalterable laws. He is sure of his Being, but equally sure that it lies within the human will to choose and change one's whole direction. So, against the static, eternal images of Being we find a language of Becoming asserted: 'Free-will cannot be debated, but only experienced, like a colour or the taste of potatoes'. A human life in this mode is like a child in a garden where the central fountain is surrounded by many different paths radiating outwards, and he can choose to go down one or another.

But how can these two modes be related? If there was freedom, how is it lost? So Sammy begins to search for an explanation of what he already knows, to review his past in order to discover how he became his being, but he cannot escape the contradictions. He has 'hung all systems on the wall like a row of useless hats', yet he desperately desires some all-embracing pattern and looks to the writing of the book, the act of communication itself, as a way of finding one. But his two modes of vision cannot but affect the writing. First, we find them reflected in different ways of experiencing time:

'For time is not to be laid out endlessly like a row of bricks . . . Time is two modes. The one is an effortless perception native to us as water to the mackerel. The other is a memory, a sense of shuffle fold and coil, of that day nearer than that because more important, of that event mirroring this, or those three set apart, exceptional and out of the straight line altogether.'

One is a mode of being, the other of becoming; and this in turn means that the historian of his own past finds himself playing different roles. Mere chronology is a 'dead thing'; to keep the life and truth, the tale must unfold as it appears to the imaginative eye, but Sammy inevitably finds himself pulled in differing directions because he has a double vision. He will see himself as a faithful transcriber of events ('I have no responsibility for some of the pictures'), when to record is simply to bear witness. But he is also a self-conscious artist, ordering his narrative with Jamesian expertise, for 'understanding requires a sweep that takes in the whole of remembered time and then can pause. Perhaps if I write my story as it appears to me, I shall be able to go back and select.' Yet again, he knows that to select is to falsify and that any pattern is reductive. He knows that communication is impossible, that each of us exists in the loneliness of a 'dark thing that sees as at the atom furnace by reflection, feels by remote control, and hears only words phoned to it in a foreign tongue'. He knows, finally, the truth of Gerontion's cry: 'After such knowledge what forgiveness?'

So the contradictions ebb and flow as the voice speaks, or, rather, as one kind of voice changes into another and back again. The novel may seem a hopeless proposition: each pattern contradicts the other, yet patternlessness is simply incoherence. But to have tuned the voices, to have got the differences and their implications clear to ourselves, is already to have begun to move beyond Sammy. His search will eventually achieve a full tuning for him, whereby the dichotomy will be revealed in utter starkness; but we can begin to anticipate, to see as Sammy does not as we watch him voyage into his past, to detect which mode is operating where and why. And there may be more than this, for we must not forget that behind Sammy's confusions there lurks a greater writer allowing him to explore different roles, juxtaposing them, playing a waiting game. The more clearly we can see what Sammy is doing, the nearer we are likely to come to Golding. Will he be able to take us beyond Sammy, to find a path beyond the dichotomy so deliberately created by the form and advertised by the title? 'Free fall' is at once the momentous choice in Eden, and the effortless being in space when all forces are balanced. Are either, or both enough? Are they reconcilable? Golding's fourth novel represents a determination to find out.

II

Rotten Row, the world of Sammy's earliest memories, is seen in the mode of Being. In common with the apocalyptic opening it shows the ordinary lit from within so that the lighting is more

important than what it plays on. The surface of Rotten Row is a
rural slum: poverty, hardship, dirt and moral delinquency. Sammy
is a bastard, his mother and Evie are 'sodding liars', Ma Donovan's
pretty daughter may have the pox, and so on. Yet this is not 'the
truth'. When Ma provides Sammy with a father from her fantasies:
a soldier, an airman, a clergyman, the Prince of Wales, 'the glittering myth lay in the middle of the dirty floor, accepted with gratitude,' because it points to something anterior to the cold world of
'reality' and 'fiction', 'truth' and 'lies'. The small boy's world is
lit with romance, beauty, drama, mystery, that are quite as 'real'
as, or more real than, the 'realities' they illuminate. Evie's uncle in
the suit of armour, the long spoons, the girl who becomes a boy
who can pee higher than the others, the lodger's Snow-Maiden
swan's feathers, all point in the same direction. The slop-pool
from a drain is iridescent with life and colour in the two-foot
world, the bogs on wash-day become a vividly dramatic setting
for epic action which wholly transcends its basis in defecation,
half-held-up bloomers and superstitions about syphilis. In Rotten
Row there is a rich vitality, a sense of community, a security, a
boozy comfort. It *is* an Eden, untroubled by dirt, presided over
by Ma and Evie, and life continues, not uniformly happy, but
'permanent and inevitable in this shape'.

Ma is not so much a person, or a relationship, as an archetypal
creature of myth permanently fixed in the eye of childhood:
'These last few months I have been trying to catch her in two
handfuls of clay—not, I mean, her appearance; but more accurately, my sense of her hugeness and reality, her matter-of-fact
blocking of the view.' Later he will see her 'as a stranger might see
her, a massive, sagging creature, mottled and dirty. Her hair was
in wisps over her brown forehead, her face was a square-ish,
drawn-down mass with a minute fag sticking in one corner of
the mouth'. But when we get there we know that this is only an
'appearance', for we have known what it is to see her and her
world through the eyes of the 'infant Samuel'.

These eyes transmute evil, suffering, dirt. When Rotten Row's
devious scrap-dealers are arrested they appear handcuffed 'between two dark pillars surmounted by silver spikes'. When death
comes to the lodger the stopping of the heart is no more than the
stopping of the clock with which it is confused; a black car with

panes of chased and frosted glass; a missed opportunity of seeing the magical cap of white feathers. The teachers at the infant school are tall trees. Occasionally a shadow falls; a Mongol child disgraces herself, 'she was taken home by one of the trees, for we watched them pass through the gate, hand in hand'. But the shadow lifts, and Sammy doesn't go through any gate, even when he passes from childhood into boyhood.

In the primary school we become much more aware of the darker side of the boy's world. Now there is violence and gang warfare. Under Philip Arnold's influence the young Sammy learns robbery with violence as he bullies smaller boys for their precious fag-cards of the Kings of Egypt. Yet Philip, belonging to a different order of Being—'clever, complex, never a child'—can only make Sammy do evil things; he does not make him evil even when, cunningly playing upon his weaknesses, he persuades him to spit upon the altar of the church. There is a collapse, but it is purely physical, not 'moral' or 'religious'. The verger's blow on the ear 'lays him open' only in the sense that it bursts a mastoid infection and puts him in hospital, no more. For the boy's Being cannot change or be changed; he can do bad things but he cannot *be* bad.*

The central episode of this section sums up the nature of the child's Being and pinpoints its implications. On the airfield, 'trespassing', Johnny and Sammy see tragedy—a plane crashing in flames. But there is no sense of transgression or suffering: only a man, tall, hatless, smeared with black, shouting: 'You kids shove off! If I catch you here again I'll put the police on you . . .'; and a sensible getaway. Then they trespass again, into the General's garden, avoiding a policeman by hiding behind a bush and disappearing noiselessly across the lawn. Having seen tragedy, they see transfiguration:

'We were in the upper part of the garden, looking back and down. The moon was flowering. She had a kind of sanctuary of light round her, sapphire. All the garden was black and white. There was one tree between me and the lawns, the stillest tree that ever grew, a tree that grew when no one was looking. The trunk was huge and each branch splayed up to a given level; and there, the

* cf. Ch. 2, p. 106.

black leaves floated out like a level of oil on water. Level after horizontal level these leaves cut across the splaying branches and there was a crumpled, silver-paper depth, an ivory quiet beyond them. Later, I should have called the tree a cedar and passed on, but then, it was an apocalypse.'

But they only *see* what is revealed; as 'two points of perception, wandering in paradise' ('we were eyes'), they see, but they do not understand.

This is an Eden because it is illuminated from within by the light of Innocence; it is as true of the whole world of childhood as it is true of the hospital ward that 'remembered, they shine'. Innocence is the nature of the Being described, and it cannot be changed—it is useless to look here for the beginning of responsibility. The grey faces have no source here and the only scar is from Sammy's operation; trespass, violence, stealing, blasphemy, do not spell out 'guilt'. It is easy to see why. The purity of vision is possible because of the total absence of self-consciousness; perception has not yet given way to reflection.* The General's garden, like all the other scenes, is a setting for Blake's *Songs of Innocence*. There is no calculation, choice, responsibility, and without these there is lacking a dimension essential to evil or guilt. Philip has it, but that is why he is never a child. Sammy makes the diagnosis explicit: 'I was innocent of guilt, unconscious of innocence.'

The infant Samuel, then, opposes to the Being described in the opening paragraph a Being qualitatively different, yet seen in the same mode. One is innocent, the other guilty. One is unconscious, the other conscious. One cannot find forgiveness, the other does not need and cannot give it, because it cannot understand. One has lost the power of moral choice, the other has not yet acquired it. Yet both are *states*, unchangeable, 'islanded in pictures', with a sheer gulf between.

Golding can be seen to have gone behind *Lord of the Flies* and *Pincher Martin* to show that there is an innocence in childhood and that the child does not automatically father the man. He has re-phrased *The Inheritors* so that, in child and man, Lok again faces Tuami across the Gap between innocence and experience.

* cf. Ch. 2, p. 81–82.

Yet the net effect is to pose all the more awkwardly the problem of Becoming, how one changes into the other.

The orthodox 'moral' way of accounting for such a change would be to look for an action, a freely chosen crossing of some moral Rubicon, which led to further decisions and actions, amounting together to a change in one's inner nature. So Sammy turns next to just such a moment: the initial action in his seduction of Beatrice.

Yet we have already noticed that innocent Being can do bad actions without becoming bad; and Sammy, looking back, sees from the start that his Rubicon found him already determined, so that he cannot be said to have chosen to do what he did. The laconic opening sentence of the new section: 'Even by the time I was on the bike by the traffic light I was no longer free', undermines at the outset the validity of a moral account.

This is Sammy's *Vita Nuova*, acridly rewriting Dante's experience of the revolution of Love. Sammy's Beatrice, first manifested to him at school in front of a picture of a Palladian bridge in the art-room, is as much a showing-forth of another world as Dante's, a miraculous Being, equally unattainable. But Sammy sets out to attain her (his Beatrice is surnamed I-for); where a greeting is for Dante a grace beyond deserving, Sammy intrigues for one as a prelude to possession. So we find him on another bridge at a traffic-light, initiating the first move in what certainly looks like a moral metaphor. The bridge is crossed, the red light of warning first breaks down and is then ignored. Yet we are told from the beginning that this cannot be so; where there is no freedom there can be no morality; the moral metaphors and language are ironic; signs and warnings as irrelevant to Sammy as the huge baked-bean advertisement to which he cries 'I didn't ask to fall in love'.

Yet it does look like a story in the mode of Becoming. It is, convincingly, an adolescent tragedy with both the poignancy and the rather tawdry absurdity of millions of such affairs in real life. The presentation catches the absurd/pathetic tang of the elaborately casual cyclist separating his girl from her knowing companions; the mechanisms of Lyons, busrides, country walks, the bed-sitter with the Van Gogh flowerpiece, the fierce high-talk to uncomprehending ears, the self-dramatization, the narrow bed, the sexual failure. It is psychologically convincing too: the obsessed, salt, boy; the unawakened, socially and sexually inhibited girl; the passionate proposals; the front of reluctance alternating between the prim and the inhibitedly neurotic. Unable either to reject or accept, Beatrice is driven first into engagement and then into an increasingly lubricious and unsatisfactory sexual relationship. Happiness is caught with the right touch of immaturity: 'I rode home, my heart molten with delight, goodness and gratitude. For it was good. She was nineteen and I was nineteen; we were male and female, we would marry though she did not know that yet . . .', but such moments are rare and the story is even more convincing in its record of how frustration turns into exploitation as Sammy tries desperately to break through to an impossible togetherness. Inevitably, disillusion becomes desertion, another woman and a more satisfying love, marriage and children.

Looked at from this angle the story does seem to have the scope and complexity of a well-observed and credible human relationship, the kind of treatment Golding never gave in *Pincher Martin*, as we can easily see by comparing it with its source in the Mary episodes. Even its vulgarities and lapses from 'good taste' have a realistic basis. Golding was clearly determined to get the peculiar tang of adolescence across at whatever cost in grace and power; so the language veers from the flat to the melodramatic, the humour can be excruciating, the experience is absurd, irritating, embarrassing, as well as pathetic, in the ways that adolescence itself can be.

This means that we are led to reflect in largely social and psychological terms. When Sammy talks of losing his freedom, we think of this as a result of his obsession with a girl whose behaviour is irritatingly provocative, and we think of that behaviour as both psychological and socially conditioned. We might consider the whole thing as a flatter, slangier, less 'poetic' version of the story of Paul and Miriam in *Sons and Lovers*. If Sammy speaks of loss of freedom he seems merely to echo the age-old lament of the anxious lover:

'For now there were rough ropes on my wrists and ankles and round my neck. They led through the streets, they lay at her feet and she could pick them up or not as she chose.'

And yet it is no less clear that Sammy, looking back, is once again aware of the tension between Being and Becoming. We have noticed how, if he is already determined at the moment by the traffic-light, he can only be said to become more strongly what he already is, and we can only read the episode in terms of Becoming in that special sense. Constantly, also, we become aware of a bed-rock of Being jutting through the surface, so that the loss of freedom acquires different and darker overtones from those we have been considering:

'Once a human being has lost freedom there is no end to the coils of cruelty. I must I must I must. They said the damned in hell were forced to torture the innocent live people with disease. But I know now that life is perhaps more terrible than that medieval innocent misconception. We are forced here and now to torture each other . . . Those who lose freedom can watch themselves forced helplessly to do this.'

We cannot see this as simply an intensification of the drama: it creates a sense that somehow, beyond or below, there is a determinism far deeper than the psychological. The terrible seduction scenes, credible as they are, reveal some sort of metaphysical dimension; the narrative carries within itself some point which only a later gloss can reveal. Or we could say that the tale has suddenly outpaced the teller's ability to explain what he nevertheless knows to be true. When he reflects: 'the descent we were now to embark upon and at my hands was one I was powerless to control or stop', we can share an impression that this is true of the story as he represents it, and yet in terms of 'character' or 'plot' there is no adequate explanation for the terrible determinism. Another kind of picture, as yet obscure in its significance, is being drawn behind the one we are watching; and across every incident, however casual, falls the shadow of an ominously larger meaning. So, for example, we begin to feel that Beatrice's repeated 'maybe' is more than the irritating and provocative revelation of her inability to say yes or no:

'I would try to explain.
    ' "I'm trying to find out about you. After all, if we're going to

spend our lives together—where are you? What are you? What is it like to be you?"

'Her arms would shake—those arms that bent in at the elbows, were so delicate that they seemed for receiving only—her breasts and her face would push against me, be hidden.

'Impatient and angry. Continue the catechism.

' "Aren't you human, then? Aren't you a person at all?"

'And with shudders of her wrists and shaking of the long, fair hair she would whisper against me:

' "Maybe." '

If 'maybe was sign of all our times', it becomes a chord sounding uneasily again and again throughout the episode, and hinting at a growing uncertainty. Sammy, continually brought up short by the word, is shown at the limit of his 'explanations'; the word blocks and undermines the psychological, the social, the behavioural certainties.

Indeed, we can see in this instance how the love affair itself is based on perceptions of Being, in a way that makes the reference to the *Vita Nuova* more than morally disparaging irony. For all Sammy's questions are Being questions: where are you, what are you, what is it like to be you? Just as much for him as for Dante, Beatrice is a revelation of Being wholly other and superior to his own—'the most mysterious and beautiful thing in the universe'—and it is *that* he longs for. The basis of his tragedy is that he confuses, as Dante never did, sharing in that Being with possession of the body that manifests it. We shall not understand the obsession which drives him to torture and exploit her unless we understand what kind of an obsession it is, and how little, basically, it has to do with the sexual act it is so readily confused with:

' "I said I loved you. Oh God, don't you know what that means? I want you, I want all of you, not just cold kisses and walks—I want to be with you and in you and on you and round you—I want fusion and identity—I want to understand and be understood —oh God, Beatrice, Beatrice, I love you—I want to be you!" '

The same uneasy sense that there is some metaphysical dimension operating below the physical, is shown in the difference between Sammy the painter and Sammy the lover. Through the paintings the story is again pushed away from questions of psychology and sex, motive and behaviour; yet Sammy the lover cannot understand this because he identifies his paintings with his lust:

' "I shan't paint your face at all. I just want your body. No. Don't rearrange it. Just lie still."

'Beatrice lay still and I began to draw.

'When the drawing was finished I made love to her again. Or rather, I repeated what my pencil had done, finished what my pencil had begun.'

In fact, however, the painting records what he has *not* done and in it, as in all his good paintings, he 'stands the world of appearances on its head'. The climactic picture to which, after a particularly degrading exploitation, he adds 'the electric light-shades of Guernica to catch the terror', reveals when he looks at it later in a public gallery no sign of the rape, the brutality, the suffering and devastation of Picasso's masterpiece:

'The electric light that ought to sear like a public prostitution seems an irrelevance. There is gold, rather, scattered from the window. There was dog faith and big eyes and submission. I look at the picture and I remember what the hidden face looked like; how after my act and my self-contempt she lay, looking out of the window as though she had been blessed.'

Does the painting reveal a reality of Being which contradicts the lover's dossier, though implied by the name itself and the reference to Dante? Maybe . . .

Finally, the tension can also be detected in the oddly double tone which governs the whole episode and gives it its peculiar flavour. Here again contradictions meet, for the tone is a mixture of sympathy and searing contempt; and the fluctuations are traceable to Being and Becoming too. The eyes that see and record the lovers are the eyes that have recognized the Being described in the opening paragraph. The knowledge that the younger self is no less determined and helpless than the older carries with it a sympathy, no matter how ridiculous the situation may be. When the young

Sammy is repulsed, and weeps, the older narrator records clearly enough an impression of 'that ridiculous, unmanly, trembling creature'—and yet the effect of the scene as a whole is so different that our predominant response is a compassion strong enough to override both ridicule and laconic amusement:

'I was trembling regularly from head to foot as if my button had been pressed. There in the winter sunlight, among the raindrops and rusted foliage I stood and trembled regularly as if I should never stop and a sadness reached out of me that did not know what it wanted; for it is a part of my nature that I should need to worship, and this was not in the textbooks, not in the behaviour of those I had chosen and so without knowing I had thrown it away.'

After the first dismissive sentence the tone suddenly warms; and though we can go on to see that the *behaviour* is ridiculous, the young man revealing the nature of his inner being, helplessly, is not. Indeed he only becomes ridiculous when he 'turned away and made a dramatic effort to master my emotion. That was a cliché of behaviour and therefore not frightening.' But it is absurd. The distinction seems clear enough. Whenever the Being of the lovers is recognized, however diminishing the context, the tone is one of understanding. Sammy looks back over the years with a sad grasp of what then was ungraspable. But the moment the narrative eye sees only Becoming, the motives and behaviour of the lovers acting out a drama produced, directed, played out as though this were all, the tone sharpens, and can flay. Indeed, the moments which we may feel are raw, embarrassing, in dubious taste, are directly traceable to the contempt Sammy feels for the blindness of the lovers, as they strut and fret in what they think are actions of their own devising and decision:

'Unconsciously we were both setting ourselves to music. The gesture with which she opened her knees was, so to speak, operatic, heroic, dramatic and daunting. I could not accompany her. My instrument was flat.'

This is more than the sour comedy of impotence, and isn't finally reducible to the slangishness, awkwardness, embarrassment and indignity appropriate to adolescence. The ultimate sourness is, as in *Pincher Martin*, directed to the posturing and self-dramatization of the 'hero' who cannot realize his inability to master himself or his situation, and whose heroics are radically false. When Sammy reveals Being he cannot but sympathize; but he cannot explain motive, decision, behaviour without conveying a sense of contempt so raw that it cares nothing for niceties of taste. If we have learnt to tune the voices in the prelude, we can detect the nature of the discord everywhere.

Yet we must not simplify: there is another side to the world of behaviour, action, and decision. The contemptuous flick lashes the Communist Party too, and the young man who thinks that Comrades Alsopp and Wimbury are a movement which knows where it is going and can explain the actions of men both past and future. Yet there is also 'a certain generosity' in the Party, 'a sense of martyrdom and a sense of purpose'; and it is through his membership that he meets Taffy, who in a few weeks becomes his wife. Taffy is hardly present in the book, yet she has a definite importance; for we can see that the relationship has real value. It neither threatens nor exploits, and it exists happily within a behavioural world. When Sammy records that: 'we achieved that extraordinary level of security when we did not expect entire truth from each other, knowing it to be impossible and extending a *carte blanche* of forgiveness beforehand', truth and forgiveness have to do with what they have done, not with what they are, with their 'histories'. This relationship does not pierce through to Being, it exists solely in terms of behaviour and in that region they can offer and receive explanations, however edited. Explanation cannot be total, but it is possible and satisfying. The lovers demand far less, but they achieve far more. When the nonsense of Party belief is swept away, there is in the clasp of these sublunary lovers something that is generous, and something that suffers to some purpose. It would seem to be, then, the dimension of Being and the determination to touch it that causes the torture. The world of Taffy and Sammy is smaller, but it does not destroy, and what it gives is real.

Yet we do not forget the deeper perspective either. There is the picture of Johnny: a 'still' of perfect, joyous Being flying into the air on the brow of a hill at 100 m.p.h., and kissing his girl in a

mode where there is no before and after, no cause and effect;
simply a revelation of love so perfectly unified that consequences
cease to matter and the eyes are turned quite away from the road
of Becoming that can lead to one thing or another. This 'remains
a measure' in Sammy's mind 'of the difference between us'.

Moreover it is Taffy's Sammy who 'explains' his relationship
with Beatrice as

'the mind's self-deception. Certainly there was no light in her
face . . . Her only power now was that of the accuser, the skeleton
in the cupboard; and in this bounded universe we can easily put
paid to that.'

But he cannot satisfy his own deeper self, let alone us. His vision
of the cat mangled by the motorcar, and the nightmare in which
Beatrice runs crying for him, through a rising water that he has
escaped, are visions in the mode of Being which will not be explained, and point to a universe that is boundless, without possibility of forgiveness or atonement.

Finally, we return to determinism. The child's world revealed
innocence, the lovers' world guilt, but in neither is there free
choice or responsibility:

'What else could I have done but run away from Beatrice? I do
not mean what ought I to have done or what someone else could
have done. I simply mean that as I have described myself, as I
see myself in my backward eye, I could do nothing but run away.
I could not kill the cat to stop it suffering. I had lost my power to
choose. I had given away my freedom. I cannot be blamed for the
mechanical and helpless reaction of my nature. What I was, I had
become. The young man who put her on the rack is different in
every particular from the child who was towed along the street
past the duke in the antique shop. Where was the division? What
choice had he?'

'What I was I had become' . . . but we are no nearer to knowing
how. We only know that looking at the guilty *action* will not tell us.

It would seem, then, that guilt must be located in Being; and
if Sammy cannot put his finger on its beginning, he can at least

pinpoint exactly the first realization of its nature. 'Becoming' questions are put aside for the while and the focus of the novel narrows again to isolation, as we find Sammy interrogated in the P.O.W. camp by a Gestapo psychologist and forced to recognize the nature of his Being in the horror of the cell. We move firmly back into the world of *Pincher Martin*; it is the 'unnameable, unfathomable and invisible darkness that sits at the centre' of Sammy that takes the attention. Halde's remark that 'there is a mystery in you which is opaque to us both' defines the nature and function of a journey into the darkest interior.

He is being questioned to extract information that will allow Dr Halde to prevent a mass escape. He is being asked to betray his fellow-prisoners; or, in another sense, he is invited to prevent a massacre in which fifty lives might be lost instead of the two who have just been shot. The situation is a cliché but the treatment is complex: the Gestapo *éminence grise* is a man of great civilization and humanity, and the moral problem a tangle of relativities in which there can be no simple right or wrong. Yet the real problem, as always, is wholly anterior to any question of moral decision.

In what sense can Sammy be said to 'know' anything? Halde wants 'to raid the camp swiftly and suddenly and with absolute certainty of what I am going to find and where'; he wants the location of the tools, tunnel, radio, and civilian clothes. Sammy does not know any of this. His fellow prisoners do not trust him enough. What he does 'know' is the result simply of his painter's eye and its perceptions of Being: the eyes which instinctively study his fellows day after day could tell at any time that out of hundreds, perhaps twenty-five are the kind of beings who would try to escape. But such 'knowledge' might be everything or nothing; it cannot be defined, verified or explained, and only an explanation would satisfy. In the interrogation Sammy is trapped again between the worlds of fact and action, and of being; asked questions in one language that he could only answer in another, and so cannot answer at all. He refuses to talk, not because he is either a hero or a 'chuckle-headed' conformist to some 'little code' of loyalty or patriotism, but because he is as helpless as the infant Sammy interrogated by the verger and facing the impossibility of communication.

So the whole interrogation becomes a parody of the temptation of Christ, where the irony lies only partly in the different
'world' the tempter offers; but far more in the hero's different
capacity to answer. Sammy, as Halde points out, 'has no health
in him':

'You do not believe in anything enough to suffer for it or be glad.
There is no point at which something has knocked on your door
and taken possession of you ... You wait in a dusty waiting room
on no particular line for no particular train.'

Christ, like the dead men, 'could say no because (He) could say
yes'; He had 'some simple knowledge, some certainty to die for',
some purposive Being. Sammy can say nothing; he is indeed, as a
tiny but significant moment makes clear ('Do you feel nothing?'
'Maybe.') in the position of Beatrice responding to the catechisms
he put her through, before he too is given over to torture.

The torture starts with the cell's darkness, for Sammy, like
Pincher, is terrified of the dark. In *Pincher Martin* we could not
ask why, or how he became so, but now Sammy proceeds to do
just that. There is a break in the narrative as he resolutely attempts
to localize and explain his fear. He thinks back to the lonely child
in the cold, loveless rectory, after Father Watts-Watt had adopted
him; remembering the rattle of the handle on the bolted door, the
draughts and tapping pictures, the timid homosexual advances,
the persecution-mania with its talk of signals and unusual happen-
ings in the middle of the night. But when all has been remembered,
the fear remains stubbornly inexplicable. Father Watts-Watt
'added nothing to the terror of the dark ... Now I have been back
in these pages to find out why I am frightened of the dark and I
cannot tell. Once upon a time I was not frightened of the dark and
later on I was.' The drift, and the significance of the narrative
break just here, is apparent. Whatever fear there is in Sammy, and
however it has influenced his actions, it is part of his Being and
cannot be 'explained' in terms of environment or behaviour. Once
again Becoming questions are blocked, this time with full delibera-
tion and purpose; but the blocking is no longer because the
questions are excluded, but because they cannot be answered before Sammy's Being has been investigated. As the darkness of the

cell begins to press on Sammy's eyeballs, we know that his 'history' can tell us nothing more. Only the revelation afforded by myth will serve.

So in Chapter 9 we find ourselves back in the characteristic Golding world of isolated man. Dr Halde, 'Doctor Slope', precipitates him into the pit of his own being so that its nature is fully and horribly revealed to him. He is not tortured, but allowed to torture himself, and his terror of the dark elucidates for him and for us the kind of mind that fears this thing rather than that thing. The fictions of his horrified imagination define the shape of what he is, stands for, believes in at the heart of his Being. The nature of his fear becomes explicit, 'it cared only to protect my privates'; and the worst thing he can imagine to torture himself is the severed penis he thinks he discovers lying in its blood in the middle of the floor. This is both a pointer to a Being in which sexuality is the central reality and value and, in the horror of the organ divorced from the complex humanity it ought to be only part of, an exact symbol of that Being.

The crux of the entire novel is, however, as with all the previous ones, not the revelation itself but the response to it. Sammy's life 'centred round the fact of the next few minutes I spent alone and panic-stricken in the dark'. He shrieks for help,

'the cry of the rat when the terrier shakes it, a hopeless sound, the raw signature of one savage act. My cry meant no more, was instinctive, said here is flesh of which the nature is to suffer and do thus. I cried out not with hope of an ear but as accepting a shut door, darkness and a shut sky.

'But the very act of crying out changed the thing that cried . . .' There is no help in the present, nor in the past, and the future holds only imaginations of increasing terror to the point of extinction. Yet . . .

'The thing that cried fled forward over those steps because there was no other way to go, was shot forward screaming as into a furnace, as over unimaginable steps that were all that might be borne, were more, were too searing for the refuge of madness, were destructive of the centre. The thing that screamed left all

living behind and came to the entry where death is as close as
darkness against eyeballs.

And burst that door.'

But Sammy does not die; instead the door of the cell bursts open
too, and he walks out into the prison camp with his innocent
vision miraculously restored.

Now at last we begin to 'cash' the apocalyptic language of the
novel's opening; and Chapter 10 (the chapter of resurrection
following temptation and torture) is perhaps its finest imaginative
achievement. The prison camp becomes the General's Garden
seen again, but now with the qualities of conscious awareness
leading to reflection that were missing from the child's vision.
The drab huts 'shone with the innocent light of their own
created nature'; the dust 'was a universe of brilliant and fantastic
crystals, that miracles supported instantly in their being'.

'Those crowded shapes extending up into the air and down into
the rich earth, those deeds of far space and deep earth were aflame
at the surface and daunting by right of their own natures though
a day before I should have disguised them as trees. Beyond them
the mountains were not only clear all through like purple glass,
but living. They sang and were conjubilant.'

And now the landscape reveals also the power and the glory of
man. The Kings of Egypt of the child's cigarette-cards take flesh,
and proclaim a wonder and beauty in the midst of suffering and
dirt. As he looks at them he cries out again, and 'this cry travelled
away and along a fourth dimension' where love flows, so naturally, powerfully, and incandescently that 'standing between the
understood huts, among jewels and music, I was visited by a
flake of fire, miraculous and pentecostal; and fire transmuted me,
once and for ever'. At last the painter's eye, always devoted to
Being, comes into its own in love of nature and man, and the
'secret smuggled sketches of the haggard, unshaven kings of
Egypt in their glory are the glory of my right hand and likely to
remain so'.

Yet we must recognize the cost of such a vision. The Kings are
of Egypt, not of Israel, and they are seen through tears, by one

who has just staggered out of a sea of death. The eyes are dead because the old Sammy Mons Veneris who could live content with himself and his world is gone for ever; yet the Being they inhabit remains, and the vision so full of love for fallen man and a fallen universe is filled with loathing when it turns inward on that Being:

'Now at last, the eyes of Sammy turned and looked where Halde had directed them . . . what they saw was not beautiful but fearsome . . . here was a point, a single point which was my own interior identity, without shape or size but only position. Yet this position was miraculous as everything else since it continually defied the law of conservation of energy, rule one as it were, and created shapes that . . . could be likened to nothing but the most loathsome substances that man knows of, or perhaps the most loathsome and abject creatures, continuously created . . . and this was the human nature I found inhabiting the centre of my own awareness . . . But now to live with such a thing was unendurable.'

In the last phrase we find the driving force of Sammy's novel, and are very nearly at the position he occupied when he began it. Looking back at Beatrice now, the ordinary eye can understand the painter's eye and bring her into focus:

'The beauty of her simplicity struck me a blow in the face. That negative personality, that clear absence of being, that vacuum which I had finally deduced from her silences, I now saw to have been full . . . She was simple and loving and generous and humble . . .'

Yet the cell which has given him insight into the value of himself and his past has done nothing to suggest that the past was anything but inevitable. We can understand with a new accuracy the violence of his self-condemnation, but also appreciate the force that makes him go on searching for a *cause*.

Now, however, we can also detect a shape that the strategy of search has fallen into. The evidence for understanding the Being revealed in the opening paragraph is almost complete, but the problem of Becoming is apparently no nearer solution. Yet this is far from the case. For to have realized that guilt cannot be localized in action but must be sought in Being, and to have discovered the exact nature of the guilty Being, is to be able to define the question of Becoming with an accuracy impossible before. The choice, if it existed, must have been *a choice of being*, anterior to action, and the question then becomes: How did I choose to be *that* kind of human being? Moreover if childhood is too early, and the start of the guilty action too late, then such a choice if it happened at all, must have occurred in the missing space—the time of adolescence. There, and only there, if anywhere. The peculiar chronology of *Free Fall* is not wilfully obscure, but logical. Insight into the beginning can only *follow* insight into the nature of what is begun, and that is far more difficult than it sounds; achieved only by the process of exclusion that we have gone through. After three necessary sighting shots, the target area is pinpointed.

There is however a difference from the earlier school episodes that goes beyond the difference in the age and vulnerability of the boy, and depends on a new position of the narrator. Coming after the cell, the account cannot be on the level of mere reminiscence; it is bound to have a new quality of explicit analysis. So Sammy recalls through his younger self, but arranges the episodes with an emphasis and definition that always demonstrate an adult understanding. We move sharply back for the second time into the mode of Becoming. Once again the voices, the actions, the psychology, are sharply observed and realistically convincing; but this time the vision is carefully ordered to bring out a pattern of choice. So the young Sammy confronts his spiritual parentage, two views of reality, artistically juxtaposed. There is the ordered universe of scientifically predictable cause and effect, taught by Nick Shales with a deep sense of its logic and beauty. And there is the miraculous world of the spirit, of Moses and the burning bush, taught with vivid power by Rowena Pringle. For a while Sammy moves easily between them without realizing their incompatibility, until the cruelty of the scripture-mistress forces him to choose. Inevitably, however, he chooses between the philosophies, not as they were, but as they were presented. He chooses Nick's instinctive goodness which is logically no part of his philosophy; he rejects the tortured and torturing spinster though what she taught had compelled his belief. Yet his own Being remains innocent, so this cannot be the determining choice. It is the good Being of Nick that is chosen; the bad Being of Rowena that is rejected: 'People are the walls of our room, not philosophies.'

There comes a time however when Sammy uses Nick's philosophy to deny the goodness for which he chose it. The wine of sex has been spilt in the children's blood and Sammy, having dashed down without thinking a portrait of a hardly-noticed girl in the art-room, finds he has been captured not only by the light in her face and her beauty, but by the body that holds them. He can never draw her again; she becomes an obsession. The idea of possessing her sexually receives dramatic formulation when the attractive French mistress and the games-master are caught together in the boiler-room—their dismissal sends a shudder of pleasure round the school. This is what sex is, the dangerous, forbidden, but utterly fascinating fruit, and Sammy is enthralled. He turns to Nick, but for him, 'if the Devil had invented man he couldn't have played him a dirtier, wickeder, a more shameful trick than when he gave him sex!'. In Nick's rational and scientific universe there is no place for the mysterious irrationality of sex; it is branded shameful, reduced to a trick, and in the wake of such diminution comes evil. Sammy is willing enough not only to see sex as the Devil's trick but to espouse it, because of his compulsion to possess Beatrice; and he converts Nick's rationalism into an egotistic ethic where good and evil become relative, the only absolutes being one's own desires and the eleventh commandment. In words recalling Milton's Satan he begins to deify his own urges: 'musk, shameful and heady, be thou my good'; and with this he begins to move into 'the world of the lads'—Mercutio, Valentine, Claudio—who made the law the servant of passion and desire. Now at last Sammy really focuses on the gap between behaviour and being that his novel has been opening up more and more: 'For this guilt', he says, 'I found occasion to *invent* a crime that fitted the punishment. Guilty am I, therefore wicked I will be ... *Guilt comes before the crime and can cause it*' (our italics). He seems to be accepting himself as irretrievably fallen, if that word can be used of someone whose 'good' is what he himself decides. All that is needed now is the conscious and deliberate decision that fixes the guilt. As he bids farewell to school Nick

tells him to commit himself totally to whatever he chooses to do.
The headmaster goes a little further:

'If you want something enough, you can always get it provided
you are willing to make the appropriate sacrifice. Something,
anything. But what you get is never quite what you thought; and
sooner or later the sacrifice is always regretted.'

Sammy's future Being is already coming into existence, already
being robed as a destiny; yet he is not finally committed to it, nor
has he clarified and accepted the cost. He is still free . . . just.

He walks out into the hot summer day, and as he enters his
'bower of blisse' the answer to the headmaster's question 'What is
important to you?' becomes clear, namely 'the white, unseen body
of Beatrice Ifor, her obedience and for all time my protection of
her; and for the pain she has caused me, her utter abjection this
side of death'. It is the crucial moment, and as he emerges from
the wood, 'so that there should be no doubt I now see', it is as
though the angel of the gate of paradise holds a sword between
him and the spices. Below the weir lies the water, the angel
breathes on it, 'it seemed to me that the water was waiting for me'.
It is a final chance of purification, an opportunity to see whole, but
he takes from the water only the experience of his own sexuality,
and when he emerges fresh, composed, self-sufficient, he faces
and chooses between the alternatives. He moves away from 'the
providential waters' and, on the hillside between 'earth and sky,
cloister and street', the free decision we have been searching for
takes place:

'What is important to you?
   ' "Beatrice Ifor."
   'She thinks you depraved already. She dislikes you.
   ' "If I want something enough I can always get it provided I am
willing to make the appropriate sacrifice."
   'What will you sacrifice?
   ' "Everything." '

It is the formal catechism of self-damnation, the deliberate choosing of a part for the whole. Sammy ratifies his guilt, determines

the course of his life, and loses his freedom. Here Being and Becoming meet as Sammy chooses his determinism. It is only in a
special sense an action . . . Sammy 'does' nothing . . . but it
determines all future action and all future being. It is his free fall.

Then, having discovered the beginning, we see what it led to in
the end. We go back to the General's Garden, now the grounds of
a mental asylum; and just as years before the eyes of the boy had
witnessed an apocalypse and manifested innocence, so now the
no less contemplative eyes of the man see his guilt made flesh:
'Beatrice sat, looking at the wall, looking at nothing. Her face was
in the shadow of her body . . .' Desperately, Sammy tries to communicate with her, but she has become what he chose, Miss Ifor,
a body without mind or spirit. Like Minnie in the infant class,
she is only minimally human; she disgraces herself and is led
away. There can be no atonement, no forgiveness. Sammy is left
to live with his Being in all the violence of his self-condemnation.
We return to the condition of the opening paragraph, recognizing
the full enormity of what it means to live in two worlds that cannot be unified:

'All day long the trains run on rails. Eclipses are predictable.
Penicillin cures pneumonia and the atom splits to order. All day
long, year in, year out, the daylight explanation drives back the
mystery and reveals a reality usable, understandable, and detached.
The scalpel and the microscope fail, the oscilloscope moves closer
to behaviour. The gorgeous dance is self-contained, then; does
not need the music which in my mad moments I have heard.
Nick's universe is real.

'All day long action is weighed in the balance and found not
opportune nor fortunate or ill-advised, but good or evil. For
this mode which we must call the spirit breathes through the
universe and does not touch it; touches only the dark things, held
prisoner, incommunicado, touches, judges, sentences and passes
on.

'Her world was real, both worlds are real. There is no bridge.'

III

This conducts us to the limits of Sammy's understanding. We come round full circle to a definition of the dichotomy implied by the first paragraph, and gradually explored and focused until it can be explicitly stated in its full starkness. He has apparently solved the problem he set out to solve. He has contrived to show how he became his being. Yet if we find it extremely peculiar and difficult to accept, it is not simply because the conceptual framework is so different from any we are likely to have met. There is brought to a head in the final section a critical problem that affects the novel as a whole.

Are we convinced by the moment of free fall to which the whole quest leads? Because it cannot be an action within a human relationship, it is curiously removed from the world of behaviour in which moral decision is usually shown in novels; but so enormous a determinism depends on it that we must be imaginatively convinced, or the whole novel surely collapses in ruin. Golding has to create a moment in which Sammy does nothing; yet it must be demonstrably crucial enough to determine all the actions and behaviour of the book. Can we truly feel that the boy wandering through the musky wood, bathing in the water, climbing the hillside, and there formally damning himself, is capable of such terrible self-determination, and that the moment convincingly represents so irretrievable a decision? There is certainly a claim to Miltonic consequence:

> *'ingrate, he had of mee*
> *All he could have; I made him just and right,*
> *Sufficient to have stood, though free to fall.'*

But at that moment—'What will you sacrifice?' 'Everything'—if we do not feel that, in the fiction, Sammy has had all he could have from Golding, and been made just and right, the novel will collapse as a novel, and reduce itself to a theological treatise which we accept or reject on conceptual grounds alone. If we felt that the episode was a construct, a text-book illustration for moral theologians indicating the exact conditions necessary for grave sin, rather than the solidly convincing achievement of a novelist, realizing dramatic truth through protagonist and scene, and capable of satisfying the full testing conditions of novels of becoming, we could only fully respond to it by a kind of faith in the theology which determines it. Or again, if we doubt the convincingness of the scene, would this not suggest that there is something wrong with the theology?

The problem however is far from simple; for it is partly a question of the way that art itself demands a localization and articulation that are not like life, and uniquely so in the situation to which Golding's explorations, and their form, have led him. In 'life' terms, whatever our philosophy, there seems to be no particular difficulty about conceiving that a boy of nineteen, before he actually does anything, might be so self-conditioned that he cannot help himself when the moment of apparent choice of action appears. In life this would be a process, only gradually becoming conscious. But just as a parabola must contain a single point which belongs neither to the up curve nor the down, but is the point where one turns into the other, so such a process would have to contain a single moment of determination. Yet to represent such a moment fully, any artist would have to give it a prominence and explicitness out of keeping with its true place in the curve; though he could try to minimize this to a greater or lesser extent by gradual preparation and consequence.

The real difficulty then is not the 'theology'; rather that Golding chooses to maximize his highlighting, and to give his scene a clarity of analysis and an explicitness of language that stretch realistic credibility to breaking point. Why is this?

Most obviously, it is because this is Sammy's book, and the whole driving force of it is his search precisely for a *moment* of choice. This must inevitably 'island' it 'in a picture', since he is not interested in the re-creation of the process, the accumulation of tiny nudges towards it, or confirming it afterwards. The process is of course implicitly there, but we do not experience it in life-like graduation because of the analytic mode that Sammy imposes on the whole section. This in turn, as we have seen, is because his search has reached after the cell a point where he knows exactly what he is looking for and where to find it. He is a man hastening to a destination, superimposing upon the features of experience a grid-map of itinerary. When he reaches the scene, we experience

it as his clarification to himself of what the boy was doing. The
boy must have been conscious and deliberate, morally speaking,
in the movements of consciousness within the mind, but not in
that way or that language; yet what is important for Sammy is not
at all to experience the boy realistically, but to get the implications
precisely clear. Finally we might quote Sammy on his own painting. He knows that 'the rectangle of a canvas' is 'a limited area
however ingeniously you paint . . . Living . . . is too subtle and
copious for unassisted thought. Painting is like a single attribute,
a selected thing.' But he sees also the peculiar nature of his success in catching Beatrice in a picture:

'I had put the girl on paper in a way that my laborious portraitures
could never come at. The line leapt, it was joyous, free, authori-
tative. It achieved little miracles of implication so that the viewer's
eye created her small hands though my pencil had not touched
them. That free line had raced past and created her face, had
thinned and broken where no pencil could go, but only the
imagination.'

This is obviously Golding on his own art too, or what he would
like it to be. (We have seen how this new novel is bound to be
about writing a novel and reading a novel because of the new
problems Golding was posing himself.) Ought we not, then, to
look at the scene of Sammy's fall in the same way, to see that it
implies what it does not need to show in detail? If it 'breaks', it
merely honestly indicates the boundary-line where—if we want
what 'really' must have occurred—art must no longer seek to
encapsulate, but rather to liberate the imagination?

Yet this will not altogether dismiss the difficulty either; because
there remains a sense in which it is part of the whole clash
of Being and Becoming in the novel. Sammy's painting, as we
have seen many times, is an Art of Being; what the portrait of
Beatrice does is 'catch this particular signature of being which
made her unique'. Yet the moment of Sammy's fall is a moment of
Becoming. And we may ask how far an *Art* of Becoming exists in
the novel as a whole?

Its 'Being' sections—Rotten Row and boyhood, the cell and the
transfigured camp—are both assured and homogeneous. There *is*

an Art of Becoming: the sections of Becoming—the affair with Beatrice and the closing section—do exhibit a strength new in Golding's work. In their richness of observed detail, speech, motivation, psychology, behaviour, they are also imaginatively resourceful and confident. Yet, significantly, they are not homogeneous. The first, as we saw, is continually shot through with intimations of Being; the second is patterned analytically as we have just been arguing. Page by page the scenes convince, but they are always felt to be in the service of some governing purpose which frames them, islands them (in that significant phrase we may now complete) '*out* of the complexities of living'. Surely, however reasonable the technical explanation, it is true that in pitting one kind of novel against another, Golding's art remains finally weighted towards an art of Being? It is much less so than in any of the previous novels; it is capable of dealing with new complexities in a new way; but it never wholly commits itself to that way without revealing a clear tendency to veer back. So, at the key moment of Becoming, we may still feel that the 'islanding' is excessive, and that some more marked move towards the Art of Becoming would have been more appropriate. The novelist's eyes which saw no need to take longer, to do far more filling in of what is only implied, to place one more firmly in the boy's consciousness, are eyes still primarily concerned with Being. Yet, on the evidence of the novel, it is by no means a question of incapacity. Golding clearly possessed the means, if he had been convinced of the need, for more 'laborious portraitures'.

IV

Yet such criticism pales beside Golding's self-criticism, once we see the significance of the novel's final page. We may object that Golding, in pitting Being against Becoming, is still caught in a too reductive pattern of Being; and that he ought to have swung over more to Becoming, where signpostings like 'Beatrice Ifor', or for that matter the obedience of Beatrice to the Being chosen for her by Sammy, Beatrice turning into Ifor, would have to be paid for in a different currency; but Golding himself is altogether more thoroughgoing.

Free Fall

In *Free Fall*, finally, he comes to see both Becoming and Being as patterns, and sees *all* pattern as reductive. What we have been discussing is Sammy's book; but it ends at the top of page 253, and for the rest of the page Golding himself takes over as we have been expecting him to do, and the effect is revolutionary. In the end neither Being nor Becoming, nor yet Sammy's attempt to adjust them to each other, will do.

Let us recapitulate Sammy's two worlds without a bridge, conceptually. There is a pattern of Becoming, where cause and effect operate, man chooses, and becomes what he chooses by acting. In Nick's language: 'If you do that sort of thing you become that sort of animal. The universe is wonderfully exact, Sammy. You can't have your penny and your bun. Conservation of energy holds good mentally as well as physically.' The exactness of cause and effect may have to be studied with greater and greater subtlety, beyond, say, the uncertainty of Kenneth on the cause of Beatrice's insanity, but behaviour is ultimately explicable. Humans are free to change, but only from one state into another, they cannot combine both states. There is responsibility, but there is also the possibility of forgiveness through understanding. There is nothing that cannot be explained.

Conversely, in the pattern of Being, man chooses to be one thing or another, and this determines all his actions. Nick's phrases are reversed. If you are that sort of being you do that sort of thing—and have no freedom to do otherwise. But here there is no conservation of energy: the bush burns unconsumed; the good shine, even if they behave badly or foolishly, continually generating light from within; the evil generate vile shapes unceasingly. Being cannot be changed. There can be a change of vision, but this only clarifies the nature of the Being it inhabits. There is responsibility, but no forgiveness. There is no 'explanation'; there is revelation, apocalypse, recognition.

Both patterns are true; hence neither can be true in itself. Sammy uses both, but he also manages to adjust them to each other at two points. Being and Becoming cross at the moment of free fall, where Sammy becomes what he chooses. They cross again at the moment of resurrection, when the lips utter the cry in the cell. This is in one sense a death and a new beginning. But the beginning is only one of *judgement*, not Being; the fourth dimension crosses the other three only to condemn.

We have also to adjust the characters to these worlds. Most live in only one pattern. Taffy, Kenneth, Sammy himself in his marriage, live purely in a world of Becoming, where forgiveness is possible and there are no grey faces. The Good, like Johnny and Nick, and the infant Samuel, live purely in Being and neither need nor can give forgiveness. The Wicked, like Rowena and Philip, also live in a single world of Being, and they do not recognize any need for forgiveness. But there is a new distinction between the Wicked and the Guilty: 'The innocent and the wicked live in one world . . . But we are neither the innocent nor the wicked. We are the guilty . . . We weep and tear each other.' The Guilty live in both worlds, so that they recognize what they are, understand how they became as they are, but can find no forgiveness. These are Sammy and perhaps his guardian, who knows what's what, and outgrows his Christian biretta. For them, most terrible of all, 'both worlds are true. There is no bridge.'

Sammy has explained how he became his Being; but if the deeper object of the search was the reconciliation of the two worlds, it is self-defeating. Both patterns are true, but their truths remain contradictory; they touch, only to condemn. Sammy fails to find what he was looking for most.

On the last page, however, Golding moves beyond him. The ending differs from those of the previous novels in that it contains no surprise or shock; indeed, it could hardly be more ordinary, less dramatic. Yet it is like them in that the author looks again at what has been achieved as a whole, and asks us to do the same; and its effect is more unsettling than ever before.

One tiny piece is missing from the jigsaw of Sammy's experience; and while the gap is emphasized by the rest, it must also in some sense give a new and final orientation to everything else. Narratively it is utterly simple: just the moment when the cell door opens and Sammy emerges to find the commandant sitting where Halde had been. Behind Sammy is an ordinary cupboard with a wet floorcloth on the concrete, and four utterly simple sentences are spoken. Yet they leave Sammy puzzling, as though they were the Sphinx's riddle, 'what is man?'.

This, indeed, is just what they are, and their cryptic density and opacity is Golding's hard-won answer to the reductiveness of *all* pattern. The puzzled Sammy of the final sentence is a wiser man than the one who penned the confident statement at the top of the page. For it is not merely that Being and Becoming are both reductive patterns. Sammy's dichotomy is a pattern too, albeit a more complex one than the twin components it tries to adjust. At the very end we are given an opportunity to see without pattern; a hint of how cryptic and intensely difficult such seeing must be, a challenge to achieve it.

For the difficulty is not that the simple sentences are meaningless; it is the opposite. They mean too much, too contradictorily, and they must mean their contradictions simultaneously. The moment that we 'explain' them as meaning one thing, or even one thing or another, we fail the challenge of seeing that they mean both at once. We fall again into pattern, into reduction.

'Heraus' is a curt, brutal-sounding order from the world of punishment and imprisonment; a command only to change one prison for another. It is also—Go out—an offer of an open door, and Compassion sitting where the Judge had been expected. It is neither; because it is and must be both together. We must also complete 'You have heard?' in two opposite ways at once. Have you heard the good news? that there is no judgement, that you are free, forgiven, have died into new life? And—we remember the same words on the lips of the lieutenant—Have you heard the bad news? The two indefatigable cricketers have been shot, the weeping Sammy tortured. 'This should not be happening. I am sorry.' 'Sorry, Sammy. They're a lot of bloody murderers.' 'Bloody swine!' But have you heard that you are a swine and murderer too, that we all are, sorry, and self-condemned? Yet again it cannot mean either because it must mean both, simultaneously. So, 'the Herr Doctor does not know about peoples'. He does of course: has he not tapped Sammy's loathsomeness, revealed him to himself? But he also does not, because he is an 'explainer', an 'either/or man' ('are you a hero or not, Sammy?'), a reducer. The moment we fail Golding's challenge and 'reduce' the cryptograms, we too are on the slippery slope. It is only in riddle, in dense opacity, total ambiguity, that things can be seen as they really are.

And what then of Sammy's book?

For Golding, it can only be a failure. Sammy's paintings of the Kings of Egypt in simultaneous misery and glory are not only his greatest work, but 'likely to remain so', for they point to where his book cannot go. At its end we see clearly why only the man who has experienced both worlds should have even the opportunity to see truly. Certainly none of the reductive characters could do so. Miss Ifor, Nick and Rowena, Johnny and Philip, Taffy and Kenneth, Dr Halde, all escape the agony, but necessarily forfeit the vision. Yet we do not see Sammy the writer achieving it, nor know whether he could, ever. From the old standpoint of Becoming we might have objected that while we can accept what Sammy sees after the cell as true for him, we never have a chance to verify for ourselves something like the 'real' radiance of Beatrice. But the criticism now is a far deeper one. We are *not* meant to substitute the painter's Beatrice for the lover's. She is both; a girl with a light in her face and a shining being; a girl sexually inhibited, frustrated and frustrating; both Beatrice and Ifor at once. So Nick is saint and devil, radiant and evilly reductive, simultaneously. But the objection is not that we do not see as Sammy sees. For Sammy does not see like this. The objection is that because Sammy cannot see truly at all, neither can we. His false vision may be only an eyelash away from meeting the conditions of true sight that Golding has come to realize by struggling in and through him. But the eyelash splits the focus. Sammy's pattern of mutually exclusive modes would only have to be altered by bringing them, superimposed, into the same focus; but this is the whole difference between single and double vision. And there is no achievement of single vision: only a cryptic challenge to try it for ourselves in its astonishing difficulty, and an obscure indication of the conditions it must meet. Self-mockingly, Golding adopts a comic German-English to tell us that Herr Doctor/Sammy/Golding 'does not know about peoples'. No criticism of *Free Fall* has been nearly as trenchant as its author's.

Yet it is surely not perverse to claim the book as a considerable achievement, not in spite of but because of all this. It is only through a huge effort of exploration, analysis, and discovery that we have been able first to recognize the problem, and then to see at least the way to overcome it.* The author of the first three Golding novels was already a novelist of real stature. To read *Free Fall* properly is to watch that novelist in the act of transforming himself, not without pain. And as *Pincher Martin* produced the problem which led to *Free Fall*, so the writing of his fourth novel clarified for Golding what he had to attempt in *The Spire*. *Free Fall* diagnoses true, single vision. *The Spire* seeks to attain it.

* The goal is strikingly similar to Iris Murdoch's in her interesting essay *Against Dryness* (*Encounter*, January 1961, pp. 16–20). Cf. our different, but related discussion of 'fable', 'history' and 'myth' in Ch. 6.

V

THE SPIRE

(1964)

I

In some ways *The Spire* reverses the psalmist's cry; the straight is made crooked and the plain places rough. Ambiguity, paradox, reversal, these are the words that come most readily to mind when we try to give an account of the book, and they seem no less just when we agree that in its purely narrative trajectory *The Spire* is the most straightforward of Golding's novels since *Lord of the Flies*. The story has none of the obscurity of *The Inheritors*, springing from the imaginative demand that we enter the consciousness of primitive people; nor the double structure behind *Pincher Martin*'s remorseless concentration on a single moment; nor the sudden shifts in time, direction and mode of *Free Fall*. The narrative is generally as clear as the spire itself; any obstruction in reading comes from the density and intensity with which its implications are investigated. For the moment we pause to make sure that we have understood the detail, the atmosphere changes. What looked like firm ground turns into a mirage, cross-lights begin to play on the scene, so that fair seems foul and foul fair.

It is useful to begin by recording this dual impression of the novel—extreme clarity accompanied by extreme opacity—because if it is part of our experience of reading, it is also part of the meaning. This curious impression is not a sequential one, we do not find light giving way to darkness. Rather, the light changes constantly as we read. We can often see, caught in a single paragraph, different reflections of the book as a whole. One such moment occurs at the beginning of the novel, when Jocelin stands at the great west door of his cathedral looking up the aisle:

'The most solid thing was the light. It smashed through the rows of windows in the south aisle, so that they exploded with colour, it slanted before him from right to left in an exact formation, to hit the bottom yard of the pillars on the north side of the nave. Everywhere, fine dust gave these rods and trunks of light the importance of a dimension. He blinked at them again, seeing, near at hand, how the individual grains of dust turned over each other, or bounced all together, like mayfly in a breath of wind. He saw how further away they drifted cloudily, coiled, or hung in a moment of pause, becoming, in the most distant rods and trunks, nothing but colour, honey-colour slashed across the body of the cathedral. Where the south transept lighted the crossways from a hundred and fifty foot of grisaille, the honey thickened in a pillar that lifted straight as Abel's from the men working with crows at the pavement.

'He shook his head in rueful wonder at the solid sunlight. If it were not for that Abel's pillar, he thought, I would take the important level of light to be a true dimension, and so believe that my stone ship lay aground on her side; and he smiled a little, to think how the mind touches all things with law, yet deceives itself as easily as a child.'

An immediate response to such a passage is likely to be to its visual brilliance, the perceptive rendering of intense sunlight in the dark and dusty nave. When we come like Jocelin to see 'near at hand', we see that the light is trapped and seen in terms of the very different element of dust. In the foreground, the individual grains dance in relation to one another; further off, the dance becomes collective; in the distance, there is a blending into 'sundust', honey-coloured against the darkness, so solid that it seems no less of a pillar than those of stone. The confidence of the eye is shaken, and the paragraph concludes by questioning the vision itself, knowing that the eye can get the angles, the certainties of horizontal and vertical, wrong.

We see that this is not simply a description of the vagaries of light in darkness. The scene has dramatic content, a subject. Cathedrals are not usually in a state of dust and chaos, and in the relation between the sunlight and the dust kicked up by Jocelin's decision to build the spire, there exists one of the main tensions in the plot itself. The novel will turn out to be about seeing in a very literal sense, seeing neither sun nor dust but 'sundust'. It will not be surprising when the comparison of individual speck and mayfly makes its reappearance as a bleak comment on human beings. Abel's pillar reminds us of something also suggested by the stained glass window of Abraham and Isaac with which the novel opens. The work of God, the building of the church, may include bloodshed, sacrifice, murder. The pillar looks straight, the window looks beautiful—but the story they tell is of crookedness and suffering. When Jocelin smiles 'to think how the mind

touches all things with law, yet deceives itself as easily as a child',
we seem to have an authorial comment; but later we shall come to
see that this reflection has a dangerous facility, that it exhibits
Jocelin's complacent handling of a truth to which, personally, he
is blind. His smile is actually the measure of his self-indulgence,
created for us also by the exalted, 'whipped-up' style with which
the book opens. This use of style has been characteristic since
Pincher Martin.

And so we come back to the paragraph, not simply as an expression of something finely seen and rendered, but as a drama-
tization of what it is to see only what one wants to see, and to see
without understanding or insight. Jocelin's vision operates at a
level of dangerous intensity: the light 'smashed through the rows
of windows in the south aisle, so that they exploded with colour',
the honey colour is 'slashed across the body of the cathedral'.
Though Jocelin may smile at 'the important level of light', *he* is in
no doubt of the 'true dimension'. The progress of the novel will
consist in the taming of metaphors of violence, the overturning
of certainties, the transformation of primary colours to depth and
shade. The book which opens with such explosive confidence
will end in puzzle, with a truth not seen so much as glimpsed from
the very corner of the eye, expressed not with the bold assumptions of emblematic metaphor, but with the tentativeness of
simile: *'It's like the appletree!'*

II

From emblem to simile—we could see *The Spire* as developing
in that way, and in saying this we would be establishing a wave-
length for reading. Golding's boldness is to make his central
character an 'alter-novelist', a patternmaker, an emblematist, a
refiner of the raw material of experience. His church is a man lying
on his back, the nave his legs placed together, the transepts his
arms outstretched: ' "We are labour" said the walls. The ogival
windows clasped their hands and sang: "We are prayer". I had
seen the whole building as an image of a living praying man . . .
inside it was a written book to instruct that man.' But the 'written
book' that Golding creates, for Jocelin's instruction and ours, tells

the price of having a meaning but missing the experience. The whole of Golding's art is concerned to create a spire in the place occupied, in Jocelin's mind, by a diagram of prayer; glass, stone and steel, not only 'the constant fabric of praise'. The two voices are clearly caught in dialogue between Jocelin and his master mason:

'We're surrounded by new things. We guess; and go on building. . . . we've come to something different because we were chosen, both of us. We're mayfly. We can't tell what it'll be like up there from foot to foot; but we must live from the morning to the evening every minute with a new thing.'

To which Roger replies:

'I don't know what you mean. But I know how much the spire will weigh, and I don't know how strong it'll be. Look down, Father —right over the parapet, all the way down, past the lights, the buttresses, all the way down to the cedar top in the cloister.
   ' "I see it." '

These eyes have to be forced to look 'down' or 'at'; their natural tendency is to look 'above' or 'through'.

This strategy of Golding's, the building into his novel of a counter-novel, is one that we examined in relation to *Free Fall*, but here it is used with a much greater consciousness of purpose. In the earlier novel it sprang initially from a degree of uncertainty on the part of the author, and issued in an exploration that belonged to life as well as to art. Here the two 'novels' continuously follow the progress of the spire itself from the beginning. They interplay rather than intersect, one is never supplanted or defeated by the other, there is genuine equipoise until they finally come together. What Jocelin makes abstract, Golding must make concrete; Jocelin's explanations must be Golding's explorations; where Jocelin sees God the Father in a glory of sunlight, Golding must see 'God as lying between people and to be found there'. In this way Golding, like the master-mason, 'barters strength for weight, weight for strength'; the novel, no less than the spire, being 'a great dare'. If it reaches its pinnacle in simile, it is because that figure maintains a tension between the things that divide, no less than the things which bring together. The two poles create a field of force only when neither takes over the other.

What exactly *The Spire* is 'like', however, takes us into an analysis of the novel as it unfolds.

III

From the outset of the novel Dean Jocelin dominates the scene and our imaginations. Our response to him is however continuously ambivalent—is he a saint or a destructive monomaniac, self-deceived? The first four chapters suggest that any answer will be paradoxical.

The first chapter is ablaze with sunlight and exaltation; but we are presented with a visionary who sees nothing. We encounter him laughing, crying with happiness as God the Father seems to explode in radiance through the stained glass; but his eyes are half-closed and the upthrust chin does not make for clear sight. The meaning of the stained glass, that story of Abraham and Isaac and the cost of faith, passes him by; and it does so because his glance is so fixedly upwards. He cannot focus on Pangall and the tear he sheds:

'There was a sharp tap on the instep of Jocelin's shoe; and as he looked he saw a wet star there with arms to it and tiny globes of water that slid off the dubbin into the mud of the yard. Impatiently, he let out his breath and looked round for something to say. But the sunlight on stone drew his eye upward, to the empty air above the crossways. . . .'

'Joy', 'love', 'patience', 'forgiveness'—such words are constantly on Jocelin's lips; but of the realities which give the words meaning he remains tragically unaware. Pangall is an irritation. Father Adam has 'no face at all. He is the same all round like the top of a clothespeg'. Jocelin is deaf to the depths of God's 'simplicities' as the choir sings the creed. He is just as deaf to the voice of Caesar when, reading the letter from his patroness in the bright light of the crossways, he refuses her any answer.

The second chapter reverses the strategy of the first. Dust

obscures the sunshine. In a thick yellow fog workmen with deformed, cloth-covered faces caked with dirt and sweat, chant obscene songs in the transepts. The pit dug at the crossways reveals that the church rests on rubble, brushwood, mud. The human instruments of the work are no more reliable. The master mason sees his assignment in the light of his own ends, and turns a blind eye to the fighting among his men and their sadistic treatment of Pangall. His wife Rachel is vulgar, 'emancipated', a ceaseless torrent of abuse. The sacristan, Father Anselm, with his beautiful head, silver-haired and saintly, has a cold unloving heart, and a mind bound by rule and prescription. On the other hand, if the first chapter was concerned to point to the pride beneath Jocelin's sunny faith, here in the dust of the cathedral we are reminded of his warmth. We are not in doubt of his superiority as a human being to the others we meet. The power of his faith is thrown into high relief by the scepticism of the master builder. His heart may be on his sleeve, but it exists as the sacristan's does not: ' "Father Anselm. Friendship is a precious thing. . . . What have we done to it?" "Is that a real question, my Lord, or a rhetorical one?" ' But, even with Anselm, Golding is fair. Amusement, a curious kindness, flicker across that pseudo-noble face and we are made, in Jocelin's words, to balance one scale against another.

Sunshine, Dust, these elements belong to the surface. The third chapter introduces another element, Water, which takes us below ground, to places which are hidden, either in the church or in the human mind. Water seeps into the pit, into the graves in the choir and arcades, and the cathedral fills with the smell of corruption. There is irrational fear among the workmen, hysteria, and one of them falls from the roof leaving 'a scream scored all the way down the air'. The old Chancellor lapses into imbecility. Plague threatens; 'and the voices rose in fear of age and death, in fear of weight and dimension, in fear of darkness and a universe without hope'. Jocelin is taken into the human cellarage. He learns of Pangall's impotence, Rachel's coital giggle that makes her incapable of giving or receiving fulfilment. Above all, he begins to be made aware of the growing relation between Pangall's wife and Roger Mason. To these intimations of mortality Jocelin's attitude is one of uncomprehending revulsion:

'(Rachel) stripped the business of living down to where horror and farce took over . . . He spoke viciously . . . "The impervious insolence of the woman!" . . . He cried out loud. "Filth! Filth!" '
His feelings toward Roger and Goody bring together the subterranean worlds of the mind and the earth:

'Then an anger rose out of some pit inside Jocelin . . . He lifted his chin, and the word burst out over it from an obscure place of indignation and hurt. 'No!' All at once it seemed to him that the renewing life of the world was a filthy thing, a rising tide of muck so that he gasped for air . . .'

The very vehemence of Jocelin's disgust is however an indication of his own 'cellarage'. When he looks at a stained glass window now it is not to see 'God the Father exploding in a glory of sunlight' but 'a dully rich story . . . and the light of the altar was a divided thing, a light in each eye'. His mind is inhabited now by the devil as well as the angel; he can no longer suppress his own sexuality; the revelation of others' begins to reveal him to himself. In the sexual dream which closes the chapter the world within and the world without are seen within one perspective. The devil masturbates the phallus/spire of his body. And the dream poses the question: is the building of the Spire a similar self-erection and self-fulfilment, a distortion and degradation of God-given creativity?
  The fourth chapter literally clears the air, and lifts us into the sky. The wind blows the rain away and dries the earth. On the roof of the crossways the lead is rolled back to reveal blue sky; and at once the explosive ecstatic language is back, the old perspective resumed. Delightedly, Jocelin climbs into the tower:

'The pit was no more than a black dot, a hundred and twenty feet below . . . It seemed suddenly to Jocelin that now he loved everybody with ease and delight . . . So Jocelin clasped his hands, lifted up his head and included the boys and the dumb man and Roger Mason and Goody in one tremendous ejaculation: "Rejoice, O daughters of Jerusalem!" '

But though the language may be back, the tone has lost its assurance since the opening chapter. The brilliant sunshine causes confusion, shadows, after-images. The church at Easter is divided: flowers in the Lady Chapel, but on the other side of the screen 'the body of the church was as secular as a stable or an empty tythe barn'.

Throughout Lent Jocelin preaches, but does not confess or repent. He cannot stay 'above' in the tower, cannot forget or ignore what he has learnt of Rachel, Roger, Goody and Pangall. The internal turmoil of visitation by angel and devil grows worse, robs him of sleep, makes his head ache and flashes of pain dart across his eyes. And suddenly those eyes are forced to concentrate on the pit at the crossways where a sheet of metal has been set up to throw light to the bottom. There he sees what it is for a building to aspire beyond the nature of its foundations:

'Then, as Jocelin looked, he saw a pebble drop with two clods of earth; and immediately a patch perhaps a yard square fell out of the side below him and struck the bottom with a soft thud. The pebbles that fell with it lay shining dully in the reflected light, and settled themselves in their new bed. But as he watched them and waited for them to settle, the hair rose on the nape of his neck; for they never settled completely. He saw one stir, as with a sudden restlessness; and then he saw that they were all moving more or less, with a slow stirring, like the stirring of grubs. The earth was moving under the grubs, urging them this way and that, like porridge coming to the boil in a pot . . .'

As the pavement splits and the pillars sing with unbearable strain, the whole army of workers become hysterical with fear. Frantically, they try to fill the pit with, amongst other rubble, the blindly ecstatic stone heads of Jocelin the dumb sculptor had been carving. The Dean himself kneels directly under the central keystone of the crossing. Defiantly he 'knelt stiff, painful and enduring; all the time the singing of the stones operated on the inside of his head. At last, when he understood nothing else at all, he knew that the whole weight of the building was resting on his back.' This is a parody of prayer in that it is dominantly self-assertion, self-will. There is no hint of penance or humility, no abandonment to the will of another. Nevertheless there are intensities of courage, faith, and vision here, and beside these the attitude of the master-mason to the building seems puny and cynical. But Jocelin is willing to sacrifice not only himself but Roger too, in his absolute determination to see the spire built: 'I'm only learning now, how terrible it is. It's a refiner's fire. The man knows a little perhaps of the purpose, but nothing of the cost . . .' The story of Abraham and Isaac is more than a picture now.

But the sacrifice which in fact follows is a terrible parody of the story of the man of faith. This is one of the few points in the novel where the narrative becomes obscure. The presentation is extremely elliptical because Golding wishes his reader, like Jocelin himself, to be made to realize only very slowly the full implications of Roger's frantic warning: 'You just don't know what'll come of our going on!' Jocelin's view of the scene is obscured, and so is ours. The full realization of what actually happens will come only much later. But for clarity's sake we may anticipate.

As so often in Golding—the murder of Simon, the sacrifice of Liku—it is panic which precipitates tragedy. The army of workmen, shattered by seeing the foundations move, are waiting for the obvious decision that they are to abandon the spire. Roger returns to tell them that Jocelin has left them no choice but to go on, in the face of what seems inevitable disaster. Their response is a 'fierce yell'. They have become used to using Pangall as their 'fool', who brings them luck because they objectify in him their sense of the misshapen and ridiculous, and neutralize it in mime and mockery. At this moment of panic and rage they turn on him *en masse*. With a victim so helpless (as with Simon in *Lord of the Flies*), tormenting turns to sadism and vilification to bloodlust. But, once again, there is more—there is primitive magic. In Pangall, Misshapenness and Impotence are ritually murdered. The sacrificial victim is built into the pit to strengthen the inadequate foundations. Across the terrible scene Roger and Goody face each other 'in anguish and appeal, in acknowledgement of consent and defeat'. Jocelin, protected against the mob by the dumb man's body, has no real idea of what he has done; but after these four chapters he, and we, will have to learn to 'count the cost' in a more terrible currency.

IV

The first four chapters are intensive, the next four are extensive, as the tower rises and permits wider and higher views. 'Up here' there is growth, certainty, happiness; 'below' is darkness, incomprehension, distraction. Or—so it seems.

'. . . he passed through the close from the deanery to the west door, hardly able to see his feet for fog; and though the nave was clear of it, like a sort of bubble, it was near enough pitch dark. He climbed, and came out of the corkscrew stair on to the beams, and in a blinding dazzle. For up here, the sun was shining . . . there was downland visible all round, but nothing else. The fog lay in a dazzling, burning patch over the valley and the city, with nothing but the spire or the tower at least, piercing it. Then he was strangely comforted, and for a time, almost at peace.'

A sense of claustrophobia gives way to relief as the novel opens out, as Jocelin climbs away from the nave. But this is only 'for a time'. The cellarage cannot be ignored by climbing into the tower. 'Up here', 'out yonder', 'down there', turn out to be part one of the other, as chapters five to eight make clear.

The terrible scene by the pillar marks a watershed for Jocelin, even though he does not understand it consciously. He emerges noticeably changed, not in his will, which is even more a 'blazing certainty', but in the disturbance of his mind, his sudden high-pitched giggles, his kaleidoscope of emotions. Prayer, confession, human relationship, are all locked out of his mind. He absorbs himself in the work. But the cellarage lies in constant wait:

'Among the rubbish at the bottom of the pillar he saw there was a twig lying across his shoe, with a rotting berry that clung obscenely to the leather. He scuffed his foot irritably; and as now so often seemed to happen, the berry and the twig could not be forgotten, but set off a whole train of memories and worries and associations which were altogether random. He found himself thinking of the ship that was built of timber so unseasoned, a twig in her hold put out one green leaf. He had an instant vision of the spire warping and branching and sprouting; and the terror of that had him on his feet. I must learn about wood, he thought . . .'

This passage catches admirably the disturbance of a mind unconsciously aware of things it does not wish to know consciously, things which insist on intruding. The odd pressure behind the word 'obscenely', the onrush of not-so-random associations, betray his subterranean awareness that his spire has become a branching and sprouting evil, sidestepped by a 'practical' thought which is nevertheless loaded with irony. In fact he is trying not to learn, not to see, what he does not wish to know. He looked straight through Rachel, 'so he never saw the astonishment under the red paint'. What had been myopia before is now a deliberate act of exclusion. When he tries to speak to Goody there is significant misunderstanding and distress, met with a characteristic evasion: 'I must climb away from all this confusion.' And so he does, but to do so he has to twist away the cassock which marks him out as a man of God and a minister. As he climbs above it all, he feels 'the same appalled delight as a small boy feels when he climbs too high in a forbidden tree'.

From the tower the landscape can be seen in a new way as a unified whole to the eye, an order which the growing, dominating spire arranges with new rationality around itself. Here there seems no confusion, though the new perspective has to include the old man seen stumbling into his privy, the cheating milkmaid, the drunk lying in the ditch, as well as the enclosed nuns behind the walls of their garth. But the view, the landscape, is not in fact just something 'out there below'. The inner eye also shapes it into pattern:

'He examined the strips and patches of cultivation, the rounded downlands that rose to a wooded and notched edge. They were soft and warm and smooth as a young body.

'He got down on his knees, hard, eyes shut, crossing himself and praying. I bring my essential wickedness even here into thy air. For the world is not like that. The earth is a huddle of noseless men grinning upward, there are gallows everywhere, the blood of childbirth never ceases to flow, nor sweat in the furrow, the brothels are down there and drunk men lie in the gutter. There is no good thing in all this circle but the great house, the ark, the refuge, a ship to contain all these people and now fitted with a mast. Forgive me.'

'The world is not like that'—Jocelin's confidence has been transposed into a different key, but it is still there, only this time in a radical rejection which amounts again to revulsion. And, prompting that revulsion, we see the pressure of the sexuality which is revealed as soon as Jocelin's consciously willed exclusions are momentarily relaxed.

He cannot live with the eagle and raven; and though he increasingly fears the descent to face life below, face it he must. In Rachel's babble he learns that Goody is pregnant, and since he knows that Pangall was impotent this can only be the result of an adultery he has condoned, and indeed exploited, in forcing Roger to stay. Jocelin's tears are of rage and disgust at sexuality, not (as he tells himself) at the drunkenness he has seen; the thick parody of the Magnificat a transparent self-deception. The learning, the 'wood' of the evil tree, the lesson of 'the height, the weight, the cost', goes on.

In the sixth chapter the metaphorical overtones these words have acquired are subjected to a new scrutiny.

We, like Jocelin, are reminded that whatever inner meanings may be released by the spire, it is first and foremost a technical fact, an exercise in building. Jocelin turns it into an emblem, an occasion for a sermon. Our lives are like the mayfly, we can never tell about the future, 'we must live from the morning to the evening every minute with a new thing'. The spire is a diagram of prayer, 'each new foot reveals a new effect, a new purpose'. Against this there is now pitched the full weight of the spire as a physical reality, the spire which Roger Mason sees:

'Let your eye crawl down like an insect, foot by foot. You think these walls are strong because they're stone; but I know better. We've nothing but a skin of glass and stone stretched between four stone rods, one at each corner. D'you understand that? The stone is no stronger than the glass between the verticals because every inch of the way I have to save weight, bartering strength for weight or weight for strength, guessing how much, how far, how little, how near, until my very heart stops when I think of it. Look down, Father. Don't look at me—look down! See . . .'

It is physical sight that Roger tries to restore for Jocelin, and we are made to feel its unquestionable rightness. And yet, just at the point where Jocelin's belief looks too simply an evasion, we are reminded of its quality, its courage, its willingness to trust: 'Roger—He isn't needlessly cruel, you know . . . A good workman never uses a tool for something it can't do; never ignores it; takes care of it . . . But build quickly . . .' It is a mark of Golding's control of this book that he never allows us to adopt a position or settle for a conclusion. A sudden delicate change of tone, the direction of criticism changes, and a new exploration begins.

Jocelin is not the only one who encourages Roger Mason to overcome his fear of heights. Goody in the 'swallow's nest', high in the tower, grips her hand on Roger's as white shows at his knuckles. She too has climbed up the tree from the terror and the shame, as her voice is heard 'pleading, ingenuous, sweet. "But I didn't laugh—did I?" ' Roger's cry 'as if from the very pit bottom' is, however, one more recognition of the guilt 'up there'. A tower built in faith, built in heavy stone, built in sin: all three perspectives are true. Hence none can be exclusively true.

The incident of the swallow's nest tugs Jocelin out of security into chaos. As far as the building itself is concerned, Roger's 'curious, valuable mind' finds a way around an apparently impossible problem, as Jocelin had foreseen. The disintegration of the spire is prevented by the invention and installation of a steel band riveted around the stonework, taking the strain. Jocelin has to take the full responsibility for the extra cost of the work upon himself alone. But though the band does its work, and imparts a 'new quality' to the stone, there is inevitably a new lesson to be learnt in the light of the new achievement. Jocelin looks down on the cloisters:

'The boys of the songschool had left their game on the sill of the arcade again. He could not see the squares of the board scratched in stone, but he could see the white, bone counters of the game that lay on it. He could see some of them; but only some, for the stone between the battlements cut off a corner of the board from his eye. There was a kind of childish security in looking at the game, the white counters, one, two, three, four, five—

'His cheek was hard against the pinnacle and he knew he had not moved. But a sixth counter had appeared, had slid into view with another square of board under it. He knew he had not moved; but he knew that the tower had moved, gently, soundlessly up here, though down there the pillars might have cried— eeee—at the movement. Time after time, he watched the white counter slide into view, then disappear again; and he knew that the tower was swaying under him like a tall tree.'

There is no secure basis for observation or escape 'up here' at all. The truest knowledge that can be gained here is of the fearful strain on the pillars below that makes them sing; and to listen to such singing is 'a penance'.

The attempt to contain the 'chaos' below is less successful still. Jocelin tries not steel, but money; but the gold with which he hopes to have Goody sent away to the garth at Stilbury comes too late. He is forced to watch one brutal exposure after another. The blood on the money (blood which comes from the abortive birth of Roger's and Goody's child) seems at first sight too crude an emblem, too insistent. Yet there is far more involved here than the blood-money of betrayal. Jocelin had insisted to Roger that God would solve the physical problem of the disintegrating spire if he would trust the promptings of his mind; and the mason duly produced the band of steel. The cost was great, the Chapter would not accept it, and Jocelin took full responsibility himself. Red sparks fly, there is a cry of pain from an injured worker, the white stone is scarred and broken, but Roger has dared to obey his inner prompting, and the steel band holds the tower.

That the 'chaos' below cannot be held is not just attributable to the greater complexity of the human situation. Jocelin, too, has had inner promptings about Goody, but he has done nothing. He seeks now not to include but to exclude her. So he has to watch red blood from Roger's head, red hair twisted round Rachel's fingers, red blood from the 'knife-pains' in the white flesh, all that pain issuing in a birth wholly abortive. The blood on the money summarizes all this and precipitates the agonized recognition, 'this have I done for my true love'—and it raises to a new level Jocelin's appalled understanding of his inadequate sense of human cost. 'I was a protected man', he cries. 'I never came up against beldame.' ('Sex' in that sense being a modern word, this is one of the very few times when Golding's medieval setting appears to have given him any difficulty.) Jocelin has been seriously ignorant of human nature, priding himself in his attempt to exclude sexuality in excessive and morbid revulsion. 'This have I done for my true love': the words of the Easter carol refer directly to the betrayal of Christ, who sacrificed himself for love of fallen man, while Jocelin has both sacrificed others and exploited their fall 'in the dreadful glow of his dedicated will'. Deeper still, and still hidden from Jocelin, the words carry a hint of the secret of his true feelings for this girl—a hinted betrayal not only of her, and of God, but of himself.

In the eighth chapter any remaining distinction between 'up here', 'out yonder' and 'down there' is finally demolished. The death of Goody loosens in Jocelin the dykes that kept the dark inner water from flowing into consciousness. Now 'he would be aware of a feeling rising in him, coming up towards the chest like a level of dark water'. With a new clarity of eye ('pain did it, pain did it, pain did it'), and a new humility ('I'm not very intelligent'), he begins to examine internal feelings and external relationships: 'What's this called? And this?' With a shock, we realize that these are the first genuine questions in the book. Anselm had a point after all; the others were merely rhetorical.

As the cone of the spire rises, the light fades within while the octagons narrow and enclose. The snaking rope that hangs from the louvre seems 'haunted', possessed of an evilly destructive spirit. The pillars can no longer take the strain of remaining upright, they bend and become crooked—though the singing stops, for good. At this discovery Roger, already sodden with drink, not only bends but breaks. The human singing to God stops too, since services can no longer be held in the cathedral. Even the godless curse Jocelin. The 'little ones', the children of God who must be suffered to come unto him, are driven out by 'the great ones, the builders'; the capstone hanging round the spire's neck reminding us of the biblical penalty. Faith at such a price becomes indistinguishable from blasphemy.

'In', 'yonder', 'below': in a swift summarizing series the perspectives are put before us, merge, and fade into one another. 'In'—Jocelin sees himself reflected in the metal sheet that had thrown light into the pit:

'For a moment he thought of exorcism, but when he lifted his hand, the figure raised one too. So he crawled across the boards on hands and knees and the figure crawled towards him. He knelt and peered in at the wild halo of hair, the skinny arms and legs that stuck out of a girt and dirty robe. He peered in closer and closer until his breath dimmed his own image and he had to smear it off with his sleeve. After that he knelt and peered for a long time. He examined his eyes, deep in sockets over which the skin was dragged—dragged too over the cheekbones, then sucked in. He examined the nose like a beak and now nearly as sharp, the deep grooves in the face, the gleam of teeth.

'The kneeling image cleared his head. Well Jocelin, he said soundlessly to the kneeling image; Well Jocelin, this is where we have come.'

It is a moment in which we are made sharply aware of the cost to Jocelin himself, his suffering, borne without self-pity; and yet at the same time the image inclines towards parody. The kneeling, the halo, the girt robe dramatize the man away into an ironic gargoyle.

Having looked 'in', his gaze turns outward towards the 'cup' of the horizon:

'The evening turned green over the rim of the cup. Then the rim went black and shadows filled it silently so that before he was well aware of it, night had fallen and the faint stars come out. He saw a fire on the rim and guessed it was a haystack burning; but as he moved round the rim of the cone, he saw more and more fires round the rim of the world. Then a terrible dread fell on him for he knew these were the fires of Midsummer Night, lighted by the devil worshippers out on the hills. Over there, in the valley of the Hanging Stones, a vast fire shuddered brightly. All at once he cried out, not in terror but in grief. For he remembered his crew of good men, and he knew why they had knocked off work and where they were gone. So he shouted aloud in anger at someone.

' "They are good men! I say so!"

'But this was only one feeling. Inside them, his mind knew what it knew.'

It is a bitter irony on the growing love between Jocelin and the men he thinks he knows better than anyone he has ever known. Moreover, the 'lesson for this height' is not just the cross 'up here' fighting the devil 'out yonder'. 'Up here' is a temple built by a David with blood on his hands; a gargoyle-priest wondering whether the loss of God has been 'included' in the cost. Now, faced with the fiery horizon, 'a host of memories flew together. He watched, powerless to stop as they added to each other. They were like sentences from a story, which though they left great gaps, still told enough.' Knowing now that his beloved men are Druidic devil-worshippers, he realizes at long last what must have happened to Pangall—the significance of the rotting mistletoe berry. But if his men are sacrificers, so is he. Evil is not just 'out yonder' in the belfries 'on the rim of the world'. It is 'up here' where 'the story, with the disjunct sentences, burned before his mind'; it is 'down there' at the crossways where 'the replaced paving stones were hot to his feet with all the fires of hell'.

V

The third and final part of the book opens with what looks like an ending. In Roger's absence his foreman Jehan loosens too quickly the cable around the wedges. The octagons come thundering down; with a breaking of stone and a splintering of woodwork the spire impacts itself into the parapet, while terrified workmen fight down the ladders. The great work still stands. Yet it openly manifests its crookedness. The novel about building a spire is over.

Following the pattern of the earlier novels, Golding alters the viewpoint when the action is completed. But the change marked by the arrival of the Visitor and his Commission is not obtrusive; and much more a starting-point for a farther journey than a milestone showing how far we have travelled. It is illuminating to compare the arrival of the Visitor with the arrival of the naval officer in *Lord of the Flies*.

At first it does look as if the pattern in the earlier novel is to be repeated. Anselm's muttered 'Why shouldn't he see him as he is' seems to prepare for an ironical scene in which appearances will be played off against realities—though it is Jocelin's 'adult' vision that sees the Chapter as a crowd of little children, growing smaller. The real change from the earlier novel lies however in the Visitor himself, and his treatment. There is no incomprehension here, no complacency. He is full-size, powerful, intuitive, sympathetic. We can have nothing but respect for his handling of Anselm and for his acceptance of Jocelin's definitions of faith and service. If we can understand why Jocelin feels the interrogation 'unfair and unanswerable', we can also see how lethal the exposure of the tainted money and the tainted workmen is, and how myopic and desperate Jocelin's answers sound when the questions are put. The Visitor retains a real sense of Jocelin's faith, and though there is a gap between his experience and ours, the interrogation is still rightly directed.

As the questioning proceeds, the direction becomes clear. Jocelin is forced into answers which sharpen his self-knowledge:

'She's woven into it everywhere. She died and then she came alive in my mind. She's there now. She haunts me. She wasn't alive before, not in that way. And I must have known about him before, you see, down in the vaults, the cellarage of my mind.'

It is these vaults that the interrogation opens for Jocelin. For the first time he becomes consciously aware of 'levels':

'. . . on the purely human level of course, it's a story of shame and folly—Jocelin's Folly, they call it. I had a vision you see, a clear and explicit vision. It was *so* simple! It was to be my work. I was chosen for it. But then the complications began. A single green shoot at first, then clinging tendrils, then branches, then at last a riotous confusion . . .'

Even now, however, this is still too crisply analytic. Metaphors block the work of understanding. Every item has now to be examined by bringing it into focused experience. The image of the Tree of Evil, burgeoning in the work, in the mind, in the heart, contains whatever 'explanation' there seems to be, but that explanation can only be earned when the image has been destroyed and replaced by physical and psychological reality. As the inquisition ends, we see Jocelin girding himself for a terrible and difficult climb, not like Simon's up an external Mountain of Truth, but within his own being.

The farewell to the old Jocelin and the embarkation on the new can be seen in the bitter ambiguity with which the chapter ends. He still has absolute faith in the power of the God he has lost. He believes in the ability of the crucified Christ to transfigure his Church and make it prevail. The driving of the Holy Nail into the capstone enacts his faith in the way the second Tree redeems the first. With the nail, the spire cannot fall.

But, for himself, he feels the Kingdom to be irretrievably lost 'for want of a nail'. The old rhyme finally opens the last cellar and reveals what he has locked away there; the essential sexuality of his feeling for Goody Pangall. Knowing 'in the cellarage' of Pangall's impotence, he had used it for unadmitted reasons, to keep her from belonging sexually to anyone else. Memory restores her girlhood to him and exposes his unconsciously prurient reaching out to her. Another sexual dream reveals to him the meaning hidden in the earlier ones, the identity of the 'devil' of his lust:

'She came towards him naked in her red hair. She was smiling and humming from an empty mouth. He knew the sound explained everything, removed all hurt and all concealment, for this was the nature of the uncountry. He could not see the devil's face for this was the nature of the uncountry too; but he knew she was there, and moving towards him totally as he was moving towards her. Then there was a wave of ineffable good sweetness, wave after wave, and an atonement.

'And then there was nothing.'

He never cared for the girl's personality, hence the facelessness. What he wanted was the dog-like devotion of the dumb man coupled with her body. Refusing to recognize this, let alone crucify it, he created the bogus marriage, which led to the adultery, which led to her death. He exploited Pangall, and, in exploiting the adultery as a hold over Roger, he caused Pangall's death. The 'atonement' contains the final irony. By Christ's Nail there is an atonement for the corrupt material and workmen of the spire. But for Jocelin there is no Nail; the only 'at-one-ment' he has ever desired is the relief of pent-up sexuality in the uncountry of dream with a dehumanized phantom. After that there is nothing. This is the 'darkness of man's heart', found within himself, rather than by the race with the Beast across the churchyard. But where *Lord of the Flies* ends with a weeping recognition, the last three chapters of *The Spire* travel on within the darkness to discover whether all is yet 'included'.

The tenth chapter knocks away the remaining props that might have supported and sustained Jocelin. Was he not 'chosen'? The Lady Alison comes to tell him that, if he was, it was not by God but by the whim of a cynical young king and his courtesan: ' "I have a sister and she has a son." . . . "We shall drop a plum in his mouth." ' Jocelin's deanship is as corrupt as Ivo's canonry. Is the Nail not holy? Lady Alison has a new perspective for this too.

' "Our bishop Walter in Rome—" . . . "I asked him for money, blind fool that I was. He did better." . . .

' "You asked him for money—and he sent you a nail!"

' "I said so."

' "*Walter!*"

' "She began to laugh, round after round of laughter that built up high, until it took away her breath, and in the silence he heard the singing of pillars in his ears. It was not that he understood anything or worked out anything by logical steps in his head; but that there was a sickness driving in and a shuddering of the body to his very fingertips.'

And then the man of faith, the dumb man who had given Jocelin such unquestioning loyalty (to the point of saving his life), arrives as the final 'messenger'* to tell him that the stone pillars,

---

* The strange word becomes accurate if it is a reminiscence, conscious or unconscious, of the role of the messenger in the *peripeteia* and *anagnorisis* of Greek tragedy.

on which his whole spire depends, are as corrupt as he had made his four human ones. The polished stone skin, gleaming and dust-repellent, covers only rubble. The 'giants' of the past, who built 'a miracle of faith', were liars and cheats without even 'Builder's Honour'. The vocation, the relic, the very material of his work—everything turns to ashes.

'Then all things came together. His spirit threw itself down an interior gulf, down, throw away, offer, destroy utterly, build me in with the rest of them; and as he did this he threw his physical body down too, knees, face, chest, smashing on the stone.

'Then his angel put away the two wings from the cloven hoof and struck him from arse to the head with a whitehot flail. It filled his spine with sick fire and he shrieked because he could not bear it yet knew he would have to. At some point there were clumsy hands that tried to pick him up; but he could not tell them of the flail because of the way his body threw itself round the crossways like a broken snake. So the body shrieked and the hands fought with him and under the heap was Jocelin who knew that at last one good prayer had been answered.

'When the pain ebbed he found they were carrying him back from the place of the sacrifice with careful hands. He lay on an absence of back, and waited.'

This is the turning-point of the novel, and it establishes itself as such when we recall not merely the continual shift and counter-shift between 'inner' and 'outer', but, more precisely, the identity of Jocelin's spine with Jocelin's spire. We recall the moment when he first realizes the absence of foundations: 'The singing of the stones pierced him . . . his will began to burn fiercely, and he thrust it into the four pillars, tamped it in with the pain of his neck and his head and his back . . . he knew that the whole building was resting on his back.' But now the very pillars are rubble, and the burning will no longer hides the secret motives which fuelled it: 'His spirit threw itself down . . . as he did this he threw his physical body down too, knees, face, chest, smashing on the stone.' Although the significance of the scene must be grasped in terms of the resolution of a radically dualistic vision into a unity, the physical 'foreground' is no less important. Jocelin is the Snake struck by the flail beneath the Evil Tree, but the tubercular spine and the body contorted in pain are not merely emblematic. The metaphor is authenticated by experience, but the physical seizure exists in its own order of reality too. The tuberculosis is itself an adequate 'explanation' of Jocelin's euphoria, the 'angel' at his back warming him, his increased sexuality. Both physical and spiritual violence are caught in the language, calculatedly shocking as the pain travels from the bottom to the top of his being. As 'head' is united with 'arse' the physiological, the psychological, the philosophical are convulsed within a single spasm.

And if the old Jocelin lies like a snake destroyed by the flail of Judgement, the snake seeks its own destruction, and it is out of this destruction that contrition and humility are to come. He is carried not from the place of judgement but 'the place of the sacrifice', and he speaks, at last, of a real atonement: 'I have given it my back. Him. Her. Thou.' There is no longer any blazing certainty, only a series of possibilities, an acceptance of truth infinitely refracted. It is true that even destruction as fierce as this can provoke a flicker of spiritual pride, playing against Jocelin's helpless turning to others: 'What can you know, Father Anonymous? You see the outside of things. You don't know the tenth of it.' But these flickers are part of pain and felt to be punished. As Father Adam kneels in prayer, Jocelin sees 'how mistaken they were who thought of him as faceless. It was just what had been written there, had been written small in a delicate calligraphy . . .' The eyes of the visionary are focusing into sight: 'He cried out to the face before he knew he was going to. "Help me!" It was as if these words were a key.'

The first thing the key turns is the lock in the chest where Jocelin's old notebook lies. Here he recorded his original 'revelation'. We can measure how far we have travelled when we hear again the old language, brash, ecstatic, ironically prophetic:

'My body lay on the soft stones, changed in a moment, the twinkling of an eye, resurrected from daily life. The vision left me at last; and the memory of it, which I savoured as manna, shaped itself to the spire . . .'

Now Jocelin can only groan: 'It's an ungainly, crumbling thing. Nothing like. Nothing at all.'

But what is most interesting about the extracts which Father Adam reads from Jocelin's notebook is that they are not destroyed by the ironic counterpoint. In the end they carry their own conviction. We *do* feel that the young Jocelin—in a phrase of Lawrence's—was momentarily 'tapping wild life at the source'. The passage asks us to respond to the genuineness of Jocelin's past as well as to his present, and to see that there was a moment when he seemed to have access to the springs of creativity. This is the moment known, however fleetingly, by every genuine artist when the wholeness and radiance of his conception flashes before him; though remembering that moment in the face of the completed object, spire or novel, he can only say: 'It's an ungainly, crumbling thing. Nothing like. Nothing at all.' (On one level, like *Free Fall* before it, *The Spire* is a novel about writing a novel.) And so, quietly and unobtrusively, the movement of the novel begins once again to turn in upon itself. For so long we have been concerned with the blindness of vision, the crookedness of the spire. Now, initiated by these extracts from the notebooks, we are made to contemplate with new insight, a degree of wonder in the spire, and the serenity of acceptance. We contended earlier that this was a novel in which we were never allowed to settle into a view. It has seemed that we were doing so, acquiring a single vision of corruption and evil. But the scene at the crossways marks a turning-point here too, because, while for Jocelin it marks a dark climax, for us it begins to undermine the darkness with reminders of excluded light. Looking back now, perhaps we should begin to wonder whether there has not been something too stark in the outlining of the gargoyle-priest, the Evil Tree, and the Hell at the Crossways.

Having learnt to see Father Adam as more than anonymous, Jocelin tries to see Anselm anew. This indeed is no case of mining a new rift of virtue. The interview follows a familiar pattern: Anselm's spiteful jealousy, his stonyheartedness, Jocelin's old emotional claims pressed home unavailingly. There can be no resolution; but again there is acceptance, even of Anselm's deliberately wounding charge that Jocelin has blight on his hands that kills or ruins everything he touches. He asks Anselm's forgiveness, not for what he has done, but for what he *is*.

Having failed to find forgiveness in a brother-priest, he turns to seek it 'from those who were not Christian folk'. Bent almost double like an old man, a 'stinking corpse', Jocelin confronts the drunken degenerate that Roger Mason has become. This is a much more complex meeting, for Jocelin has a real respect for Roger; they do to some extent understand each other; and Roger does at first respond to Jocelin's appeal.

'I'm a building with a vast cellarage where the rats live; and there's some kind of blight on my hands. I injure everyone I touch, particularly those I love. Now I've come in pain and shame to ask you to forgive me.'

In a burst of emotion, Roger does. Then, however, Jocelin probes deeper, and suddenly he seems to Roger a missioner of vengeance come to remind him of the terrors he has tried to escape in drink, and the punishment that awaits him. Questions about Goody, questions about the folly of the building, these can be contained. But not this:

'What holds it up Roger? I? The Nail? Does she or do you? Or is it poor Pangall, crouched beneath the crossways, with a sliver of mistletoe between his ribs?'

Evil and terror banish forgiveness, and the two men destroy each other. After Jocelin is thrown down the stairs his death agony begins, as he crawls in the gutter, mocked and reviled. On the other hand his words, 'there's still something you can do, Roger, my son', misunderstood as a demand for atonement, lead directly to Roger's abortive suicide and the helpless imbecility which follows. Jocelin seems to have failed utterly, first with Anselm, now with Roger. He can find no hope through others.

There has been, however, something embedded in his own experience which is both true to Vision and true to the blindness of Vision, true to the love of human beings and true also to their murderous cruelty.

To find it, we need to return first to the moment when, shuffling through his own back-yard on his way to Roger, Jocelin saw an appletree and a kingfisher, glimpsed suddenly from the corner of the eye:

'He twisted his neck and looked up sideways. There was a cloud of angels flashing in the sunlight, they were pink and gold and white; and they were uttering this sweet scent for joy of the light and the air. They brought with them a scatter of clear leaves, and among the leaves a long, black springing thing. His head swam with the angels, and suddenly he understood there was more to the appletree than one branch. It was there beyond the wall, bursting up with cloud and scatter, laying hold of the earth and the air, a fountain, a marvel, an appletree; and this made him weep in a childish way so that he could not tell whether he was glad or sorry. Then, where the yard of the deanery came to the river and trees lay over the sliding water, he saw all the blue of the sky condensed to a winged sapphire, that flashed once.

'He cried out.

' "Come back!"

'But the bird was gone, an arrow shot once. It will never come back, he thought, not if I sat here all day. He began to play with the thought that the bird might return, to sit on a post only a few yards away in all its splendour, but his heart knew better.

' "No kingfisher will return for me."

'All the same, he said to himself, I was lucky to see it.'

This flash of sudden unalloyed beauty in the midst of so much that is crooked, dark and sordid, has a striking dramatic effect. It is right to talk of 'effect' rather than 'meaning', because the passage comes to us, as the experience does to Jocelin, directly and without conscious reflection. It simply happens. Appletree and kingfisher establish themselves as part of his universe. It is only *after* the experience he is about to undergo that his sight will become insight.

These experiences begin with the scene with Roger. There, as we have noticed, Jocelin achieves an act of contrition that is wholly convincing and has it accepted in real love, if only for a moment. He lays aside the last remnants of his priesthood because he knows he is unworthy of them. He cannot remove his tonsure, but he sees it as a mark of heresy and blasphemy, and considers himself as a dead-dog gargoyle through which no clean water could run. Now, however, as he experiences the reality of human love, 'he found himself babbling foolish things about an appletree, saying foolish, nursery things and patting a broad, shaking back. He is such a good man, he thought, so good— whatever that is! Something is being born here under the painted, swinging sign.' The beauty he had glimpsed in the world is un- consciously fused with the goodness he finds in the man. The sign is the sign of Letoyle, that moment when the robes of the priest and visionary are laid aside for a 'birth' in the dying sinner. True love is born into Jocelin's world beneath that starry sign. If it does not last; if, indeed, so little later the arms that have em- braced, expel to death . . . that, too, carries a reminiscence. Jocelin meets the fate of Simon and all those who remind men of their guilt; but the gap between the two novels is nowhere clearer than in the dimension of his realization, by comparison with the enigmatic little boy's.

Jocelin's encounter with the mob is much more obliquely pre- sented than Simon's. Motivation is never made clear, and even their identity is obscure. If the mob is the townspeople, do they continue to hate and curse Jocelin for what he has done to the Cathedral? If the mob is the 'army' of workers, do they hate him for what he has done to Roger, without whom they are nothing? It could be either or both. But the significance of the mob-scene is to be sought in another direction altogether. What Jocelin hears, above everything else, is laughter. He has become a re-embodiment of Pangall, re-enacting his death. We are in at the beginning of another hunt to the death as the clown becomes the scapegoat: 'The noises began to bray and yelp. They created their own mouths, fanged and slavering.'

The naked perception of physical beauty, the acknowledgement of love, and now the manifestation of the Beast: in these rhythms we have the coda which is to lead into the final pages of the novel. It is important to notice that it is the experience that comes over to Jocelin, and the meaning to us. He has now become a perceiving eye, a generous heart in a broken body. And if the mob break away from him, stopping short of Simon's fate, it is because the work of torture and death is already done. The spire stands crookedly. Jocelin's back is one vast suppurating tubercular lesion.

He does not merely know about Pangall now, he has become him; and he becomes also, in a way that is carefully hinted at, another follower of the Via Dolorosa. In his agony he manages the Christ-like response to his murderers: 'My children, my children.' There is only acceptance; not a trace of anger, bitterness, self-pity. 'Here I show what I am', he thinks, as he falls into the filth of the gutter. He does indeed show himself, but not as he thinks. It is through indifference to self that his new sanctity is revealed. But this sanctity comes about not, as in the case of Simon, by statement, but through the deliberate balance and counterbalance of the action as Golding has taken it beyond the Inquisition and the crooked spire.

VI

It is to the spire itself, moreover, that we finally return. We could say of the last chapter that Golding replaces Vision by vision, the physical eye's ability to see things as they are. It can only do so when the Visionary himself ceases to come between us and what he sees.

The 'eye' of the last chapter is capable of examining with the same objectivity and exactitude a face, or a fly cleaning its legs on the vault of the ceiling. It sees the 'self' it inhabits with clinical clarity, beyond all feeling. Jocelin orders Gilbert to sculpt him for his tomb as he is, far removed from the ecstatic bird-heads of the visionary, 'stripped in death of clothing and flesh, a prone skeleton lapped in skin, head fallen back, mouth open'. The dumb man draws 'with a face of fascinated disgust', but to Jocelin this is merely the objective memorial of what he has become.

With Father Adam summoning him to the last rites, the moment of death arrives. With it some three complete 'explanations', but the last is the decisive one, and on it his eyes close.

The endings of Golding's novels are always extremely important, and contain vital shifts of meaning. Analysis must become more detailed here, where 'all things' really do 'come together'.

Formally, the action of the closing pages can be swiftly described. Father Adam summons Jocelin by name, to help him into heaven. He must however assent to his faith. With growing urgency, as the moment of death approaches, the priest tries to get him to say the words 'I believe', or, if he cannot, to make a gesture of assent. But there is nothing. Only, at the very end, 'he saw a tremor of the lips that might be interpreted as a cry of: *God! God! God!* So of the charity to which he had access, he laid the Host on the dead man's tongue.' Since we know that it was *not* 'God! God! God!', the stark irony seems to be that the Man of Faith, the Visionary, has died seeing nothing but despair. The gift of the Redeeming Body is useless, a mark only of the Christian charity of the giver.

To see whether this is true, however, we have to enter and understand the incoherences of Jocelin's mind at the moment of its extinction.

On the first call of his name, knowing how near he is to death, Jocelin's freewheeling mind gives him the first of the three 'explanations':

'He looked up experimentally to see if at this late hour the witchcraft had left him; and there was the tangle of hair, blazing among the stars; and the great club of his spire lifted towards it. That's all, he thought, that's the explanation if I had time: and he made a word for Father Adam.

' "Berenice."

'The smile became puzzled and anxious. Then it cleared.

' "Saint?" '

This is the 'psychological' explanation. Berenice dedicated her hair, her 'crowning glory', to sexual love, and erected it to the stars. So Jocelin's spire can be seen as an erect phallus lifted towards the girl he lusted after. The whole thing was a substitute gratification for a need he would never consciously acknowledge, a self-erection for self-fulfilment. 'That's all, he thought.' If it is all, it turns Father Adam's response into a macabre joke. He doesn't understand, but he desperately wants Jocelin to be 'saved', and there *was* an obscure early Christian martyr called Berenice. Jocelin, 'when he was properly balanced' after the racking desire to laugh, falls in with the deception because 'he had a sudden liking for Father Adam and desired to give him something'. But there could hardly be a less saintly 'explanation' than the first one.

Unless it be the second. As the little man taps his forehead, Jocelin sees him as dying too, and his own *memento mori* vision of himself intensifies into a vision of the universal Adam:

'he saw what an extraordinary creature Father Adam was, covered in parchment from head to foot, parchment stretched or tucked in, with curious hairs on top and a mad structure of bones to keep it apart. Immediately, as in a dream that came between him and the face, he saw all people naked, creatures of light brown parchment, which bound in their pipes or struts. He saw them pace or prance in sheets of woven stuff, with the skins of dead animals under their feet and he began to struggle and gasp to leave this vision behind him in words that never reached the air.

'*How proud their hope of hell is. There is no innocent work. God knows where God may be.*'

The world of man is wholly absurd, irrational, and evil. For in his absurdity and irrationality man is proud. There is no hope of good or beauty; only hell awaiting pride. His own aspiration towards heaven destroyed the man and the woman who alone could make heaven meaningful, since God is to be found 'between people'. His Faith 'traded a stone hammer for four people'; built a crooked work on the breaking strain of four human pillars. The propositions: 'There is no innocent work' and 'God knows where God may be' sum up despair with bleak finality.

But only now, when the italics on the penultimate page seem to proclaim the 'message' of the novel, does the *literal*, *physical*, *seeing* occur. Looking back now, we can perhaps realize in a new way what Golding's real purpose has been. Behind all the endless complications of the book we could measure its progress and establish its basic structure in terms of stages of physical seeing: First, the explosive light through Abraham's window. Then, the vertically divided light above the altar, one light for each eye, and the horizontal division between the light above and the darkness below. After that came a single Vision of uniform evil, when 'all things came together': the work 'a plant with strange flowers and fruit, complex, twining, engulfing, destroying, strangling . . . the anguished faces that cried out from among it'; and the universal Adam in his pride of hell. But this is Vision not vision; the mind and imagination reading itself into the world, not the objective eye. The Vision of universal Adam is 'a dream that came between him and the face' of Adam himself. The whole strategy of the novel, its basic form, has been to manoeuvre us through the obsessive world of Jocelin's mind, emblem-haunted, until we reach the point at which we now stand.

In the final split second the physical eye opens anew. The physical double vision and the mental single one are focused anew, at the point where Jocelin's selfhood is extinguished. Having come through confusion we are brought to the right opening for the light to impinge, in a moment of sheer perception. The 'whole truth' at last impacts upon the retina:

'There were two eyes looking at him through the panic. They were the only steady things, and before them, he was like a building about to fall. They looked in, an eye for an eye, one eye for each eye. He bit more air and clung to the eyes with his own as the only steady things in living.

'The two eyes slid together.

'It was the window, bright and open. Something divided it. Round the division was the blue of the sky. The division was still and silent, but rushing upward to some point at the sky's end, and with a silent cry. It was slim as a girl, translucent. It had grown from some seed of rosecoloured substance that glittered like a waterfall, an upward waterfall. The substance was one thing, that broke all the way to infinity in cascades of exultation that nothing could trammel.'

We return to the physical beauty of the 'sundust' vision, so long ago. Since then we have seen the sun, known the dust only too well. We have seen how the individual grains 'bounced together', and have inspected the mayfly lives in their blind ignorance. In a more distant perspective we have seen how the four human relationships made a collective, mysterious shape, the Tree of the Knowledge of Good and Evil, with anguished faces crying out from among the dark overripe fruit. But we have lost sight of what Jocelin's eye then told him, when he was 'absent-minded' enough to follow it. There remains the ultimate perspective: that dust gives solidity to sunlight and softens it to sweeter colour, that light gives life to dust, that 'sundust' to the human eye is a beautiful and solid phenomenon, though it is ephemeral, and though it may involve the upsetting of apparent certitudes and angles of vision if we are to see it.

So now, after the confusion, the flowering of emblematic meanings, the complexities, we still have to see for the very first time the completed spire as a thing in itself, whole and one. We have plumbed heights and depths which show conclusively enough that the spire must go down as far as it goes up, and vice versa, and we have developed deeper and deeper understanding of man and his work. But the whole has to be rehabilitated, seen objectively and inclusively, with an eye cleaned of Jocelin. It is *one* thing, a unity that moves the eyes into focus. We do not have to be reminded that it is askew, leaning to fall. But it is also 'slim as a girl', with an upward 'fall' rushing like a fountain, cascading, exulting, as it connects 'above' and 'below', the earth and infinity. We have got to a sufficient distance to see 'crooked beauty' as Jocelin saw 'sundust'. It has a colour too, the colour both of human flesh and of the mystic rose.

In that moment of perception the certainty of Jocelin's despair is demolished: 'Now—I know nothing at all!' But through all his amazement and terror, the 'wild flashes of thought' that 'split the darkness' seize on a truth which directs the irony away from Jocelin to the language of Father Adam. 'Our very stones cry out.' The spire itself and Jocelin's inevitable response to it proclaim a Belief and an Assent on a different and altogether deeper level than an abstract credal statement like 'I believe in one God'. Stones and flesh and blood cry out, proclaim, because they *must*.

But no 'message' is announced. We get a glimpse of something out of the very corner of our eyes because we have been put in the right position to catch the flash of truth if we can. It cannot be decoded, conceptualized, explained. It can only be conveyed at all, not in the form of a statement, but first a question, then an outcry

without a verb, and finally 'words of magic and incomprehension'
—something suggested only by analogy.

'What is terror and joy, how should they be mixed, why are they
the same, the flashing, the flying through the panicshot darkness
like a bluebird over water? . . .

'In the tide, flying like a bluebird, struggling, shouting, screaming to leave behind the words of magic and incomprehension—
  '*It's like the appletree!*'

The whole weight has to rest on what our eyes took in un-
wittingly of that casual moment in Jocelin's back-yard. It is a
weight of being, not of 'meaning'. Yet it is more than what is seen
with the eye. If Vision has had to give way to sight, this in turn
has to be assumed into insight. We cannot do this by translating
imaginative analogies into conceptual terms. The physical remains primary, and the similes insist that analogy remain on the
level of suggestion rather than 'explanation'. Nevertheless there
is the 'magic' of revelation as well as 'incomprehension'; we have
to keep the balance right. We need to explore the imagination
which not only sees, but 'sees into the life of things'.

The first analogy works in the dimension of time. The kingfisher flashes just once, like an arrow shot over sliding water,
concentrating into utmost intensity all the blue of the sky, but so
transiently that one cannot take it in until it is gone—and it never
comes again. There is a 'panicshot darkness' before and after man's
time on earth that is 'like' the sliding water, the tide, over which
the bird flies (and into that darkness Jocelin's life is on the point of
vanishing). There is a transient moment of purposeful being that
is 'like' the bird, concentrated infinity, intensest bluefire, flashing
light. Jocelin sees the life of the spire as a fusion of utmost
intensity with utmost transience; one thing, revealed in one
glimpse, like kingfishershotoverslidingwater. The 'elements' are
meaningless apart.

The second analogy works in space. The appletree goes on
being there, dancing. It unites the flashing pink, white, and gold
'angels' of the blossom, filling the air with vivid colour and scent,
with the 'long black springing thing' of the branch, like a snake;
unites them into a single organism. There is more of it than the

one branch, it spans walls and barriers, bursts up and out, lays hold of earth and air like a fountain, miraculously. It remains the Tree which was the source of all our woe. It remains also a scatter of clear leaf and blossom, a marvel.

So, framed by the window, caught in one glimpse of the perceiving eye, are the intensest blue transience seen for one instant and the rosecoloured beautyskew cascading to infinity: the spire as one thing, 'like' the kingfisher and the appletree. *All* the 'meanings' are enfolded within the concrete being. That is the 'magic'. They can never be fully or satisfactorily expounded, defined, or conceptualized. That is the 'incomprehension'.

But they do amount to a statement of Faith. Although it is not 'God! God! God!' in the way Father Adam means, it is, one suspects, God! God! God! in the way Golding means, and in its love and exultation it has its own inclusive charity.

Free Fall diagnosed the reductiveness of pattern; *The Spire* takes up the challenge to see without it. Golding sets a whole series of patterns at war in order to convince us that none will do. The Spire is built in heavy stone, in faith, in sin; all three things are true, and contradictory. For Jocelin there are explanations physiological, psychological, moral, religious, social; all are convincing in themselves, and none is satisfactory. But we have to be made to know and understand them all, in wrestling with twelve complex and difficult chapters, before we can be brought to the right position, with sufficient breadth and depth of knowledge, to receive from the corner of the eye in the deliberate tentativeness of simile a single glimpse of what it is to be human. The 'idea' of the novel might seem trite and obvious, but the 'world of difference' is the novelist's world of experience and insight.

VI

PERSPECTIVES

He holds him with his glittering eye—
The wedding guest stood still,
And listens like a three years' child:
The Mariner hath his will.

Ultimately, the appeal of every literary artist must be that of
Coleridge's Mariner. He is there for us to talk about only because
he has caught and held our imaginations. So far in this study of
Golding we have been trying to describe the effect of the
'glittering eye' as it has revealed itself in the particularities of
individual works; in this final chapter we hope to shift the perspective and see the particular kind of 'will' that Golding has
exerted over us. How, in other words, do we judge the imaginative
features of the Golding novel?

To put the question like that is to feel a special sympathy for
Blake's dictum that to generalize is to be an idiot, and reasons for
this feeling are not far to seek. The trouble lies initially in the concept of 'the novel' itself. Over the two and a half centuries of its
existence, the novel has come to cater for so many different needs
and pressures of the imagination that it cannot accommodate them
meaningfully under a single label. Nevertheless the range and
disposition of a particular imagination tend to elude us if we
concentrate our attention exclusively on its specific manifestations.
A novelist's *oeuvre* becomes something more than an aggregation
of books; it can reach a point of definition where seeing one book
in the light of another gives us new insight into the nature of the
imagination which is operating. To describe this body of work
takes us immediately into describing the kind of novel which this
imagination instinctively offers. And at once we have to deal in a
vocabulary which has had to do duty for so many purposes that it
can be used only if it is buttressed by closer definition and example.
We hope to distinguish Golding's particular kind of novel by
bringing together the terms 'fable', 'history' and 'myth', and trying
to make clear our understanding of them and their relevance to
the five books we have discussed.

Literary concepts are precipitated by impressions, so we might
turn first to the impressions made by a Golding novel. We might

think of it as something heavily patterned, uniformly intense, severely exclusive. The patterning can be observed even in the externalities of length and chapter division, virtually the same in every novel. The general form is so markedly dialectical that we are invariably led into describing each novel in terms of different worlds brought into stark confrontation. The moment of confrontation is of high dramatic intensity, though as the novels progress the 'moment' becomes less precise, and consequently less stark in its effect. The books are uniformly intense in that the mood in which each is written hardly changes; though there may be violent shifts in the point of view. The central characters may interrogate themselves remorselessly, may indeed alter, but always they remain the eye of a storm. Related to this homogeneity of mood is the dominant impression of exclusiveness. The shaping spirit of the imagination seems always at work in the foreground of our attention. There is a determination to follow what is thought to be the main road, so that we can only glimpse the possible extensions of a relationship, a place, a sub-topic. Hence we feel that, however densely imagined a particular character or episode may be, everything has been pared down, stripped of irrelevant detail. Bringing these impressions together, we might say that a Golding novel gives the effect of something dedicatedly made, every strain and stress calculated and overcome, so that the final product leads us to think in terms of a sculpture.

This however is only half the story. Our impressions are formed not only by the shape of the fiction but also, where its movement takes us—and here we seem to be faced with paradox. These books, so emphatic in pattern, so exclusive in structure, have as an increasingly dominant theme the limitations of the pattern-maker and the tragic consequences of his vision. This is already present in *Lord of the Flies*. Piggy and Jack try to press their patterns of human nature into action; but neither can bear to see man as he is. Only Simon achieves a vision more inclusive and accepting, but he is destroyed by the excluders who translate the boy into the Beast. The problem of pattern becomes the overt theme of *Free Fall*, it is Sammy's obsession:

'I have hung all systems on the wall like a row of useless hats. They do not fit. They come in from outside, they are suggested patterns, some dull and some of great beauty. But I have lived enough of my life to require a pattern that fits over everything I know; and where shall I find that? Then why do I write this down? Is it a pattern that I am looking for?'

It is there most complicatedly in *The Spire*, where Jocelin seeks explanation or comfort in one pattern after another, until, 'knowing nothing', he is left staring at an object, seeing it, as it is, for the first time.

Our general impressions are founded on paradox: books of calculated and obtrusive design work towards the creation of a mysterious centre, visionary eyes have to learn to see, novels of purpose insist on the importance of discovery. Basically a Golding novel grows through the tension between its form and his imagination. To describe this tension we must enlarge the context of discussion and the terms 'fable', 'history' and 'myth' help to establish a useful perspective.

Fable brings Aesop to mind as a point of departure. Broadly speaking, the fabulous world is one that is made up. It exists deliberately outside the world which we inhabit, and fidelity to common experience is a very minor or even an irrelevant consideration. Aesop's world is inhabited by animals with human traits; other fabulists may write of giants and monsters, or, if they write of men, it is in the mode of dreams and vision, or of an 'uncountry' where the boundaries of probability can be crossed and recrossed at will. Yet if the world of fable is quite unlike the world of everyday, it has direct bearing on it. We enter the other world to analyse our own with greater clarity and freedom. We look continually for point; so that the process of reading involves a continuous need for translation. Our awareness of meaning depends on our awareness of correspondence. Nothing is offered for its own sake. Situations, relationships, protagonists, figures, are selected, controlled for a purpose beyond themselves, serving an analytic design or debate.

Curiosity rather than analysis is the motive behind the imagination we describe as history. This is the imagination which Virginia Woolf sketches in her essay on Arnold Bennett:

'Mr Bennett would keep his eyes in the carriage. He indeed would observe every detail with immense care. He would notice the advertisements; the pictures of Swanage and Portsmouth; the way in which the cushion bulged between the buttons; how Mrs Brown wore a brooch which had cost three-and-ten-three at Whit-worth's bazaar; and had mended both gloves—indeed the thumb of the left hand glove had been replaced. And he would observe, at length, how this was the non-stop train from Windsor which calls at Richmond for the convenience of middle-class residents, who can afford to go to the theatre but have not reached the social rank which can afford motor cars, though it is true, there are occasions (he would tell us what) when they hire them from a company (he would tell us which).'

Virginia Woolf is polemical; but setting this aside, we can see the kind of imagination involved. History recognizes no other level of 'reality' than the phenomenal or contingent. It is anti-formal; not in the sense that it attempts to escape form, which would be impossible for art, but in the sense that it rejects any idea of imposing form on multifarious experience. It seeks always by complicated interrogation to expand, extend, or even subvert what it feels to be the restrictions of pattern. It wishes to include everything and willingly pays the price. It cheerfully accepts 'bagginess' and 'monstrosity' in the service of faithful representation. Since its horizons tend theoretically to infinity, its ending—a death, a marriage, a birth—will be an arbitrary pause rather than a conclusion. By definition, history can never tell all there is to be told, there is always another story. History as fiction begins with historians themselves filling in the lacunae between facts, writing scene or dialogue by inference to lend plausibility to 'what must have been', while remaining true to the facts as they have found them. Fiction as history tries to persuade us that it is merely a transparency through which we view a complicated phenomenal world, its persons and places empirically 'true'. Such fiction may be weighted towards the portrayal of individuals, or societies, or epochs. In the first case we have fictive biography whose basic shape is the shape of a man's life. In the others, a number of such biographies are made to interact. But whatever the weighting there is the same fundamental drive towards inclusiveness—'Mr Bennett would observe every detail with immense care'.

Perspectives

Of the structure of anthropological myth we can predicate nothing; each story of Gods and their dealings with men has the shape of its own vision. But literary myth so deals with men as to reveal an archetypal 'truth' hidden below the surface of everyday life. This cannot simply be 'made', it must be discovered. If fable suggests Aesop, myth takes us back to Aristotle and his citation of *Oedipus Rex* as the perfect tragic *mythos*. In *Oedipus* we have an imaginative mode quite different from either fable or history. The rhetorical structure is not designed for translation into correspondences; equally, it is not concerned with the self-sufficiency of the phenomenal world. Rather, we begin with the world we know, and examine it in such a way that we no longer seem to know it. The essence of literary myth is process, and, more precisely, reversal and discovery. *Oedipus* opens with the assertion of a stable world (I am Oedipus of Corinth, saviour of Thebes, this is my wife Jocasta, these are my children), but it dissolves in the acid of a different truth. Swellfoot of Thebes, deformed bringer of plague, patricide, incestuous husband and father-brother, puts out the eyes which had persuaded him that the world was the explicable world of man and not the inscrutable world of the gods. Myth is history seen through an X-ray lens which reveals a more basic structure than that of the surface body of life.

Fable, history, myth—it is important to insist that nothing qualitative is implied in these terms. They are three different ways of looking at life, each of which has a different stance towards 'truth'. Myth may seem to make larger claims than the others, but there are as many realities and truths as there are ways of looking; and we are concerned with modes of imagination not philosophical views. Each has a fundamental strength of a different sort, but when looked at from an angle other than its own, each has also fundamental limitations. From the viewpoint of history, myth and fable seem too rigidly patterned, taking too exclusive a grip on the complex processes of life. From the viewpoint of fable, history is a baggy monster, capable of testifying only to its own muddle; while myth is mystification, depriving itself of intellectual freedom through its pretensions to a historical reality. From the viewpoint of myth, history tries to include too much, fable too little. Each mode affords a definably different satisfaction as it proceeds from a different imaginative urge. Fable offers the pleasures of analysis, history those of recognition, myth those of revelation.

To see the varying treatments of character in these different modes is to see from another angle their distinctive emphases. It is history that gives us our normative idea of fictional character, an idea typified, for example, in the opening of *Emma*:

'Emma Woodhouse, handsome, clever and rich with a comfortable home and happy disposition; seemed to unite some of the best blessings of existence; and had lived nearly twenty-one years in the world with very little to distress or vex her. She was the youngest of the two daughters of a most affectionate, indulgent father; and had in consequence of her sister's marriage, been mistress of his house from a very early period. Her mother had died too long ago for her to have more than an indistinct remembrance of her caresses; and her place had been supplied by an excellent woman as governess, who had fallen little short of a mother in affection. Sixteen years had Miss Taylor been in Mr Woodhouse's family . . .'

The mode is established: the heroine is put before us, age, disposition, upbringing. Her relations with her family, the indulgence of her father, the early death of her mother, the maternal affection of her governess—it is out of this material that the novel will be woven. The assumptions governing fictional character here are almost too familiar for us to be able to recognize them. There is no theoretical limit to the facts that we ought to know, and our knowledge of characters presented in this way (in terms of family, relationships, education, outlook) is analogous to our knowledge of people in daily life. Or, more strictly, it is analogous to a convention of expressing that knowledge to ourselves or to others. A character-sketch such as Jane Austen gives us of Emma, and the 'reference' we might be asked to give for such a person, assume a similar structure, a similar vocabulary.

We could not say the same for the presentation of Mr Gradgrind.

' "Now what I want is, Facts. Teach these boys and girls nothing but Facts. Facts alone are wanted in life. Plant nothing else, and root out everything else. You can only form the minds of reasoning animals upon Facts: nothing else will ever be of any service to them. This is the principle on which I bring up my own children, and this is the principle on which I bring up these children. Stick to Facts, sir!"

'The scene was a plain, bare, monotonous vault of a schoolroom, and the speaker's square forefinger emphasized his observations by underscoring every sentence with a line on the schoolmaster's sleeve. The emphasis was helped by the speaker's square wall of a forehead, which had his eyebrows for a base, while his eyes found commodious cellarage in two dark caves, overshadowed by the wall. The emphasis was helped by the speaker's mouth, which was wide, thin, and hard set. The emphasis was helped by the speaker's voice, which was inflexible, dry, and dictatorial . . .'

We are immediately presented not with character, but with attitude, a stance deliberately posed for purposes of argument and analysis. We sense that every detail of scene and speaker, no matter how tiny, is not descriptive but pointed; and we begin at once to translate them into their point. The predominant impression is of the artifice of the author. The rhetorical performance rivets our attention to his design. We know that action will be important, but will not be the inevitable outcome of character so much as of careful plotting; and that the total pattern will be created not by the way the characters act upon one another but by the way they fit in with one another as functional components of a single informing analysis. With this we know that we are in the world of fable.

Interestingly, and of necessity, myth eludes such brief illustration. It begins in a way indistinguishable from history; but its underlying structure is only gradually discovered by the special ordering of the narrative. Like history, myth has to persuade us that its characters are real people in real places, but it has links with fable in that it persuades us to question the nature of this reality. Unlike fable however, the revelation of myth will be gradual, unobtrusive, taking shape beneath the surface. As far as the presentation of character is concerned, this means that individual features fade to reveal archetypal forces, like those classified by the great psychologists. But just as these forces, however archetypal, cannot be truly conceived apart from this and that individual, so myth can only be expressed in personal terms, and never in the abstract terms of fable. It is possible to go further and say that the more myth is concerned with isolating the archetype, the more banal it becomes, because it has lost contact with the complexities of the individual, without whom this imaginative process can have no life. Oedipus again will indicate the kind of interest in character we find in myth. He begins in a world of history, so that we can talk of his character in terms of leadership, assurance, hot temper; but then this alters to reveal the 'character' or 'signature' inscribed upon him by the gods, one not peculiar to him but a part of the human condition. The complexity of Oedipus is refocused in the light of the sphinx's riddle 'what is man?', but it is this man in this situation which gives the riddle all the imaginative life it has. If we try to see myth in terms of its 'message', it trembles on the edge of the received, or even the trite. But it is a sense of the powerful imaginative resonance of the archetypal that drives an author to seek to capture it in fiction, as it is the imaginative power and richness of the capture that makes the fiction valuable and not the thesis we could abstract from it.

Perhaps these varying treatments of character are sufficiently distinct to require a different terminology, so that 'character' might be reserved for history, 'type' or 'attitude' for fable, and 'archetype' for myth. But this terminology should be purely descriptive in purpose. If we see the mode of history dominant in *The Prelude*, *War and Peace*, *A la Recherche du Temps Perdu*, the mode of fable in *The Faerie Queen*, *The Pilgrim's Progress*, *Gulliver's Travels*, the mode of myth in *Oedipus Rex*, *The Ancient Mariner*, *Moby Dick*, then it becomes clear that by no earthly standard could we want to rank imaginative works of this order. We have been using history, fable, and myth in an attempt to characterize certain modes of the imagination, hence they are anterior to specific literary genres. They may be found in poetry, drama, and fiction. Further, there is no reason why these modes should not co-exist within a single work of art, and they often do. The imagination, though it may travel one line more than another, is not confined to a single track. (Allegories, for example, often combine fable and myth, novels—like Jane Austen's—history and fable.) Nevertheless, the recognition of these varying predilections of the imagination, whatever labels we pin to them, should prevent us from applying to one predominant mode criteria appropriate to another.

With these terms in mind we can return to our general impressions of a Golding novel. If his five books are considered collectively, they seem to constitute a phase of work which we might reasonably consider complete. This is not to say that they are a step-by-step achievement in which each step must be 'higher' than the last. Rather, they provide a series of variations on a problem, which within his own terms he now seems to have resolved, and this series of variations can be plotted in terms of fable, history, and myth; the twelve years' work can be seen as an exploration of the problem of disengaging myth from fable, and of giving it a sufficiently historical location.

To think of *Lord of the Flies* is to think of the qualities of immediate accessibility, clarity of design and intention, which mark it off from the novels which followed, and explain its popular success. The island setting, isolated from the complexities of society; the exclusiveness of its characters, not merely children but boys before puberty; the firm direction of its plot; all minister to that creation of a deliberate artefact which is the hallmark of fable. It affords the satisfaction of a ship-in-a-bottle, it is a world of equivalences, of meticulous scaling-down. We seem to be able to review it in its detail and in its total design simultaneously. The author seems in conscious control, doing with virtuoso skill and success what he has obviously set out to do. *Lord of the Flies* is in fact the closest of Golding's novels to fable.

Our criticism however has attempted to show how much the novel differs from any such account. There is an important openness in the presentation, especially of Piggy and Simon, which raises questions about the overt design of the book; in one sense making it considerably less definitive than it seems, in another, giving it a new dimension of interest. Looking back now, we can see that this dimension is the stirring of myth imagination in a world primarily fabulous.* Golding's imagination is more

---

* In 'Fable', *The Hot Gates*, pp. 98–9, Golding records how his imagination seemed to him to 'get out of hand' in the first episode with the pig's head. What he there regards as a fault 'of excess', however, we regard as a point of growth.

complex and less articulate than his design and structure. His basic art is already one of revelation rather than demonstration, and what is eventually revealed is more mysterious than author or reader expected. Also, although the novel is calculatedly isolating both in setting and in its characters, it depends on our acceptance of a psychological reality 'true to life'. The boys have to be entirely credible as boys if we are to respond to the novel's vision, and in the imagination of the island and its inhabitants there is a pronounced drive towards the mode of history which plays against the thesis, the translation and the analysis of fable. *Lord of the Flies* in retrospect reveals the myth-imagination already seeking to liberate itself from a mode which, from its viewpoint, is too confidently analytic, too restrictive.

In that respect *The Inheritors* is a long leap forward. In one sense, at the level of 'subject', Golding takes a world so completely 'other' that it might seem unequivocally to invite the description of fable, taking its place with Utopia, Brobdingnag, Erewhon. Moreover he seems to have begun from a thesis-quarrel, a conscious design to demonstrate the inadequacies of Wells. But Golding establishes the novel's 'otherworld' by employing all his imaginative resources, not as More, Swift and Butler do, to manoeuvre analytically between 'their' world and 'ours', but rather to make us forget our world and become imaginatively immersed in the dense mystery of his. The essential element in the writing is the discovery of a procedure which inhibits analysis and judgement, becoming for the first time essentially exploratory and tentative. In other words, the datum of *The Inheritors* seems to belong to fable, but its whole realization belongs to history in which myth is located by imaginative exploration. This is not to say that Golding's interest is that of the historical novelist trying to recapture the past, though his anthropological knowledge continually tethers his imagination to fact. His mode is not history but myth, in that it seeks to reveal archetypal truth within history; it is not fable, in that the myth is demonstrably discovered by the process of writing the novel, could be discovered in no other way, and turns out to be far more complex and difficult to grasp than the novelist thought when he started.

In *Lord of the Flies* we are continually made to look *at* a scene in order to pinpoint its significance within the whole analysis; in *The*

Inheritors we are drawn into the scene, incapable of seeing where we are going, but immersed in a mysterious act of discovery. A comparison of the death of Simon with the death of the Old Woman may illustrate this better than a general statement can do:

'The water rose further and dressed Simon's coarse hair with brightness. The line of his cheek silvered and the turn of his shoulder became sculptured marble. The strange, attendant creatures, with their fiery eyes and trailing vapours, busied themselves round his head. The body lifted a fraction of an inch from the sand and a bubble of air escaped from the mouth with a wet plop. Then it turned gently in the water. Somewhere over the darkened curve of the world the sun and moon were pulling; and the film of water on the earth planet was held, bulging slightly on one side while the solid core turned.'

Although, as we argued, the total imaginative context of this surrounds it with a more ambiguous suggestiveness than is apparent, the first response is to its clarity and the certainty of its design, the serene confidence with which Golding relates the fraction of an inch and the wet plop with the ordered and beautiful processes of the cosmos. At this moment he seems exactly sure of the placing of Simon's death against the 'darkened curve of the world' and the phosphorescent tide pulled by sun and moon. In contrast with the two scenes with the pig's head, Golding seems to tell us exactly how to see. What we are most aware of is the conscious artistry of the novelist.

In *The Inheritors*, Lok is confronted suddenly by the dead body of the Old Woman coming up at him as he hangs 'upside down' over 'deep water':

'The weed tail was shortening. The green tip was withdrawing up-river. There was a darkness that was consuming the other end. The darkness became a thing of complex shape, of sluggish and dreamlike movement. Like the specks of dirt, it turned over but not aimlessly. It was touching near the root of the weed tail, bending the tail, turning over, rolling up the tail towards him. The arms moved a little and the eyes shone as dully as the stones. They revolved with the body, gazing at the surface, at the width of deep water and the hidden bottom with no trace of life or speculation. A skein of weed drew across the face and the eyes did not blink. The body turned with the same smooth and heavy motion as the river itself until its back was towards him rising along the weed tail. The head turned towards him with dreamlike slowness, rose in the water, came towards his face . . . She was ignoring the injuries to her body, her mouth was open, the tongue showing and the specks of dirt were circling slowly in and out as though it had been nothing but a hole in a stone. Her eyes swept across the bushes, across his face, looked through him without seeing him, rolled away and were gone.'

The immediate effect of this is to create an experience of bewildered incomprehension. We are no longer looking at a dead body so much as entering a mind for whom violent death is inconceivable. Hence detail, unrelated, finely particularized, is everything, pattern nothing; the rhetoric keeps 'significance' at bay. There is significance, but it comes to us unstated and unstatable, released in our imaginations with the rhythm of nightmare. 'Upside down', 'deep water': the disorientation involved here will be stabilized only at the end of the last chapter. And the writing in this passage strikes an obsessive note* quite unlike the conscious artistry of *Lord of the Flies*.

Paradoxically, however, it is *The Inheritors* which first focuses Golding's attention on the nature of his art—so much so that it is given an almost conceptual description in the closing chapter,† as Tuami prepares to carve his ivory, and in the particularity of that 'shape' senses the destiny of the People and of the Inheritors. But the explicitness with which this is done shows that Golding is in danger of slipping back into fable, this time the fable of the artist as myth-maker. For what *The Inheritors* as a whole has made plain is that the novel as myth, unlike the novel as fable, can never be aimed at directly. If it is, it will tend to become fable. The three

---

* P. N. Furbank in a review of *The Spire*, *Encounter*, 22 May 1964, pp. 59–61, observes that the image of a broken or suffering body in water is found in all the novels. Here, as in *Pincher Martin* (especially p. 96, pp. 144–5), *Free Fall* (p. 130), and *The Spire* (pp. 64–5), but not in *Lord of the Flies* (pp. 189–90, 222–3), the image occurs in a context connected with dream.

† See our mention of the difference between the manuscript and the final version, Ch. 2, p. 117.

novels that follow are increasingly profound recognitions that Hamlet's plan, by indirections to find directions out, must be Golding's also. More and more clearly, we shall find conscious artistry replaced by an art of discovery.

In *The Inheritors* Golding tried to reveal the nature of man by imagining his origins; in *Pincher Martin* he looks at his end. There is a significant change, however, which prevents these accounts from being complementary. In *The Inheritors* he is concerned with a group; in *Pincher Martin* he comes for the first time to look at individual man, not mankind. A sense of 'shape' has to be found, not in the emblematic figure of the artist carving the ivory, but in the particularities of a personal life. With *Pincher Martin* Golding confronts for the first time the problems that 'character' presents for the writer of myths.

In *The Inheritors* Golding was concerned with the way things 'fit', and consequently with a moment of discovery—not in the sense of a fleeting moment, but rather that given the right moment, a whole lifetime can be caught within it. Obviously, no moment offers itself more dramatically than the moment of death, and Golding avails himself of this to show 'what we are'. Choosing an individual character, however, inevitably raises the past and the question of its relation to the present. Man may be the sum of his actions, but we need to know how. So Golding writes on two levels, giving us Pincher's struggles on the rock in the mode of history, and giving us also the background to his being in the series of flashbacks from his past. Because he is so concerned with being, however, these flashbacks are in the mode not of history but of fable.

Neither of course represents the true mode of the novel. On a second reading the myth is discovered beneath the encounter of history and fable, with its own hidden structure of days and nights behind the chapter divisions, its own tentativeness of explanation behind the clarities of Chris-Greed, or the self-dramatizing of Prometheus-Faust, its disclaimer of official views.

This myth is a powerful and extraordinary achievement. But the clash of history and fable on the surface raises explicit problems for the reader, and also raises implicit questions about the myth's exclusive concern with being, as we tried to show. In this retrospective summary we need only emphasize again how the difficulties spring from Golding's first encounter with the precise problem of character. Dissatisfaction arises from the insufficiency of the 'stills' in the mode of fable to explain how the man on the rock becomes his being. For Golding, Martin's past has only an emblematic and analytic connection with his present, but this translates itself for the reader into Golding's indifference to the character of the man whose struggle he creates so marvellously. The design is now unhappily at odds with the imagination. Although Golding has moved from the group to the individual, he treats Pincher as an attitude, capable of being rendered in a series of analytic vignettes. Though he has realized, properly enough, that the myth-writer must come to terms with the individual, the individual he presents us with is allowed to breathe only in an oxygen chamber of the author's devising. The glass jar is a world, but the more Golding has tried to get a character into it, the more it becomes clear that the atmosphere is too rarified for human life. It could not be extended. It will have, somehow, to be broken open.

The three years that separated *Pincher Martin* from *Free Fall* obviously constituted an artistic stocktaking. As he moved away from fable towards myth the treatment of character had become of crucial importance. Abstractly, it was a question of reconciling the essential being of a character with that process of becoming without which no character can satisfactorily exist. However much the myth-maker may be concerned with a moment of definition, he must include in his process of discovery a past for his character that has the reality of his present, and can satisfactorily account for it. These are the considerations that shape *Free Fall*. The ambiguity of the title itself suggests the abandonment of all claim to the certainty implicit in the title of its predecessor. The new novel is explicitly about the problems of writing a novel. 'How shall I understand my art?' becomes for Golding both his subject and his object.

Golding chooses a central character who can be an *alter ego*: a successful artist in one mode trying to understand himself, in another, a pattern-maker resolutely interrogating his own experience. With Sammy Mountjoy, the crucial 'moment' of his life is now something to be searched for, not merely shown. Consequently he is genuinely involved from the outset in his own

history. But his search is to explain a pattern of being already
definite and known to him. So Sammy's purpose and Golding's
seem more or less the same; but both the difficulty and the way
forward lie precisely in that 'more or less'. For Sammy the
novelist remains always, inescapably, a pattern-maker. Although
Golding succeeds in creating a character of a depth and resilience
that were lacking in *Pincher Martin*, the world of Sammy's novel
never frees itself from the collision of differing patterns. The
dominant experience of the novel he writes is of learning to 'tune'
the differing frequencies, until in his 'conclusion' the worlds of
being and becoming are starkly opposed, irreconcilable. But 'two
worlds without a bridge' is itself a pattern; the last of Sammy's
'hats' and the only one that will fit for him. The imagination of
myth is there in Sammy's novel in the mysterious experience of
revelation in the 'being' sections. The imagination of history is
there in the particularized experience of the 'becoming' sections.
But, because Sammy always seeks an explanation, both are always
stratified by the patternings and analytic formulations of fable. As
we argued, Golding can use the painter's eye or the myth experience to take Sammy beyond his conscious knowledge; but in
Sammy's novel there is no fusion of an art of becoming with an
art of being into one vision. Of that novel, as much as of Sammy's
paintings, we must finally say that the art is one of 'islanding in
pictures' out of the complexity of living.

Golding's long and difficult exploration of the problem through
his *alter ego* does however show him, at last, a way beyond, though
he can only indicate its direction, not follow its path. His purpose
does eventually separate itself from his protagonist's. The final
page of the book tries to challenge us to glimpse the complexity
of living, upsetting Sammy's certainties. Not only is all hope of
an inclusive pattern abandoned, but all pattern is seen as reductive.
In other words, Golding in *Free Fall* comes to realize that myth
cannot be satisfactorily located in history until a way is found to
circumvent fable altogether. There can be no 'answer' to the
Sphinx's riddle; what myth must aspire to is the revelation of the
nature of the riddle. It is not enough to create a character who can
lead a fictive life free from mere author-manipulation. The myth-
writer must also create a historical world fit for him to live in; a
world similarly free from reduction.

In *The Spire* Golding finds such a world. Once again he takes as central figure the artist as pattern-maker, though with a much greater assurance than in *Free Fall*. Jocelin is less self-conscious than Sammy and there is no danger of identifying his explanations with Golding's. There is a return to third person narration with a corresponding gain in objectivity. Jocelin doesn't talk about seeking patterns, his whole behaviour enacts them. Golding is now quite clear about the nature and limitations of the world of fable—and it is this world he gives to Jocelin. But the world of fable is circumvented, neutralized, in two different ways. It is tethered to the world of history because they have a point of common reference—the spire itself. Seen from one point of view, the spire is the diagram of prayer (or the tree of evil); but from another it is 'a skin of glass and stone' . . . with the builders 'bartering strength for weight or weight for strength, guessing how much, how far, how little, how near'. And as soon as we think about the spire, built in faith, in heavy stone, in sin, the very diversity of explanation means that an explanation is impossible. By the end of the novel fable disappears, as Jocelin dies. We look at the spire the novel has built, and glimpse its mythic revelation because we know all we need to know.*

The building of the spire pierces every level of the novel, so that fable is taken up into history. To look at the spire is to see Jocelin, to look at Jocelin is to see the spire:

'The singing of the stones pierced him and he fought it with jaws and fists clenched. His will began to burn fiercely and he thrust it into the four pillars, tamped it in with the pain of his neck and his head and his back, welcomed in some obscurity of feeling the wheels and flashes of light, and let them hurt his open eyes as much as they would.'

There is no question now of self-consciously feeling for the shape

* This would not be true if the mode *were* history. For example, we know virtually nothing of Goody, not even her name, and little of Jocelin's early relationship with Anselm. Golding cut out, as irrelevant, an account of the latter. Without seeing this, it is impossible to know whether he was right, but it seems likely. We know all we need to know for myth *in* history. By 'historical' criteria myth will always be seen as exclusive, but our argument is that we must not blur the differing criteria. Golding may have set out to subvert Trollope, as he had done Ballantyne and Wells.

in the ivory. Jocelin is shaped by the spire as surely as he shapes it. This perfect fusion between the inner and the outer world is what gives the novel its immense solidity. The building of the spire becomes different at every level, and presents new problems both physically and metaphysically. It is not history, for it seeks the revelation of archetypal truth, but it founds itself satisfactorily in historical process, gradually unfolding.

It is in the process of discovery within history that the essence of the myth also lies, using the insights of fable, but allowing its clarities and exclusions to cancel one another out. There is no final analysis or formulated wisdom, the emphasis is on the journey and not on the arrival. Hence again and again in *The Spire* we balance faith against the cost of faith, and explanation against explanation. Is it tubercular euphoria that drives Jocelin on? Is it religion—the saint's vision? Is it psychological—sexual sublimation? Is it moral—the blindness of human pride? Is it social—the privilege of secular advantage? As the questions mount and cut across one another, the answers become a matter of increasing indifference to us. What matters is to realize, in Sammy Mountjoy's words 'the unnameable, unfathomable, and invisible darkness that sits at the centre'. But, as Golding's novels have developed into this stage, the 'darkness' has also lost its definite label, it is opacity rather than blackness. It is no longer simply associated with evil and violence, but also with good. It is shrouded in mystery, alien to definition, the most we can hope for is momentary insight. Yet mystery is not muddle. The spire against the sky is a solid object with a solid history, and it reveals, though we cannot 'explain' what it reveals. It leans askew, in constant danger of falling. The myth-maker has realized that he can present, no longer a moment of absolute definition, but only a transitory moment of revelation glimpsed from the corner of the eye. But it also cascades to infinity, 'fixing' the otherwise incomprehensible in a moment of time. In one way it is 'nothing like' the novelist's original conception, a failure; in another it is a successful discovery of a far more difficult and complex truth. Golding has rid himself of fable and achieved, not history, but that satisfactory location in history without which myth is still fabulous.

Looking back over the novels we can see the change not only in form, but in the nature of the insight which has required formal development to express it. The fable-like structure of *Lord of the Flies* insisted on the darkness of man's heart. In *The Inheritors* the darkness is no longer simply evil, though it is still fearful. Yet Tuami's eyes, unlike the officer's resting complacently on the trim cruiser, or Ralph's weeping, 'peer forward . . . to see what lay at the other end of the lake (but) there was such a flashing from the water that he could not see if the line of darkness had an ending.' It is the strength of *Pincher Martin* that there is no definite 'official view' about where the line of darkness is to be drawn. From one point of view, Pincher lies awake in the night 'helpless on the stone floor, trying to run back, run away, climb up', a victim of his own nature; from another, his darkness is the darkness of depravity; from yet another, he is not Judas but Prometheus struggling against extinction. Though on the level of its flash-backs it is more simply fabulous than *Lord of the Flies*, on others it is more mysterious than anything Golding had written. The new feeling for character it gave him is built on in *Free Fall*, dramatizing his new problems. The door of the cell where Sammy had entered into himself in darkness, eventually opens onto a genuinely ambiguous world. 'There is a mystery in you which is opaque to us both', Dr Halde had remarked, but the psychology of the cell itself is the too simple design of the Herr Doctor who does not know about peoples. The spirit of the remark however shapes the art of *The Spire*. Where Sammy's novel had been programmatic about 'mystery', *The Spire* reveals it, and we can no longer talk of 'darkness'. All of Golding's novels have been concerned in one way or another with the Sphinx's riddle, but, as they have developed, the emphasis has shifted from the necessity of getting the right answer to the necessity of posing right questions, setting the riddle in the right way. As explanations have given way to explorations, fable has gradually been assumed into myth located in history.

Put in these terms, we might incline to regard Golding's achievement from *Lord of the Flies* to *The Spire* as a continual progress, in that in his last novel he seems to have found a satisfying shape for myth. In a way this is true, but we are saying less than we might think about the actual achievement in fiction. The solution of artistic 'problems' is something that can be seen only in retrospect, and consequently it is an abstraction from the individual works of art. To think of 'solutions' as synonymous with 'achievements' would be to misunderstand the nature of the artistic process—to become, in fact, a pattern-maker without the imaginative strength of the art of fable. All we can say, as we look at the various transformations which Golding's imagination has undergone in the last twelve years, is that it would seem that *The Spire* marks the end of a phase in his work; the resolution established in that work is of such a kind that it is not easy to see how it can be extended. In saying this, the critic can claim no foresight. He can only try to learn to see what is there already, and what is there in Golding's case seems to be a body of work which has resolved what seem to have been its predominant tensions, leaving the artist free for further exploration. Criticism itself constantly aspires to the condition of fable. It is the lesson derived from working on Golding's novels that it should recognize the limitations of its patterns and welcome opacity, remembering Eliot's words:

> *. . . knowledge imposes a pattern, and falsifies,*
> *For the pattern is new in every moment*
> *And every moment is a new and shocking*
> *Valuation of all we have been.*

Criticism can speak only of 'all we have been'; but in doing so, it seeks to prepare us to understand the 'new and shocking valuation' when it comes, as it surely will for a writer who has shown the imaginative vitality and resourcefulness of Golding.

VII

THE LATER GOLDING

One is one and all alone...
Old song

I

When it appeared, *The Spire* seemed not so much a fifth novel as the destination of the preceding four. We remarked in 1967 that it seemed to mark the end of a phase, and a resolution 'of such a kind that it is not easy to see how it can be extended'. For *The Spire* appeared both to fulfil all those paradoxical demands of the Golding imagination—that the fiction be clear yet mysterious, realistic and mythic, 'islanded' but representative, straightforward and complex, fully formed yet open-ended and tentative—and to do so with an exact, complete and intricate match of substance with form. The building of the spire kept pace at every step with the building of the novel; every height revealed a new depth; patterns multiplied to defeat patterning; and everything came together at the end to make possible a unifying glimpse of irreducible mystery beyond. Moreover, *The Spire* seemed the purest instance in Golding of the work of art acutely *aware* of itself taking up, bringing together and unifying the paradoxes which had emerged from the earlier novels. And Jocelin's intense nature ensured a greater intensity of vision than ever before.

Yet in this very completeness, self-consciousness, intensity, was there not a problem, at least for its author? How was he to go on beyond? He certainly seemed in difficulties. *The Pyramid*, which he described as a step backwards in order to leap further, was not a success. There followed a long silence of more than ten years—except for the two new stories in *The Scorpion God* whose very assurance related them more to *The Inheritors* than to any new departure in terms of art. Then the silence was broken dramatically: two novels in rapid succession written, it would seem, in tandem, but of startlingly different kinds and producing very different responses.

How had Golding managed to go beyond *The Spire*? It would seem, in hindsight, by two different, even opposite, strategies.

If the 'completeness', and self-conscious intensity, were what seemed to block the way, then a form would have to be found that was less monolithic and a texture lighter and brighter. (In *Lord of the Flies* there had been an insouciance, a sense of imaginative energy with resources in reserve, a lightness of touch. As the novels had become more and more intensely truth-seeking, the artistry had become less zestful, though more highly-wrought.) The 'step backwards' seems to have come from the sense of unfinished business left over from *Free Fall,* both in content and in form. There Golding had set out to deal more fully than in *Pincher* with a contemporary world, but in Sammy's search for the pattern of individual self-determinism, what had never really come into focus was the social determinism of the English class-system, about which, as we now know, Golding felt strongly.

'I think an Englishman who is not aware of the classic disease of society in this country, that is to say, the rigidity of its class structure—he's not really aware of anything, not in social terms.'*

In English life, as the public-school motto insists, 'Manners maketh man', and Golding had never tried the novel of manners, those 'three or four families in a Country Village' which Jane Austen described as 'the very thing to work on'. But perhaps it should be in a fractured form? As a reader looks forward towards *The Spire,* the distillation of Sammy's split vision in *Free Fall,* called in question by the mysterious ambiguity of the final fragment, can seem a stage towards unity, bringing the eyes together, at the culmination of *The Spire.* But, looking back now, once the 'monolithic' unity had become the very thing blocking the way, there might seem much to be gained by splitting even more diversely into different kinds of story, especially if it were not by metaphysical stance (as with Nick Shales and Rowena Pringle) but by genre. For that would also circumvent self-conscious intensity by trying something lighter and brighter: ironic comedy of manners, even comic opera, and tragi-comedy that sharp-edged the vision as it darkened. So a step back to the world of *Free Fall,* with its adolescent lust and sense of loss but with a new sharp and ironic focus on the class structure of English society and a new diversity of form (a spire ironically recast into three surfaces, yet still coming together into figurative form), might allow Golding to move forward again. It did—though unsatisfactorily at first, as it seems to us. Yet the attempt in *The Pyramid* at least to overlook, in fractured twentieth-century terms, the territory of Jane Austen, also led directly (by a deeper sense of forms and concerns behind her) to the success of *Rites of Passage.* From his partial failure, Golding eventually learnt to succeed in a new way.

*Interview, *Twentieth Century Literature,* Summer 1982.

The Later Golding

On the other hand, the critical reception of *The Pyramid*, suffering inevitably by comparison with *The Spire*, must have sharpened his sense that the main road of his fiction still led through *The Spire*, however difficult it might seem to get beyond. Surely it was still possible to see further and more clearly? Admittedly, the novel had been essentially concerned with the immense difficulty of seeing whole. All that structuring and patterning had been only the necessary preparation for a single moment of perception at the very end. It had been necessary to exhaust all the 'languages' of the spire, to know in every way, in order that Jocelin at the point of self-extinction should become able to focus its wholeness momentarily, and cry, 'Now I know nothing at all.' Only in the tentativeness of simile—'It's like the apple tree'—had it been possible to create a suggestion of something glimpsed beyond words. The tentativeness bore eloquent witness to Golding's sense of the mysteriousness of human being (in its fusion of dark energy and bright abundance) and of the limitations of language. Nevertheless, it surely had to be possible to get deeper insight, to turn glimpsing into seeing, to make darkness (and brightness) more visible? Here too, perhaps, a fracturing of form might enable both the dark story and the bright story to be focused more clearly in separation before attempting to bring different ways of seeing together in a third 'book'. And here too the move forward might come from taking up the challenge of an even more contemporary world, both to make darkness visible and to see whether (in the words of *The Inheritors*) it had an ending. What would pose the darkest challenges? That infamous photograph of the burnt Vietnamese child? The news of some outrage by a middle-class terrorist? The back-page item about the one case even liberals find 'dirty', the pederast who interferes with little boys and refuses to be cured?

Hindsight simplifies both the difficulty and the multitude of possibilities—it will not have been that straightforward. Yet it is now possible to see how the two strategies began to clarify themselves. One would have to work with *surfaces*, trying to make fragments imply a whole, genres, a form beyond, surfaces, a depth. The other would have to go directly for an exploration of the *depths*, an attempt to built the entire *oeuvre* again, and push it one stage further, but at the same time confronting even more directly than *The Spire* the limits of language.

The Later Golding

II

In *The Pyramid*, then, Golding's aim differs radically from the massive inclusiveness, the steady and continuing concentration, of *The Spire*. By juxtaposing three comic and ironic stories, he sought a different kind of dramatic fluency, more casual in its linkages, more varied in its tones. If there was to be a unifying principle, it would—as the title indicates—express a wry irony and be not a single inclusive and solid physical structure so much as varying structurings of feeling. Most noticeably, his novel would stress the presence of class divisions, the social pyramid marked out in terms of rank, position and property. The communication of those divisions, moreover, would be largely a matter of signals, expertly sent and received, the crystal set behind the closed curtains tuning in precise wavelengths. More insinuatingly (it is an element in all three stories), there is music, providing an inner commentary on the absence of concord, of measure, in the places in which it is played—a metronome cast, finally, on a rubbish heap. These elements are colourings in the general mode of perception behind the novel: the comedy of manners, which itself is varied throughout the novel, associated in the first story with irony, in the second more with farce, and in the third with tragedy.

It is in the opening story (first published separately under the title 'On the Escarpment'), however, that the dominant note of the novel is struck: its concern with the divisiveness of class and, in direct consequence, the inability of the protagonist to see in Evie anything other than a sex object. Sammy Mountjoy, thinking of his rootless background, 'boasted, with rudimentary feeling for the shape of our social pyramid, that I was the rector's son', but Oliver has no need for such deception; he is the chemist's son (though not, significantly, the doctor's) and is on his way to Oxford. His eyes are cast upwards and are riveted on the unattainable figure of Imogen Grantley, and when he looks down it is with adolescent lust on Evie Babbacombe, 'the town crier's daughter...from the tumbledown cottages of Chandler's Close. But of course we had never spoken. Never met. Obviously.' Oliver's eventual seduction of Evie is the substance of the tale, but we are gradually made aware that Evie's background is more complex than Oliver could have imagined.

The Later Golding

One irony comes into view behind another. We watch Oliver, at the bridge or in the bushes (since his social position makes any real relationship literally unthinkable), use 'not telling' as blackmail for seduction; we watch, in counter-point, Evie forcing him into the open, in full view, and exposing him in the pub by telling all, and more. But behind this are the several suggestions of what an Oliver, 'telling and laughing', cannot tell and can hardly even glimpse behind bucolic comedy, what it is like to *be* Evie near the foot of the pyramid.

The story has considerable vivacity and is presented with a sharpness of remembered detail, both for adolescent feeling and for place, that makes it (within the terms of ironic comedy of manners) a fair success. But it is where Golding wishes to use comedy to catch sight of a darker world behind that the opening story falters. Through an adolescent Oliver, Evie cannot be sufficiently imagined for us, so that the gap between the girl with the lopsided sneer, the village tart, and the Evie who may have 'a life-long struggle to be clean and sweet', remains unbridgeable. Oliver may talk of her as 'an undiscovered person', but that has to be the reader's report too. On the other hand, the story also falters because of the uncertainty in the narrative voice. Formally, that voice is young Oliver's—the excitements, the exasperations, the callowness are registered with economy and assurance—but accompanying these is another *tone*, of knowingness, almost of condescension, as if Golding is uncertain whether his tale is sufficiently self-declaring, and he has to guide it home with a barely concealed commentator. The difficulty the story presents him with is illustrated by the seduction itself. Understandably, Golding presents it in terms which correspond to Oliver's attitude, that is to say, in a manner which is perfunctorily blind to almost everything but the physical. But Evie's attitude, 'I wanted to be loved, I wanted somebody to be kind', exists only as an assertion—there is no room for it in the imagined world of the narrative. So far as the first story is concerned, the epigraph of the novel, 'If thou be among people make for thyself love, the beginning and end of the heart', can act only as a wholly ironic and marginal note to the main text, a purely negative index.

Matters are taken up more sharply in the second story; comedy hardens into farce, hint gives way to statement, explicit judgement is called into play. A group of amateur actors are rehearsing a sub-

Novello operetta, *King of Hearts*. Oliver, on vacation from Oxford, is forced into taking part, so that he is half-participant, half-observer. The producer, Evelyn De Tracy, is a 'camp' figure, exercising amusingly his authority on stage; but once away from it, he becomes a lonely and rather desperate figure. We first focus this picture of De Tracy in a conversation with Oliver during an interval in rehearsals. Flattered by De Tracy's attention, Oliver is moved to give his views of Stilbourne: 'Everything's *wrong*. Everything. There's no truth and there's no honesty ... the things we daren't mention, the people we don't meet....' And he concludes with rhetorical force: 'Evelyn, I want the *truth* of things. But there's nowhere to find it.' De Tracy accepts the tacit invitation and promptly proceeds to give Oliver at least one instance of 'the truth' about things. He takes out a number of photographs, in one of which he is dressed as a ballerina, 'supported by a thick, young man ... they gazed deep into each other's eyes.' For Oliver, the offered moment of 'truth' is a moment of blank incomprehension: 'I laughed until it hurt.' The critical edge of the story is much sharper than in the first one. De Tracy becomes a way of focusing the hopeless pretentiousness of Stilbourne, its vanity, its petty conflicts, its atrophy of imagination. We recognize in De Tracy's situation something much bleaker than Evie's.

The story as a whole, however, is not a success. Golding seems to be trying to do too much too quickly. Perhaps for economy, he has taken a familiar situation, almost cliché-ridden—amateur dramatics, temperamental tenor, supercilious producer, bewildered outsider—and hopes to make us see through the cliché, to the genuine feeling behind it. But Golding's narrative is trapped within the cliché-world it seeks to criticize. In hindsight, however, we can now see that the story, however unsuccessful in its own terms, is an interesting prefiguring of the dramatic situation which Golding is to take up, with strikingly different results, in *Rites of Passage*. The world of theatre is to become the ship of the line; Oliver's incomprehension and the producer's revelation are to become immensely expanded and transformed into the relationship between Talbot and Colley. 'I want the *truth* of things': Golding is to return again to *that* request, and paradoxically, through a heightened awareness of surface, scene, character, language, he is to reveal a depth beyond the imaginative reach of anything in *The Pyramid*.

The Later Golding

Where the novel does succeed is in the third story. Although linked to the comic mode of the first two stories, it is closer in mood to tragic pathos. Loneliness and desolation find dramatic resonance, and Golding is much surer in his use of narrative voice. For the first time in *The Pyramid* we have events seen through an adult eye— Oliver returns to Stilbourne over thirty years after the events previously recounted—but allowing now the child's sensibility with the adult's understanding to create a glimpse of the depths, through the surface, in a way not possible before. Such a moment occurs, ironically, when the young Oliver, fearful and bored with his piano lesson, says 'I want to go.' Bounce interprets this genteely, and there is comedy—but the child's eye takes in desolation too.

'... she went through the hall, then up dark, angled stairs, where the candlelight was no more than a puddle. We came to a long corridor and there were doors on either side, some open, to show a bare floor and a glimmering window. At the end of the corridor was a step up and a glass door. Bounce opened the door.

"There you are."

She handed me the candlestick and shut the door behind me. I advanced fearfully and saw a water closet of brown earthenware.... I stayed where I was against the wall and the ice of that darkness and remoteness formed on my skin and in my hair.'

There is this kind of innocent irony, but it can be accompanied by the irony of the experienced eye. For instance, Henry's inscription on her tombstone, 'Heaven is music', vibrates throughout the story: music, which doomed Bounce to a life of frustration; music, which in its formal properties of harmony and proportion, mocked the discord in Bounce's heart; music, which she had first learnt from her egotistic father, to the accompaniment of a ruler beating across her knuckles. These ironies come together in the climactic scene in the tale when Bounce, in a final bid for Henry's attention, walks down the main street of Stilbourne, quite naked—except for those emblems of respectability, her hat and gloves. Comic, and tragic; shocking to the boy's eye to see Miss Dawlish appear in this way, shocking to the recollecting eye of the adult, when he perceives the emotional desperation in the gesture—this climactic scene exemplifies Golding's success in the story. He has found a double voice and a technique of implication which have allowed him to work within the comic mode of perception, but to keep faithful to the serious intent conveyed by the epigraph by creating a character who is really *there*. 'If thou be among people make for thyself love, the beginning and end of the heart.' Bounce's startling appearance makes eloquent the hidden reality, and Golding achieves a success which is present neither in Evie's seduction on the escarpment nor in Mr De Tracy's revelatory conversation, 'between the fireplace and the potted palm'.

Successful as the final story is, however, it is limited by Bounce's eccentricity. The reader responds to the modulation between tragic and comic, but feels that it remains intractably personal. It italicizes 'for thyself' too heavily in the epigraph, and has little resonance for the sentence as a whole. And so we see Golding's achievement in *The Pyramid* to be interesting, but severely qualified. In the first story he has focused a society where class divisions are admirably conveyed; in the second story he is heightening the implications of those divisions through the calculated use of theatre, of artifice; in the third story, he seeks to juxtapose these elements and to make us look more disturbingly at a single figure, whose behaviour at one level seems incomprehensibly absurd, at another comprehensibly tragic.

The art is of the surface, comic, but the haunting concern is to make it reveal 'the undiscovered person'. Hindsight allows us to detect in *The Pyramid* the shadowy outlines of what will become *Rites of Passage*.

III

Rites of Passage had a precise source in Elizabeth Longford's *Life of Wellington*. She describes an episode which occurred in 1797, when Wellington, then Colonel Wesley, was preparing an expedition for Manila:

'William Hickey had persuaded Arthur to take on as chaplain to the 33rd the nephew of his friend Mr Scawen, a young man named Blunt. They sailed in August. After only three days at sea the unfortunate clergyman got "abominably" drunk and rushed out of his cabin stark naked among the soldiers and sailors "talking all sorts of bawdy and ribaldry and singing scraps of the most blackguard and indecent songs". Such was his shame on afterwards hearing of these "irregularities" that he shut himself up and refused to eat or speak. Colonel Wesley was informed. He instantly rowed across to Blunt's vessel and sent for him. The wretched man declined to appear. Wesley then descended to Blunt's cabin and talked to him like a father:

"...what had passed was not of the least consequence as no one would think the worse of him for the little irregularities committed in a moment of forgetfulness... the most correct and cautious men were liable to be led astray by convivial society, and no blame ought to attach to a cursory debauch...."

Colonel Wesley's broad-minded and kindly attempts to "reconcile Mr Blunt to himself" were not successful. In ten days he forced himself to die of contrition.'[*]

To Golding, this was 'so horrific that I had to invent human circumstances to make us understand how a man could die of shame'.[†]

The first impression of the novel is its immediate accessibility. Not since *Lord of the Flies* has a Golding novel enjoyed such happy recognition; indeed, it is difficult to resist the thought that part, at least, of the success of *Rites of Passage* came in the form of reassurance that the author of the earlier novel was alive and well and that the quarter-century which separated the two books had not diminished his narrative power. There is a similar re-creation of detail and atmosphere, the South Sea island replaced by a ship of the line. The smell, the cramped quarters, the clanking pumps, the sand and gravel in the bilge, the constantly tilting decks, the wind in the ropes—the cumulative effect is to make us think not so much of vivid description as of an 'on-the-spot' report. This, Golding makes us feel, is just what it must have been like to have been aboard such a ship at the turn of the last century.[**]

But the ship's surfaces provide, even more concentratedly than the village, a model of a hierarchically structured society, and we are no less aware than in *The Pyramid* of how its inhabitants exist in the

[*]Elizabeth Longford, *Wellington*, vol. I, *The Years of the Sword*, London, Weidenfeld and Nicolson 1969, p. 51.

[†]Interview, *Literary Review*, October 1981.

[**]Golding suggests 1812 or 1813. Interview, *Twentieth Century*, Summer 1982.

medium of social discrimination. The quarterdeck above, the gentlemen passengers, the dividing line painted at the mainmast, the lower passengers, the crew: the ship as traditional literary microcosm is here specifically a class structure. The society of officers and gentlemen is an extension of its counterpart on land, ever mindful of rank, courtesies, amorous strategies and unseen paymasters. 'Below' there is the mob of sailors, crowded, noisy, dangerous when roused and (for those on the upper decks) living a life as remote as any native tribe. Between the two, marking the surface, is the first of the lines it is perilous to cross. What is striking—and the 'line' is a good instance—is how effortlessly the precisely observed detail releases the wider perspective. But the structure is filled with a tissue of social assumption (effortlessly understood by English readers, foreign to Americans) that is of the very life of the book. Talbot exists unthinkingly as the child of privilege and patronage, able to beard the very captain on his quarterdeck. Colley, raised by his cloth from the lower orders—also through patronage—betrays the *parvenu* in every detail of appearance, manner and speech and, like his counterpart in Jane Austen's Mr Collins, is riding for a fall even before he ignorantly exposes himself to the prejudice of the captain, and reaps the social resentment he has had to bottle up over the similar offence of Talbot. On the other hand, it is a very Austen-like ironic education, learning to detect the person beneath the social exterior, that Talbot undergoes in the first phase: to distinguish between Deverel, Cumbershum, and Summers; and to learn from Summers the responsibilities and obligations that go with rank and privilege. But we are also aware—as never in Jane Austen—of the instability of the hierarchy, the reverberations of a wider context in which the old world of Reason and Order has to be set against an age of revolution. The crew are turbulent. It will be to divert and appease their hostility (as well as the contempt of the officers) that the *parvenu* 'gentleman' will be sacrificed as scapegoat in the 'crossing the line' ritual, which seeks to appease forces rising from below the surface, and achieve an 'equatorial' balance. And it will be in blind ignorance of social reality that Colley proceeds to offer, in his uniform of rank, an opportunity for further humiliation directed at the 'gentlemen' above him. To compare Golding's novel with *Billy Budd* is to mark how very much more concerned with social discrimination and resentment this English novel is. It is not difficult to infer that the name of the ship is *Britannia*.

So the 'surface' world of manners is no less important than in *The Pyramid*. Now, however, behind Jane Austen as it were, Golding *opposes* the world of Fielding, Smollett and Lord Chesterfield to that of Samuel Richardson (and Coleridge). Richardson's formal invention—the epistolary method—banished the author and allowed dramatic characters to create themselves in their own voices, since 'styles differ too, as much as faces, and are indicative, generally beyond the power of disguise, of the mind of the writer'.* Instead of the merely ironic lens of Oliver, the letter-journals of Talbot and Colley create two vivid characters, 'done' through their styles. Yet their opposition, in creating *minds,* does more than merely oppose a late Augustan idiom of Taste, Enlightened Good Sense and Benevolence, to a Romantic idiom of Feeling. Talbot and Colley realize for us what is involved in the opposition of two modes of perceiving the nature of life itself. For Richardson, reality was ultimately private and psychological. Diderot praised him for taking the candle to the back of the cave of the mind, venturing into the depths as it were to make darkness visible. But Smollett and Lord Chesterfield, coming after him, used the letter form as an essentially social medium again, for travellers through worlds of men and manners, and for educating a gentleman. The assumption, ingrained in language itself, that life is *essentially* social, opposes the assumption, no less ingrained, that it is essentially private and psychological. Each man in his world. So, in Golding's invention of languages, and the proclamation of 'literariness', the triumph is that we are never aware of mere realistic pastiche of late Augustan or Romantic idiom. Indeed, what comes across is a zest of invention, a linguistic energy and exuberance which can openly admit what it is doing and delight in the skill. With considerable ingenuity, also, Golding provides an analogy and a naturalization within the book itself. As Talbot self-consciously acquires a third idiom, tarpaulin language, its arcane and archaic phrases throw into contrast his own 'natural' mode. Golding boldly heightens our awareness of languages, but in the interests of making us feel them to be of the essence of the opposed worlds they create.

The observed life of the ship, the microcosm of class-ridden society, the wider perspectives the voyage affords, the languages, all

*John Carroll (ed.), *Selected Letters of Samuel Richardson*, Oxford, Clarendon Press, 1964, p.64.

do better what the ironic comedy of manners of *The Pyramid* had attempted. We have a richness of characterization it lacked, and a juxtaposition of genres far more startling and suggestive when farce meets tragedy at the sound of Prettiman's blunderbuss. But it is when we seek to pin down the nature of our understanding of that moment, and its aftermath, that difficulty arises. We are familiar with the problem of the drastic simplicities entailed in any formulation of complex imaginative effects, but this is more disturbing. We have an uneasy feeling that we are responding so sharply to certain features of the book as to be lured, like Talbot, into false 'understanding'. The very clarity of the undertaking would seem to lead to a position where we have not only to revise our interpretation, but more radically, to ask what is the nature of interpretation? We can, uneasily, begin to feel the ground shifting as soon as we put the question which, from one point of view, seems so appropriate.

What *is* at issue in *Rites of Passage*? How Mr Talbot went to sea and learned to know himself? How Mr Colley was made to encounter the 'reality' of his own temperament and was overcome? As soon as the questions are put, we seem to hear that hidden laughter which echoes in the novel, and feel that we have been tempted into a kind of 'understanding' that it is the veiled purpose of the book to subvert. In a rather curious way, *Rites of Passage* seems to reverse the experience of being in a maze. We enter full of purpose and interest and are delighted immediately by the precision and variety of the detail, by prospects, far and near; we expect to be taken further in—then, quite suddenly, we find ourselves on the outside. We seem to have taken a wrong turn, a re-entry seems called for, and perhaps that is also part of this particular maze. To look at two crucial and related scenes is to see something of the nature of this 'turn'.

The first section, headed BETA, begins with a sentence which might serve as a warning to the reader as much as to Talbot. 'Wrong again, Talbot! Learn another lesson, my boy.' This leads into a description of Talbot's visit to Colley, at Summers's plea, to try and persuade him to give up his fast and return to the life of the ship. It is the moment when the novel is closest to its source, Colonel Wesley's words to the chaplain:

'What had passed was not of the least consequence as no one would think the worse of him for the little irregularities.... the most correct and cautious of men were liable to be led astray....'

becomes in Talbot's exchange with Colley:

'this is an unfortunate business, but believe me sir, you are refining too much on it. Uncontrolled drunkenness and its consequences is an experience which every man ought to have once in his life or how is he to understand the experience of others?... In a day or two we shall all laugh at your comical interlude... Depend upon it, you will soon see things differently.

There was no response. I glanced enquiringly at Summers....
"Well, Summers?"
"Mr Colley is willing himself to death."' (pp. 152-3)

Talbot, an eighteenth-century man believing in Reason and Good Sense, sociably makes his appeal and it falls on deaf ears. Puzzled and disturbed, Talbot recalls seeing Colley's journal, returns again to the cabin, fails to find it at first, but then discovers the pages stuffed into a crack in the wall. Eagerly he returns to his room, thrusts 'the spoils of his burglary' into his writing desk, when there is a knock on the door. It is an invitation to dine with the captain.

In retrospect, the episode would seem to offer obvious ironies: the indictment of Talbot for his failure to understand imaginatively what worries Colley, the guilty seizure of Colley's papers, and—the implication would seem to run—the fearful illumination the papers will cast on Colley's behaviour. 'Depend upon it you will soon see things differently'—the sentence seems to mobilize the ironies, and like Talbot, the reader awaits enlightenment. The narrative momentum seems that of the detective story working towards a solution. With Colley, we have two related mysteries: what happened to him on the lower deck, and why has he taken to his cabin, willing himself to death? We have a first enquiry by Talbot, which fails, and then the discovery of Colley's papers. At this point the reader has every reason to feel something of Talbot's confidence: the problem has been posed; the answer is, literally, in hand. But the reader is made to wait, because before he can turn to Colley's letter, there is Talbot's dinner engagement with the Captain. And it is this scene which is to bring a different modulation into the narrative, and alter expectations.

When Talbot arrives, elegant banter is exchanged about the Captain's 'garden', and his triumph of growing plants from seeds in his cabin. There are fleeting references to Eden and the Fall, a geranium has a diseased leaf—and Anderson remarks, 'But then, sir, he who gardens at sea must accustom himself to loss.' The conversation is vivid, the occasion a little bizarre, and ever so faintly, the aphoristic cadence of the captain's remark has an ominous undertone.

Summers arrives and the captain takes the opportunity to ask about Colley. Hearing that Brocklebank is a doctor, he tries to arrange for him to visit the sick man. Brocklebank is brought to the cabin, the worse for drink. 'Now there occurred', Talbot writes in his journal 'a scene of farce.' Quite apart from his present condition, the company learns that Brocklebank no longer has any wish to practise medicine; his interest is in art, and he lays claim to have painted the first lithograph of Nelson's death.

> '"You were not present!"
>
> "Arm's length, sir. Neither was any other artist. I must admit to you freely that I believed at the time that Lord Nelson had expired on deck."
>
> "Brocklebank," cried I, "I have seen it! There is a copy on the wall in the tap of the Dog and Gun! How the devil did that whole crowd of young officers contrive to be kneeling round Lord Nelson in attitudes of sorrow and devotion at the hottest moment of the action?"....
>
> "You are confusing art with actuality, sir."
>
> "It looked plain silly to me, sir."....
>
> "And imagine sir, Lord Nelson died down below in some stinking part of the bilges, I believe, with nothing to see him by but a ship's lantern. Who in the devil is going to make a picture of that?"
>
> "Rembrandt perhaps."' (p. 169).

The passage, for all its lightness of tone, is a crucial one in our understanding of the novel. The artist may keep reality at 'arm's length' in order to see what he wishes to see. We want the act of dying to have style and order, so that 'meaning' can be given to it. It is an act of theatre—Nelson, his heroism made manifest, surrounded by the company of his officers, and loving, grief-stricken friends. The lithographer, so skilled in reproducing the visual *surface*, can catch this 'reality' to perfection. But death (not only Nelson's) is always hidden, and alone. Suddenly, the whole conversation is interrupted by a knock at the door. 'One by one we turned. Summers stood in the doorway. "Sir. I have been with Mr Colley, sir. It is my belief the man is dead."' (p. 175). Actuality has not been kept at arm's length. Another man has died alone, his face turned to the wall, with only a lamp for company. The news of Colley's death marks the narrative climax of the book, and what follows is an extended meditation on how we are to understand that 'hidden' event. Earlier, when he was in Colley's cabin, Talbot leaned over the silent figure. 'It was then that I perceived without seeing—I knew, but had no real means of knowing.' (p. 156). It is the aim of *Rites of Passage* to give imaginative life to that perception, that mysterious kind of 'knowing', but it is not an aim which will be fulfilled in the way that Talbot—or the reader—expected it to be.

'so I have drawn a veil over what have been the most trying and unedifying of my experiences' (p. 186)—Colley's letter begins in mid-sentence and thus does not present a whole truth. This turns out to be in line with the narrative strategy of the last part of *Rites of Passage*, with this crucial difference, that it will seek to make the reader aware of what 'truth' can be told, and what can never be.

Yet when the reader settles down with Talbot to read Colley's letter, the 'truth' seems available. The documentary 'evidence' is in his hands. And in some important senses this turns out to be right. Colley's letter does enable us to see incidents in the story in a new way; his meetings with Talbot, with Anderson, with the other officers, appear in a very different light. Above all, we are introduced to a mind and sensibility in marked contrast to anything in Talbot's journal. It is not just a matter of an arrogant complacency being replaced by a nervous self-abasement—Colley also has a patron, to whom he refers in tones reminiscent of Mr Collins—but rather that Mr Colley being 'a man of feeling' extends our whole sense of the life of the ship and the voyage. After Talbot's Augustan idiom with its constant emphasis on men and manners, it comes as something of a shock to read of 'The sunlight is warm and like a natural benediction' (p. 187), of 'the white-flecked blue of the broad ocean' (p. 189), of 'terror at the majesty of this huge engine of war' (p. 189). It is, above all, the note of awe that reminds us most forcibly of a dimension totally excluded from Talbot's diary. Hearing that the ship may be sailing over waters two miles deep, Colley writes, 'I was almost overcome with faintness. Here we are, suspended between the land below the waters and the sky like a nut on a branch or a leaf on a pond' (p. 192). Colley sees his whole voyage as a spiritual one, a succession of trials and temptations to be overcome, and when, crossing the line, he sees in the sky at once the setting sun and the rising moon, he sees them as the scales of God. Again and again, we feel Coleridge's presence in Colley's voyage. Like the Mariner, able to bless the water snakes, Colley looks over the side of the ship and, no longer terrified by the unplumbed depths, sees the foam and the green weed, and is consumed 'by a great love of all things, the sea, the ship, the sky, the gentlemen and the people and of course *Our Redeemer* above all!' (p. 247).

Yet when we come to the end of the letter we find that, at least in terms of our expectations about 'what happened', nothing has been explained. What it has done is to dramatize a way of thinking, a mode of sensibility, which takes Feeling as its criteria for authentic experience, and sees the world in terms of signs. Colley does not see the world, so much as see through it.

But there remains a public necessity for explanation. A court of enquiry is set up to examine the case and to identify responsibility. Verdicts are sought: Colley's intemperance? Indifference by the officers? Indecent assault? Sexual self-disgust? With each, it is possible to see the sketch of 'what happened' taking on a clearer outline—but as this becomes clearer it releases for the reader (if not for Talbot) an overarching question about what would count as an 'explanation' at all. 'What happened' begins to fade into a more universal questioning. Talbot, however, remains committed to event. When the language of the court, of public cause and effect, is thwarted, he is able 'to piece together', by private inference, a plausible sequence of events of what must have happened to Colley. But there, for Talbot, the matter must rest; life has to continue, the ship must sail on. Courts of enquiry, like funerals, are ends in themselves.

Colley, however, is disdainful of ceremony. He fails to read the Captain's Orders, he does not carry his credentials, and when he goes to meet the men it is in clothes which he describes as 'the ornaments of the Spiritual Man', confident that they sufficiently proclaim the Truth of his mission. Impatient of the surface, indifferent to its significance, he takes on the darkness directly and seeks to overcome it. Against all advice, he goes to the lower deck, disappears from view, reaches only to the black hole of his cabin from which he never emerges. It is not *what* happened which has destroyed his life, nor is his suffering merely a matter of depression. For Colley, as for Coleridge in 'The Dejection Ode', 'Joy' was the power to make the universe anew, and when that was desecrated, then the universe turned into something monstrous.

To see Colley simply as a 'character' would be to find such a claim exorbitant. The objection would run: here is no more than a young man who takes himself intensely seriously. Duty is too easily defined, the Almighty's Will too easily accessible, judgement a decision too readily called into play. Golding has given us, if only by way of hints and guesses, a sexual explanation for Colley's behaviour, of a kind only too familiar. He has no idea of God's mercy.

The first comment to be made about such a criticism is that Golding himself makes it of Colley and assigns the comfort of it to Talbot and the Captain. For them, Colley is easily categorized—a man of desperate extremes, viewing himself passionately in one way, then being forced to see himself in quite another, intolerably. He is torn apart by contradiction and by shame, and he wills himself to die.

The judgement on Colley passed by *Rites of Passage*, however, cannot be summarized in this way. One reason is that Colley is characterized more deeply by his language than by his behaviour. He exists for us, and indeed for himself, more inwardly in terms of his journal, and while this is an inescapably personal record, it is also, in every nuance of its prose, a document of Romantic Feeling making clear that his view of the self is also a view of the universe. The name of Coleridge, invoked directly and obliquely in *Rites of Passage*, is there to indicate a map of metaphysical feeling, and when Colley exclaims 'Joy!', or gazes into the water and blesses 'the blue, the green, the purple, the snowy, sliding foam' we feel the presence of 'The Dejection Ode' and 'The Ancient Mariner', not as discrete poems, but as extensions to Colley's sensibility, giving it precision and utterance. If 'we receive but what we give, and in our life alone does Nature live', then to have reversed the Ancient Mariner's blessing is not to have damaged a character, or betrayed a priesthood, but to have made *all* vision monstrous in death-in-life. The silence of the journal is what Coleridge feared: that language becomes meaningless. Colley matters not as a character, but because he cares on that scale. He turns his back, and we are left looking at a hand enigmatically clutching a ringbolt. Language gives way to uninterpretable gesture. Despair? Hope? The mystery that attends his death, if it is to be expressed at all, cannot be—in Anderson's words—a matter of witnesses, enquiries, accusations, lies, courts martial. Perhaps there is only the shrill sound of the Bosun's pipe, 'the simple sound of life mourning death'—a voice beyond language and explanation.

However, unlike both Talbot and Colley, Golding seeks to create a rite of passage more encompassing than the occasion of its duration, more committed to a prospect of survival. *His* enquiry into Colley's death takes the form of a sustained paradox—to describe a world so vividly that we are moved to regard it as 'holding the truth', and yet, simultaneously, to make us aware that such a world has been shaped, invented,—a triumph of artifice. 'The ship of the line' is also 'a floating theatre'; the Captain's Orders are 'lines to be learnt'; the whole ship indulges in 'theatricals'; the central action—the crossing of the line itself—is described variously, as 'a tragedy', 'a farce'. The whole novel echoes with the sound of other men's art—Melville, Conrad, Richardson, Coleridge. The cumulative effect of this self-conscious insistence is to make the reader constantly aware of a structure, a dazzling surface through which a depth can be glimpsed. But—there is an inevitable loss in 'gardening at sea'—it can only be a glimpse. Partly, this is because life must indeed go on, and the depths are dangerous. So, when Colley is buried, a bracketed sentence takes the pathos out of the occasion ('At these necessarily ritualistic moments of life, if you cannot use the prayer book, have recourse to Shakespeare! Nothing else will do'), and there is always a weather-eye on the ship. When the 'end' of the novel comes, it is headed simply with an ampersand; this is a novel which resists conclusion. Yet depth is dramatically defined by the surface which encloses it.

For Golding the resources of art have to be drawn upon to communicate a 'truth' more mysterious than Talbot's, more provisional than Colley's; they have crossed the line too easily. Golding's novel is a rite which holds 'the line' itself in respect—ever mindful of the depths, but no less mindful of the human need for passage, for survival.

The Later Golding

IV

Yet Golding has always been committed to exploring beyond the line, into the depths, where the world of social behaviour and character gives way to hidden dimensions of good and evil, joy and horror—which *Rites of Passage* refuses to explore but will only call attention to, as a stage defines an open trapdoor, or a picture puzzle the shape of its missing piece. It is that 'darkness' that the other strategy, after *The Spire*, insists must be made *visible*, cost what it may in a different kind of art that may be caviare to the general. Greenfield may set us again in the twentieth-century England of *The Pyramid*, indeed even more up to date, 'what with the jets soughing down every minute to London airport and the monstrous continental trucks doing their best to break down the Old Bridge'. But now author and reader must cope from the start with visions of extremity, beginning with the twentieth-century experience of inferno. The exploratory imagination is willing to risk the outrageous, the obscure, the contorted, the farcical, in order to reveal not a brightly worked surface but the underside, 'the seamy side where the connections are'. Where *The Pyramid* and *Rites* ask us to see through a worldling like ourselves, the other strategy seems to need distorted lenses—a saintly idiot, a pederast, a terrorist—to overturn our ordinary sense of human nature and make its warp and woof unmistakable. Whereas *Rites* delights in language, *Darkness Visible* calls language itself in question. Above all, where *Rites* depends on artful *juxtaposition* of scenes and pictures, it is only a continous process of deeper and deeper *exploration* that can hope to make darkness finally visible, beyond paradox and different points of view, through some sequence of focusings. (The critical account, then, must also shift emphasis, become exploratory and sequential.)

First, what is it, to 'see'? That twentieth-century man has perpetrated 'darkness visible', in hells unimaginable to Milton, is a fact—London, Dresden, Hiroshima—but in the astonishing overture to the novel Golding not only makes his readers realize inferno, but also see what he means by seeing. It must, first, be pure perception devoid of sign, all the more terrible in this case for being objective:

'...the light of the great fire was as bright as ever, brighter perhaps. Now the pink aura of it had spread. Saffron and ochre turned to blood-colour. The shivering of the white heart of the fire had quickened beyond the capacity of the eye to analyse....' (p. 13)

Yet, focusing again, it is out of *that* shivering glare that the 'something' which seemed to have moved turns into a child—reminiscent of that most infamous of all Vietnam photographs—whose survival is, again simply, miraculous. It should not be possible, but 'they saw him plain': the brightness on his left side; why he moves as he does; the burn. The child walks out of the fire. We 'see', as no more and no less a fact than the twentieth-century inferno, the apparent miracle of survival; but it is as dark as it is bright, a horrible brightness, a scrap of humanity saved and maimed, a glimpse of terror and wonder (like Jocelin's at the end of *The Spire*). 'What had seemed impossible and therefore unreal was now a fact and clear to them all.'

But 'seeing' must now take in one dimension more. The captain of the fire crew is forced to see 'quite clearly in a kind of inner geometry' the direct connection between his moment of cowardice and inhumanity, before he could nerve himself to go to the child's rescue, and his own survival. (Now the horror is like Pincher's.)

'He shut his eyes and for some sort of time saw that he was dead or felt that he was dead; and then that he was alive, only the screen that conceals the workings of things had shuddered and moved.... He came, silent and filled in an extraordinary way with grief, not for the maimed child but for himself, a maimed creature whose mind had touched for once on the nature of things.' (p. 16)

'Seeing', then, is a threefold process of focusing: first, and essentially, concrete perception; through perception then to insight, fusing darkness and brightness, horror with miracle; then through insight to revelation of 'the workings of things', the existence of a terrifying field of force and design to which our normal experience is a concealing screen—through seeing to skrying, through skrying to vision.

Matty's book follows that process. If vision comes through fact, it is clear why the child of the burning city must be as literal as the flames. Burnt all down the imaginative side of the brain, he is so literal-minded as to be almost a 'natural'; not only un- but anti-symbolic. He knows himself merely the seventh of a number, undisguisably repulsive. Yet the only person in his terrible childhood to show him any affection brings out the instantaneous response of an essentially loving heart. And that young nurse also realizes that 'Matty believes I bring someone with me', a perception about another dimension, which perhaps is idiotic, and perhaps is not. Matty's experience, then, is remarkably concrete, is of deep division, senses dimension beyond. His 'gospel' is a deeper and deeper focusing, told mostly from the outside, objectively unsentimental.

In boyhood, social trauma succeeds physical tragedy. Out of deep need, and incapable of deception or irony, he naturally believes the 'letter', and the words about being Mr Pedigree's treasure and telling the truth; but love and truth bring destruction and repulse. Like the psalmist in the good book—only literally—he casts out his shoe at 'evil', and causes the death of Henderson and the arrest of Mr Pedigree. Now he must face not only the familiar physical revulsion of the girls, and the alienation of the boys, but the traumatic judgement of the man he loves: 'You horrible, horrible boy! It's all your fault!'

Yet there is no 'accident' in the connection of love with remorse and guilt, darkness with light. Level by level, Matty must ask deeper questions of identity and purpose. If one side of him agonizes over Mr Pedigree, the other fills with the girl and the 'roses'—and with a skrying that is not 'artificial', or even human at all. In the window of Goodchild's bookshop lie a scrap of ancient music, a hornbook Lord's Prayer, and a skrying glass:

'Matty looked at the glass ball with a touch of approval since it did not try to say anything and was not, like the huge books, a whole store of frozen speech. It contained nothing but the sun which shone in it, far away. He approved of the sun which said nothing but lay there, brighter and brighter and purer and purer. It began to blaze as when clouds move aside. It moved as he moved but soon he did not move, could not move. It dominated without effort, a torch shone straight into his eyes, and he felt queer, not necessarily unpleasantly so but queer all the same—unusual. He was aware too of a sense of rightness and truth and silence.' (pp. 47–8)

But this 'feeling of waters rising' and 'still dimension of otherness' shows 'the seamy side, where the connections are', the balance between love (Mr Pedigree, the girl) and accusation, how light, love and beauty bring out the dark deformity of the self. To the question in the empty church—'Who are you? What do you want?'—come answers through tears: the Man in Black, the guilty and remorseful man who must offer up all he wants, in penance, and can live only on the underside of the world.

But out of the skrying comes a new question—no longer 'who' but 'what' am I?—a question no longer of identity but of nature. Australia's answer, to his literal mind, is as horrible as it may seem farcical or pathetic to us. Only between the lines of the objective narrative and apparent farce can we see through Matty's eyes how the darkness is not merely in him; how the 'Black' springs viciously out of the desert air, crucifies, renders impotent, turns the whole sky black, a revelation of aboriginal nature. (Matty knows the 'facts' about Harry Bummer, but sees more than they explain.) And yet a man may become a eunuch for the Kingdom of God, and Matty's 'portions' in Australia have been much concerned with vessels of sacrifice in the temple. Now his sufferings from the crucifarce point a further question: not merely 'What am I? but 'What am I *for*?' Out of sacrifice comes prophecy—again apparently farcical: those antics with matchboxes, the pot and twigs (setting the park on fire), the weird night ritual. But it is now into a vast gap, between the narrative and Matty's consciousness, that awareness must well. He has found his purpose and is telling his wordless truth with reverberant echoes of the great truthtellers: Elisha on Baal, Ezekiel showing forth the destruction of Jerusalem, Ecclesiastes warning laughing cobbers (and readers). We begin also to glimpse the depth of feeling behind the still face. In the wilderness he enacts in silence the agony of the psalmist as the waters of affliction close over his head. He submits, shuddering, to a horrible baptism into primeval darkness and slime; but he not only bears witness to a light that shines on, transcending the passage through the underworld—he also proclaims the eternal glory of the wheeled cherubim of Ezekiel and Apocalypse. And as he leaves Australia, the essential goodness and lovingness of Matty come out unmistakably (like Lok's), when a little dust and a drop of water reveal something beyond words:

'He stood for a while looking up at the side of the ship. At last he looked down at his feet and appeared to be lost in thought. At last he lifted the left foot and shook it three times. He put it down. He lifted his right foot and shook it three times. He put it down. He turned round and looked at the port buildings and the low line of hills that was all a continent could muster from its inside to bid him farewell. He seemed, or would have seemed, to look through those hills at the thousands of miles over which he had travelled and at the hundreds of people that for all his care he had, if not met, at least, seen. He stared round the quay. In the lee of a bollard there was a pile of dust. *He went to it quickly, bent down, took a handful and strewed it over his shoes.*

He climbed the ladder, away from the many years he had spent in Australia, and was shown the place he had to sleep in with eleven others, though none of them had arrived. After he had stowed his one suitcase he went back up again to the deck and stood again, still, silent and staring at the continent he knew he was seeing for the last time. *A single drop of water rolled out of his good eye, found a quick way down his cheek and fell on the deck. His mouth was making little movements, but he said nothing.*' (p. 77. Our italics)

But finally, closing Matty's book like one of Golding's, a surprise ending challenges us to look again. We have seen between the lines of a blind narrative, and sympathized, but Matty's own words present the challenge of the literal again. He may have come from seeing to skrying to vision, but can we accept his Revelation, his world of spirit ('the red spirit with the expensive hat')—that is, John of Patmos utterly divested of poetic symbolism—that certainty of Apocalypse, that cranky fundamentalism, beyond even the Brethren in discarding Scripture and taking his Mission only from direct messengers of God? Matty's language permits no figurative compromise. The world for him is literally governed by a spiritual force, a wind that roves through him, a spell that is God's. From questions of identity, to nature, to purpose; now Matty knows that the world which began for him in Inferno will end in Judgement, but the news is good. Or else it is idiotic, Matthew's gospel; not truth of nature but the foolishness of a 'natural'. Which? There can be no ducking the question.

Sophy's book is apparently the opposite of Matty's, but follows the same process, from seeing to skrying to vision. He is repulsive, half-educated, deprived; she is beautiful, sophisticated, 'has everything'. He may be a kind of idiot, but is loving, sacrificing, faithful, saintly. She is highly intelligent, but cynical, nihilist, sadistic, deadly. Yet the apparent opposites of 'good' and 'evil', on deeper inspection, turn out to be more alike than either is like 'ordinary humanity'. After loveless and traumatic childhoods both long to be accepted but are rejected again and again. Both know themselves dual (the two sides of Matty's face; 'inside' and 'outside' Sophy) and are aware from childhood of forces beyond them acting through them. Both are 'seers', forced themselves and forcing us to see deeper and deeper into the nature and working of things. And as soon as we attempt to recall the significant moments of the two stories we detect how remarkably they are parallel, contrasting modalities of the same process of discovery. A shoe cast and a stone; a skrying glass and a transistor; a man in black and a dark creature; one stabbing and another; a dark pool and an ink blot; the parallels are as striking as the differences. Darkness and brightness become visible in people, but are also powers stretching beyond and behind them. Both look forward to a final unravelling of complexity, indeed to the end of the world as we know it.

If the burnt child is first aware of himself as mutilated and only one of a number, the dark-haired little girl in the meadow is aware both of her prettiness and of her ego and its jealousy. Though she has everything in some senses, she can't have what she wants most: Daddy. But the metaphysic nature of the story soon becomes more compelling than character conditioning or psychology, as her seeing of the dabchicks fuses ecstasy into something darker. Darkness becomes visible in her response to brightness: her possessive seeing, the excitement of imposed will and power, an answering force working through her, the 'complete satisfaction' as the stone finds its target. Before her eleventh birthday she becomes aware of herself (like Pincher) as being at the mouth of a 'dark direction' like a tunnel (p. 113), looking out into the world. She begins to see how the dark being can manipulate the outer little girl, to understand that she is alone and can belong to no one but herself. She becomes piercingly aware of a 'weird' power, uncanny, like a fate (pp. 124–6).

As she grows she begins to see how inside-Sophy is connected to something in the world. After she and Toni have got rid of their father's mistress, Sophy finds Win's transistor, and hears two talks which speak directly to the dark creature. One is about how the world is running down, the other on ESP. The first she feels she has always known; the second she mocks because its scientific statistics miss just the dark excitation, the 'other end of the tunnel, where surely it joined on' (p. 132). Now she feels not only 'a hunger and thirst after weirdness' but that 'something pushed her, shoved her, craved'. With puberty comes the sense of a new dimension of power, but the daylight beauty only makes the dark direction more visible. It is as if 'other eyes opened in the back of her head and stared into a darkness that stretched away infinitely' (p. 134), as if she were an 'expression ... of the darkness and running down' (p. 135). She explores sexuality, but the experience of intercourse seems trivial. Behind vagina and womb she feels the turd working its way, and reacts with a convulsion of hate. Sex becomes at best the 'faint ring-shaped pleasure' she knows with Roland. Until, that is, she stabs him with a penknife in a moment of rage—and finds orgastic release. The inside darkness finally joins on to the force that is running the world down to simplicity. She finds her *being*, not merely in defiance, power, or even the excitement of inflicting pain, but in being part of that destructive force. So she stops pretending; finds what she thinks is complete acceptance with feckless Gerry and his killer pal; begins to plan not petty crime but the abduction of the child, which has even more exciting possibilities should they 'have' to kill him.

Even now a dual potential remains. When she gazes into the ink blot the sensation of immersion and extinction in darkness, like the wave in childhood, produces hysterical screaming and a dead faint. Something deep within her revolts. And when she has her last inter-view with her father we may see more in her hopeless passion than the outrage (to her) of its sexuality and its grief. But finally it is the certainty of her self-commitment to the darkness and the deadliness of her nihilism—'The way towards simplicity is through outrage'—that seem the news of Sophy's book.

'"Everything's running down. Unwinding. We're just—tangles. Everything is just a tangle and it slides out of itself bit by bit towards something that's simpler and simpler—and we can help it. Be a part ... *The way towards simplicity is through outrage....*"

... And she was there; without the transistor she was there and could hear herself or someone in the hiss and crackle and roar, the inchoate unorchestra of the lightless spaces.' (p. 166–7)

Like Matty, she brings someone or something with her ('I was speaking to—of—I was someone—'). We know there will be outrage. Presently.

It would seem, then, that the effect of juxtaposing Matty's book with Sophy's is a Manichean division. Darkness is visible. So is its opposite. Matty and Sophy were dual, but each seems resolved now, and looking to the resolution of the world. As at the end of Sammy Mountjoy's autobiography, there seems to be no bridge. Indeed, the final book of *Darkness Visible* seems at first to say just that, in several ways. 'One is one,' says the title ... and all alone presumably, and ever more will be so.

So narrative is broken into several points of view: Sim Goodchild, Matty, Sophy, Sim again, Mr Pedigree, all seeing differently. Sim even thinks of himself as a committee of discordant members, and of everyone as separated by barriers of adamant from everyone else. The new seer is sardonic, disillusioned. As Matty's challenge was his literalness, so anything Sim sees must pass the test of scepticism, which believes nothing but experience. That tells him, certainly, of the uncontrollable 'thing' inside, impelling him to hurt others, and of the 'unruly member' of his private committee, still active in the elderly man's feelings for little girls. But to Edwin's good news of charismatic vision Sim reacts with the weary disillusion of one who has heard it all before, many times, and with the mockery of a bookman for a teacher who now wants to give up language in order to find the truth.

Yet Edwin's experience was of words made visible; not meanings, but a sense of shape, of sevenness, of light. Again the emphasis falls on physical seeing. Vision of something*ness* depends on seeing some *thing*. So what breaks through Sim's scepticism is no idea or belief in religion or the occult, but rather two sharply realized visual experiences, which we are made to share (albeit in words). The first is to *see* Matty, as we have never done, and descry, welling through the physical realization, both the extraordinary grief and how he is outlined against his background so that he himself, and not his history or behaviour or ideas, is the point. The second, when Matty becomes a medium for Sim to see into his own palm, distinguishes seeing from the interpretation of signs, and skrying not only from charlatan fortune-telling, but from any idea that significance can be read off from lines in words. Revelation is in seeing itself, and seeing whole, or nowhere.

'The palm was exquisitely beautiful, it was made of light. It was precious and preciously inscribed with a sureness and delicacy beyond art and grounded somewhere else in absolute health ... Sim stared into the gigantic world of his own palm and saw that it was holy.' (p. 231)

Now it seems possible that 'it all hangs together', without Edwin's superstition, and against Manichean division. In the 'place of silence' Sim, making full allowance for the dirtiness of the world, experiences not only the connectedness of opposites, farcical and holy, mundane and miraculous, but their harmony. The physical world contains the itchy nose and the compulsion to scratch which makes the seance comical, and Matty's tear which makes it tragic. But it also (in an astonishing passage) opens a 'speech' which is not 'words' but music, vision, spirit.

'There was, surely, no mere human breath that could sustain the note that spread as Sim's palm had spread before him, widened, became, or was, precious range after range beyond experience, turning itself into pain and beyond pain, taking pain and pleasure and destroying them, being, becoming. It stopped for a while with promise of what was to come. It began, continued, ceased. It had been a word. That beginning, that change of state explosive and vital had been a consonant, and the realm of gold that grew from it a vowel lasting for an aeon; and the semi-vowel of the close was not an end since there was, there could be no end but only a readjustment so that the world of spirit could hide itself again, slowly, slowly fading from sight, reluctant as a lover to go and with the ineffable promise that it would love always and if asked would always come again.' (p. 233)

It does not matter that ordinariness returns. Nor does it matter what word Edwin actually spoke. (It was probably 'joy'.) For we are concerned not with what the word 'means' but what it *is*, being, and becoming. And the barriers are broken. The three 'rivals' of the old song have become one, for a moment.

To plunge back into Matty's journal is, of course, to mark difference again. When Sim saw the word and rejoiced, Matty saw evil spirits clawing at the circle and wept. Yet the structure of seeing grows the same. When he saw the light and the deformity before, Matty thought he had to choose. But now, to his puzzlement, the wicked deceiver Sophy offers the sign of union. The Whore of Apocalypse torments him in a wet dream, but gives him the priceless gift of his manhood back, which turns a world of black and white to colour and of silence to the rejoicing of Beethoven's 'Seventh'. But the Manichean is finally healed by seeing, beyond words, how good comes into the world through evil, and light and love through human deformity: 'between the word book and the word since I have been shown a great thing. It was not the spirits and it was not a vision or a dream it was an opening. I saw a portion of providence...' (p. 237). It is not the language of Matty's book nor its sense of 'since' that matters. What opens out—from seeing to skrying to foreseeing, pro-vidence, of joy incorporating horror— can only be glimpsed in the space between the telling and the sense of cause or consequence, wordlessly.

But when Sophy comes up through the trapdoor all that unity is called in question. Without Matty, disillusion floods back. The light is harsh, or brothel-pink. Sim's sense of 'the dust and dirt and stink' behind the pretty girl deflates not only romanticism but also the newly won sense of transformation and design. Each is all alone again, behind a blank wall of indifference, meeting to no purpose.

Moreover, Matty will come no more—and the neutral voice which describes his terrible end (so much more horrible in imagination, recalling his beginning) will not allow us to know whether he had any idea of what he was doing, as he died on fire. Was there purpose—a bad man running, a boy's rescue? Or only frantic and accidental whirling, in wordless agony and horror, unable to escape?

Sophy too, hearing a rabbit in a snare, is chilled with a sense that she may be trapped rather than purposeful. But then the fire fills the sky and she rejoices at 'an outrage, a triumph!'. Moreover, she finally sees what the 'last outrage' might be, and knows herself capable. Passionately, convincingly, she imagines murdering the kidnapped child by stabbing through his genitals, the ultimate act of darkness.... But *her* sense of cosmic force and purpose also comes apart. The plan fails; Gerry escapes with Toni; Sophy the user has been used and fooled. Once again she collapses into hysteria and oblivion. But as she picks her way back along the towpath, the darkness no longer holds a triumphant sense of cosmic Evil—only emptiness, nothing.

Afterwards the TV pictures (including the lilywhite boys in their greenness) are artfully juxtaposed, but do not add up. 'No one will *ever* know what happened.' All are guilty, but at the heart of darkness now 'the horror' (there is a modern Kurtz) is a farce of madness, ignorance, solitary confinement. The novel might have ended there, pointing to that continual worry of Golding's that always makes ending problematic. How can one satisfactorily conclude without seeming to claim a final knowledge? Fearing the pattern-making of the seer's vision, he has increasingly sought both to tell and to question the telling to the end. Here the questioning seems to have won and destroyed any possibility of final unity.

Or is it, as another Man in Black said, that 'we know what we are, but not what we may be'? Does what we are determine what we become? At the end Golding summons a witness. Mr Pedigree has been woven in and out of the web since the beginning, torn between his love of the bright sons of morning and his dark obsession, the helpless victim of his 'rhythm', yet neither consenting to it nor to be cured. He too might kill a child in the end. Could such seamy material finally show us 'where the connections are'? Whether man can choose what he may be no matter what he is? Whether in the end there is darkness or light or nothing?

Of course, this means that Golding has to make us 'know' what Pedigree experiences at the moment of his death. But what is most extraordinary about the rendering of his consciousness in those last moments is again the sensuous physicality of perception ... the sun on the skin ... the sea of light ... and Matty coming. Indeed, only now that Matty is dead and he himself dying (like Jocelin) can he *see* Matty, see beyond the 'horrible' appearance and the question of who was at 'fault' in the death of Henderson and the martyrdom of Sebastian. Now he can also see the nature of the name that nobody got right, though it shows the operation of the spirit, 'the extraordinarily lively nature of this gold, this wind, this wonderful light and warmth that kept Windrove moving rhythmically' (p. 264). Finally he sees the Mattyness, the love and forgiveness that was always 'popping up', always 'connected with everything else', that he tried to throw away, but it wouldn't go ('Who are you, Matty?'). To him he can not only speak of the hell he knows and fears, but *cry for help*.

'It was at this point that Sebastian Pedigree found he was not dreaming. For the golden immediacy of the wind altered at its heart and began first to drift upwards, then swirl upwards then rush upwards round Matty. The gold grew fierce and burned. Sebastian watched in terror as the man before him was consumed, melted, vanished like a guy in a bonfire; and the face was no longer two-tone but gold as the fire and stern and everywhere there was a sense of the peacock eyes of great feathers and the smile round the lips was loving and terrible. This being drew Sebastian towards him so that the terror of the golden lips jerked a cry out of him—"Why? Why?"

The face looming over him seemed to speak or sing but not in human speech.

Freedom.' (p. 265)

But Pedigree, who (like Sammy Mountjoy) cried for help, cannot bear (like Pincher) to let go, and clutches closer to him the many-coloured ball, his life, his heart, himself. 'But the hands came in through his. They took the ball as it beat and drew it away so that the strings that bound it to him tore as he screamed. Then it was gone.' (p. 265). Do we 'know' or not? We remember Matty:

'What good is not directly breathed into the world by the holy spirit must come down by and through the nature of men. I saw them, small, wizened, some of them with faces like mine, some crippled, some broken. Behind each was a spirit like the rising of the sun. It was a sight beyond joy and beyond dancing. Then a voice said to me it is the music that frays and breaks the string.' (pp. 237–8)

If so, man can choose, can cry for help at the last, in order not to be what he is and has been. Though the pluck at the string be terrible, the death of the self, what is made is music. It is not darkness that is visible in the end, it is brightness. One is one-and-all, alone, and evermore shall be so....

And yet we cannot be *told* this, in words. Words can only bring us to the point where we ourselves can 'see', for a moment, something opening through them, in the space beyond them.

And Golding must still allow for those who cannot believe that the 'filthy old thing' that is our pedigree can ever be 'cured'. For both sets of readers there has to be a gap between 'book' and 'since', between the telling and the final sense of cause and consequence. It is there on page 265: an empty space. It rather seems as though Golding, like Aeneas, might be holding a golden bough (*Sit mihi fas audita loqui*). But the space must fill with each reader's vision. Some will see only emptiness after the word 'gone'.

V

It would seem that the two novels in tandem enabled Golding to express different potentials of his art more fully than had been possible in any single book. One kind of art deftly disposes scenes on the surface to define a gap; the other plunges beyond the line, over the edge, into the very depths—Rembrandt to Brocklebank or Picasso. One book is the most powerful of all his metaphysical explorations, seeming to contain and extend the whole *oeuvre* since *Lord of the Flies*: an astonishingly original work but difficult, contorted, obscure. The other dances along, much more light, bright and sparkling, literary, linguistically inventive, the work of a craftsman and comedian who has always been around; yet the dark gap on the stage is all the more obvious for the animation and evasiveness which surround it. Only—to admirers of *Darkness Visible*—the book must then seem necessarily lightweight and superficial because of its refusal to explore what it reveals, and in spite of its offering the literary pleasures of *passage*. Indeed, each book is weak where the other is strongest. When *Darkness Visible* approaches the social world—as soon, for example, as Sophy enters the disco—the imaginative pressure drops, the language goes brittle, the interest wanes. (Who can be bothered with Gerry, let alone Fido?) Conversely, it is when we realize what is at stake offstage, what we shall never be shown, that Talbot's language and his transitory concerns can seem most superficial and escapist. Yet each book defines the nature and integrity of the other by the vividness of contrast. Because the one is social, it must see the nature of the novel as a rite of passage, enabling worldlings to *negotiate* dark initiation and death, to cope with the 'monstrous' which comes up from underneath, to get past the 'horror' of the dying in the darkness and the human left all alone in a wide, wide sea. The narrative is sewn up, the cover story prepared, the ship goes on, the reader returns to the world—though, winds being what they are, the line may have to be crossed again! The other, because the concerns are ultimate, must begin by insisting that we stare into holocaust, and pursue to the end the metaphysical questions raised by tragedy and apocalypse. Its extraordinary protagonists, saintly 'natural', pederast, terrorist, must be taken to points of no return so that the reader, too, is taken to where ultimate questions cannot be negotiated or sailed past. One book delights in language and affirms the power of writing as a rite of passage. The other calls language in question, and strives to open up the mysterious space between words and make what is hidden there visible, wordlessly. Each tries for a different way of being true to the paradoxes of Golding's imagination and his truth-telling urgency: how from the real and the clear, contradictions always (for him) spread and proliferate into multiplicity, opacity, mystery, but also how art must continually find ways to clarify, to focus into unity. It is the great pleasure of the old song of our epigraph that from the singular it keeps opening out into greater and greater multiplicity and suggestiveness and growth, yet keeps no less concentrating back triumphantly into one. But now, by giving us 'two-oh', almost simultaneously, Golding has achieved an extraordinary effect. It is not that we can possibly think of them as somehow one work, for each is too uniquely itself. Yet manifestly they deepen the focus on the same area of preoccupation by coming from such different angles. And they seem to have liberated each to be more itself, its kind of thing, than it could have been if it had simultaneously been trying also to be the other.

And this has liberated readers too, who may have found in one or the other book more of the Golding they really like, in a purer state than usual. The reception was certainly very different. In England one novel instantaneously won widespread praise and a major prize; the other remained relatively unheralded, apparently unprized. In America it was the other way round.

It seems likely that the newly 'extreme' art, refining out elements first one way and then another, will divide Golding's admirers in their preferences, without preventing a common recognition of what has been achieved.